CRYPTOGRAPHY AND NETWORK SECURITY

—A Practical Approach

CRYPTOGRAPHY AND NETWORK SECURITY
—A Practical Approach

By

K. Haribaskar

M.E., Assistant Professor
Department of Computer Science & Engg.,
Mount Zion College of Engg. & Tech.,
Pudukkottai
Tamil Nadu

UNIVERSITY SCIENCE PRESS
(An Imprint of Laxmi Publications Pvt. Ltd.)
An ISO 9001:2008 Company

BENGALURU • CHENNAI • COCHIN • GUWAHATI • HYDERABAD
JALANDHAR • KOLKATA • LUCKNOW • MUMBAI • RANCHI • NEW DELHI
BOSTON (USA) • ACCRA (GHANA) • NAIROBI (KENYA)

CRYPTOGRAPHY AND NETWORK SECURITY—A PRACTICAL APPROACH

Printed and bound in India
Typeset at ABRO Enterprises, Delhi
First Edition: 2015
ISBN 978-93-81159-63-7

Branches

Bengaluru	080-26 75 69 30	
Chennai	044-24 34 47 26,	24 35 95 07
Cochin	0484-237 70 04,	405 13 03
Guwahati	0361-254 36 69,	251 38 81
Hyderabad	040-27 55 53 83,	27 55 53 93
Jalandhar	0181-222 12 72	
Kolkata	033-22 27 43 84	
Lucknow	0522-220 99 16	
Mumbai	022-24 91 54 15,	24 92 78 69
Ranchi	0651-220 44 64	

PUBLISHED IN INDIA BY

UNIVERSITY SCIENCE PRESS
(An Imprint of Laxmi Publications Pvt. Ltd.)

An ISO 9001:2008 Company
113, GOLDEN HOUSE, DARYAGANJ,
NEW DELHI - 110002, INDIA
Telephone : 91-11-4353 2500, 4353 2501
Fax : 91-11-2325 2572, 4353 2528
www.laxmipublications.com info@laxmipublications.com

C—
Printed at : Repro Knowledgecast Limited, Thane

CONTENTS

APPENDICES

(Pages 223-232)

PREFACE

The explosive growth in computer systems and their interconnections via network has increased the dependence of both organizations and individuals on the information stored and communicated using these systems. The internet as a world wide communication network has changed our daily life in many ways. The internet, as an open forum, has created some security problems.

Network security is a set of protocols that allows us to use the internet comfortably without worrying about security attacks. The most common tool for providing network security is cryptography, an old technique that has been revived and adopted to network security. In this Universal electronic connectivity, virus and hackers, electronic eavesdropping, and electronic fraud, security is paramount. This book provides a practical survey of the principles of cryptography and network security.

This book is organized with the following styles:

- **Symmetric Ciphers:** A detailed examination of Classical Encryption Techniques, Block Ciphers, Data Encryption Standard and Advanced Encryption Standard.
- **Asymmetric Ciphers:** A detailed covers of Number Theory, Public Key encryption algorithms and principles, including a discussion of Key Management Techniques.
- **Cryptographic Data Integrity Algorithms:** A detailed examination of Authentication Requirements, Elliptic Curve functions, Hash Functions and its algorithm and Digital Signature.
- **Mutual Trust:** Looks at network security tools and applications including Kerberos, X.509 certificates, PGP, S/MIME, IP Security and SET. Looks at system-level security issues.

Suggestions for the improvement of the book will be gracefully acknowledged.

—Author

ACKNOWLEDGEMENTS

My sincere thanks to the Chairman of Mount Zion Christian Educational Trust Mr. Jayabarathan Chelliah and Mount Zion College of Engineering and Technology Director Prof. Jayson Keerthy Jayabarathan.

I would like to thank the following mentors who provided detailed technical reviews of many chapters: Dr. R. Krishnamoorty Dean, Anna University of Technology Tiruchirappalli India. Dr. S. Palani Dean, Sudharsan Engineering College, Pudukkottai, India; Dr. R. Raghavan Director, Sethu Institute of Technology, Virudhunagar, India.

The following people contributed for syllabus and course content: Mrs. S. Malarvizhi and Ms Seema Dev Akshtha.

My heartful gratitude to my parents and family members for their passionate support throughout the preparation of the book.

—Author

PART 1
SYMMETRIC CIPHERS

Chapters

1. Introduction to Networking
2. Classical Encryption Techniques
3. Block Ciphers and the Data Encryption Standard
4. Advanced Encryption Standard

CHAPTER 1

INTRODUCTION TO NETWORKING

1.1 STEP TO INFORMATION SECURITY

The network security and information security are often used interchangeably. Network security is generally taken as providing protection at the boundaries of an organization by keeping out intruders. Information security, however, explicitly focuses on protecting data resources from malware attack or simple mistakes by people within an organization by use of data loss prevention (DLP) techniques. One of these techniques is to compartmentalize large networks with internal boundaries.

Comparison with Computer Security

Securing network infrastructure is like securing possible entry points of attacks on a country by deploying appropriate defense. Computer security is more like providing means to protect a single PC against outside intrusion. The former is better and practical to protect the civilians from getting exposed to the attacks. The preventive measures attempt to secure the access to individual computers—the network itself—thereby protecting the computers and other shared resources such as printers, network-attached storage connected by the network. Attacks could be stopped at their entry points before they spread. As opposed to this, in computer security the measures taken are focused on securing individual computer hosts. A computer host whose security is compromised is likely to infect other hosts connected to a potentially unsecured network. A computer host's security is vulnerable to users with higher access privileges to those hosts.

1.2 NETWORK SECURITY CONCEPTS

Network Security consists of the provisions made in an underlying computer network infrastructure, policies adopted by the network administrator to protect the network and the network-accessible resources from unauthorized access and consistent and continuous monitoring and measurement of its effectiveness (or lack) combined together. Network security involves all activities that organizations, enterprises, and institutions undertake to protect the value and ongoing usability of assets and the integrity and continuity of operations. An effective network security strategy requires identifying threats and then choosing the most effective set of tools to combat them.

Network security starts from authenticating the user, commonly with a username and a password. Since this requires just one thing besides the user name, *i.e.,* the password which is something you 'know', this is sometimes termed one factor authentication. With two factor authentication something you 'have' is also used (*e.g.,* a security token or 'dongle', an ATM card, or your mobile phone), or with three factor authentication something you 'are' is also used (*e.g.,* a fingerprint or retinal scan).

Once authenticated, a firewall enforces access policies such as what services are allowed to be accessed by the network users. Though effective to prevent unauthorized access, this component may fail to check potentially harmful content such as computer worms or Trojans being transmitted over the network. Anti-virus software or an intrusion prevention system (IPS) help detect and inhibit the action of such malware. An anomaly-based intrusion detection system may also monitor the network and traffic for unexpected (*i.e.,* suspicious) content or behaviour and other anomalies to protect resources, *e.g.,* from denial of service attacks or an employee accessing files at strange times. Individual events occurring on the network may be logged for audit purposes and for later high level analysis.

Communication between two hosts using the network could be encrypted to maintain privacy.

1.3 ELEMENTS OF COMPUTER SECURITY

This general approach to computer security is based on eight major elements:

1. Computer security should support the mission of the organization.
2. Computer security is an integral element of sound management.
3. Computer security should be cost-effective.
4. Computer security responsibilities and accountability should be made explicit.
5. System owners have computer security responsibilities outside their own organizations.

6. Computer security requires a comprehensive and integrated approach.
7. Computer security should be periodically reassessed.
8. Computer security is constrained by societal factors.

1.4 SECURITY MANAGEMENT

Security Management for networks is different for all kinds of situations. A small home or an office would only require basic security while large businesses will require high maintenance and advanced software and hardware to prevent malicious attacks from hacking and spamming.

Small Homes

- A basic firewall.
- For windows users, basic Antivirus software like McAfee, Norton AntiVirus or AVG Antivirus. An anti-spyware program such as Windows Defender or Spybot would also be a good idea. There are many other types of antivirus or antispyware programs out there to be considered.
- When using a wireless connection, use a robust password. Also try and use the strongest security supported by your wireless devices, such as WPA or WPA2.

Medium Businesses

- A fairly strong firewall.
- Strong Antivirus software and Internet Security Software.
- For authentication, use strong passwords and change it on a bi-weekly/monthly basis.
- When using a wireless connection, use a robust password.
- Raise awareness about physical security to employees.
- Use an optional network analyzer or network monitor.

Large Businesses

- A strong firewall and proxy to keep unwanted people out.
- A strong Antivirus software package and Internet Security Software package.
- For authentication, use strong passwords and change it on a weekly/bi-weekly basis.
- When using a wireless connection, use a robust password.
- Exercise physical security precautions to employees.
- Prepare a network analyzer or network monitor and use it when needed.
- Implement physical security management like closed circuit television for entry areas and restricted zones.
- Security fencing to mark the company's perimeter.
- Fire extinguishers for fire-sensitive areas like server rooms and security rooms.
- Security guards can help to maximize security.

School

- An adjustable firewall and proxy to allow authorized users access from the outside and inside.
- Strong Antivirus software and Internet Security Software packages.
- Wireless connections that lead to firewalls.
- Children's Internet Protection Act compliance.
- Supervision of network to guarantee updates and changes based on popular site usage.
- Constant supervision by teachers, librarians and administrators to guarantee protection against attacks by both internet and sneakernet sources.

Large Government

- A strong strong firewall and proxy to keep unwanted people out.
- Strong Antivirus software and Internet Security Software suites.
- Strong encryption, usually with a 256 bit key.
- Whitelist authorized wireless connection, block all else.
- All network hardware is in secure zones.
- All host should be on a private network that is invisible from the outside.
- Put all servers in a DMZ, or a firewall from the outside and from the inside.
- Security fencing to mark perimeter and set wireless range to this.

1.5 OSI SECURITY ARCHITECTURE

Introduction

The OSI security architecture is useful to manage, as a way of organizing the task of providing security. It defines a systematic way of defining and providing security requirements. It was developed as an international standard.

The OSI security architecture focuses on security attack, mechanism, and services. These can be defined briefly as follows:

- **Security Attack:** Any action that compromise the security of information owned by an organization.
- **Security Mechanism:** A process that is designed to detect, prevent or recover from a security attack. And security mechanism is a method which is used to protect your message from unauthorized entity.
- **Security Services:** Security Services is the services to implement security policies and implemented by security mechanism.

1.6 SECURITY SERVICES

Security Services is the services to implement security policies and implemented by security mechanism. And security mechanism is a method which is used to protect your message from unauthorized entity.

There are five types of services regarding security services:

1. Authentication
2. Access Control
3. Data Confidentiality
4. Data Integrity
5. Non Repudiation.

1. Authentication

Authentication is any process by which you verify that someone is who they claim they are. This usually involves a username and a password, but can include any other method of demonstrating identity, such as a smart card, retina scan, voice recognition, or fingerprints. **Authentication** is equivalent to showing your drivers license at the ticket counter at the airport.

Two specific authentication services are defined in the standard

- **Peer entity authentication** used in association with a logical connection to provide confidence in the identity of the entities connected.
- **Data origin authentication,** in a connection less transfer, provides assurance that the source of received data is as claimed.

2. Access Control

The prevention of unauthorized used of resources (*i.e.,* this service control who can have access to a resource, under what conditions accesses can occur, and what those accessing that resource are allowed to do).

In other way access control can be defined that the ability to permit or deny the use of something by someone.

3. Data Confidentiality

The protection of data from unauthorized disclosure.

The following four specific level of data confidentiality are defined in the standard.

Connection Confidentiality: The protection of all user data on a connection.

Connectionless Confidentiality: The protection of all user data in a single data block.

Selective-Field Confidentiality: The confidentiality of selected fields within the user data on a connection or a single data block.

Traffic Flow Confidentiality: The protection of the information that might be derived from observation of traffic flows.

4. Data Integrity

That ensure that data received are exactly as sent by an authorized entity (*i.e.,* contain no modification, insertion, deletion, or replay).

Various level of data integrity:

Connection integrity with recovery: Provide integrity of all user data on a connection and detects any modification, insertion, deletion, or replay of any data within an entry data sequence, with recovery attempted.

Connection integrity without recovery: As above but provide without recovery.

Selective-Fields connectionless integrity: Provide for the integrity of selected fields within the user data of data block transferred over a connection and takes the form of determination of whether the selected field have been modified, inserted, detected, or replayed.

Connectionless integrity: Provide for the integrity of single connectionless data block and may take a form of detection of data modification. Additionally, a limited form of repay detection may be provided.

Selective-Field connectionless integrity: Provides for the integrity of selected field within a single connectionless data block; take the form of determination of whether the selected fields have been modified.

5. Non Repudiation

Provide protection against denial by one of the entities involve in communication of having participated in all or part of the communication.

Non repudiation, Origin: Proof that message is sent by the specified party.

Non repudiation, Destination: Proof that message is received by the specified party.

1.7 SECURITY MECHANISMS

The OSI security architecture distinguishes between specific security mechanisms and Pervasive security mechanisms.

Specific Security Mechanisms

Specific security mechanisms may be incorporated into an appropriate layer. Eight specific security mechanisms as followings:

1. Encipherment
2. Digital Signature mechanisms
3. Access control mechanisms
4. Data integrity mechanisms
5. Authentication exchange mechanisms
6. Traffic padding mechanisms
7. Routing control mechanisms
8. Notarization mechanisms.

1.8 SECURITY ATTACKS

Network security attacks are a major concern in today's networked world. Software hackers and crackers are only part of the online security and privacy problem. Computer security threats can come from within.

The private or internal computer networks are vulnerable to the network security attacks either from internal or external attacks. Internal attacks generally come from the insiders who do something stupid that threaten the network resources such as introducing virus via a USB flash disks which are infected by viruses. External attacks are typically introduced via network entry point from the internet.

There are four general categories of attack:

- Interruption, an attack on availability
- Interception, an attack on confidentiality
- Modification, an attack on integrity
- Fabrication, an attack on authenticity

A distinction into active and passive attacks is explained by Fig. 1.1 and Fig. 1.2.

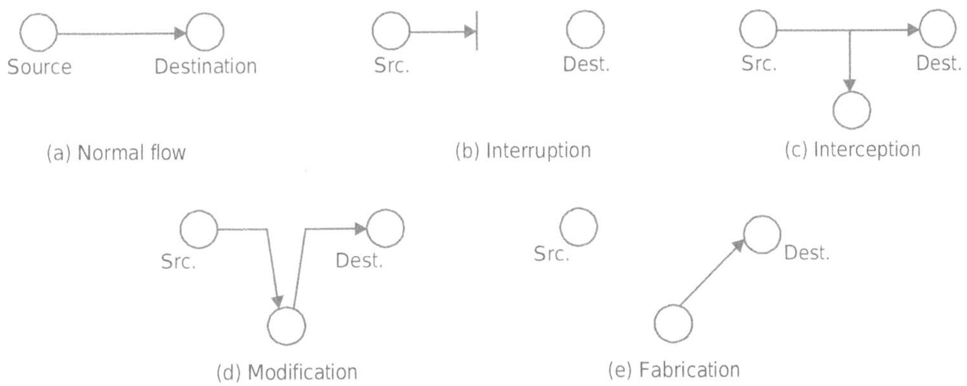

Fig. 1.1. *Security threats.*

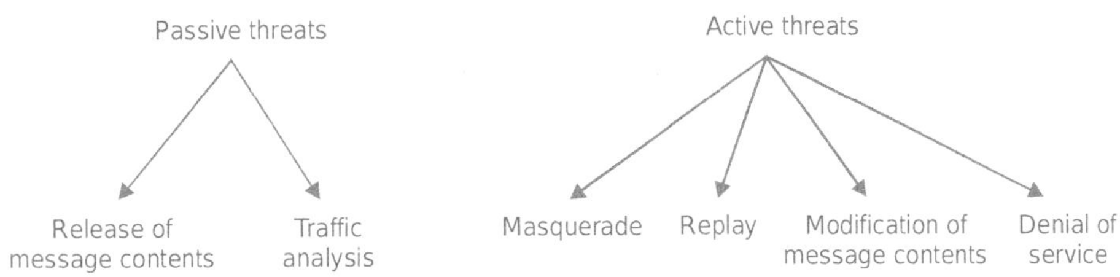

Fig. 1.2. *Active and passive network security threats.*

1.8.1 Passive Attacks

Passive attacks are in the nature of eavesdropping on, or monitoring of, transmissions. The goal of the opponent is to obtain information that is being transmitted. Two types of passive attacks are release of message contents and traffic analysis.

The **release of message contents** is easily understood. A telephone conversation, an electronic mail message, and a transferred file may contain sensitive or confidential information. We would like to prevent the opponent from learning the contents of these transmissions.

The second passive attack, traffic analysis, is more subtle. Suppose that we had a way of masking the contents of messages or other information traffic so that opponents, even if they captured the message, could not extract the information from the message. The common technique for masking contents is encryption. If we had encryption protection in place, an opponent might still be able to observe the pattern of these messages. The opponent could determine the location and identity of communicating hosts and could observe the frequency and length of messages being exchanged. This information might be useful in guessing the nature of the communication that was taking place.

Passive attacks are very difficult to detect because they do not involve any alteration of the data. However, it is feasible to prevent the success of these attacks. Thus, the emphasis in dealing with passive attacks is on prevention rather than detection.

1.8.2 Active Attacks

The second major category of attack is **active attacks.** These attacks involve some modification of the data stream or the creation of a false stream and can be subdivided into four categories: masquerade, replay, modification of messages, and denial of service.

A **masquerade** takes place when one entity pretends to be a different entity. A masquerade attack usually includes one of the other forms of active attack. For example, authentication sequences can be captured and replayed after a valid authentication sequence has taken place, thus enabling an authorized entity with few privileges to obtain extra privileges by impersonating an entity that has those privileges.

Replay involves the passive capture of a data unit and its subsequent retransmission to produce an unauthorized effect.

Modification of messages simply means that some portion of a legitimate message is altered, or that messages are delayed or reordered, to produce an unauthorized effect. For example, a message meaning "Allow John Smith to read confidential file accounts" is modified to mean "Allow Fred Brown to read confidential file accounts."

The **denial of service** prevents or inhibits the normal use or management of communications facilities. This attack may have a specific target; for example, an entity may suppress all messages directed to a particular destination (*e.g.*, the security audit service). Another form of service denial is the disruption of an entire network, either by disabling the network or by overloading it with messages so as to degrade performance.

Active attacks present the opposite characteristics of passive attacks. Whereas passive attacks are difficult to detect, measures are available to prevent their success. On the other hand, it is quite difficult to prevent active attacks absolutely, because to do so would require physical protection of all communications facilities and paths at all times. Instead, the goal is to detect them and to recover from any disruption or delays caused by them. Because the detection has a deterrent effect, it may also contribute to prevention.

1.9 KEY POINTS AND REVIEW QUESTIONS

Key Points

- A "network" has been defined as "any set of interlinking lines resembling a net, a network of roads.
- Computer security is more like providing means to protect a single PC against outside intrusion.
- A computer host's security is vulnerable to users with higher access privileges to those hosts.
- Network security starts from authenticating the user, commonly with a username and a password.
- Anti-virus software or an intrusion prevention system (IPS) help detect and inhibit the action of such malware.
- Computer security is an integral element of sound management.
- System owners have computer security responsibilities outside their own organizations.
- The OSI security architecture focuses on security attack, mechanism, and services.
- Security Services is the services to implement security policies and implemented by security mechanism.
- Authentication is any process by which you verify that someone is who they claim they are.
- The private or internal computer networks are vulnerable to the network security attacks either from internal or external attacks.

Question with Answers *(2 Marks)*

Q. 1. *What is the OSI Architecture?*

Ans. Security architecture for OSI, define such a systematic approach. The OSI security architecture is useful to managers, as a way of organizing the task of providing security. The OSI security architecture focuses on security attack, mechanism, and services.

Q. 2. *What are the aspect of information security?*

Ans. There are three aspect of the information security, *i.e.,* security attack, security mechanism, security service.

Q. 3. *What is the difference between passive and active security threads?*

Ans. **Passive Attacks:** Passive attacks are in the nature of eavesdropping on, or monitoring of, transmissions. The goal of the opponent is to obtain information that is being transmitted. Two types of passive attacks are release of message contents and traffic analysis.

Active Attacks: The second major category of attack is **active attacks.** These attacks involve some modification of the data stream or the creation of a false stream and can be subdivided into four categories: masquerade, replay, modification of messages, and denial of service.

Q. 4. *Define categories of security services.*

Ans. **Passive Attacks**

- Release of message contents
- Traffic analysis

Active Attacks

- Masquerade
- Replay
- Modification of messages
- Denial of service

Q. 5. *What is an active attack?*

Ans. An active attack involves some modification of the data stream or the creation of a false.

Q. 6. *What is an passive attack?*

Ans. Passive attack are in the nature of eavesdropping on, or monitoring of, transmissions.

Q. 7. *What is Encipherment?*

Ans. The use of mathematical algorithms to transform data into a form that is not reality intelligible. The transformation and subsequent recovery of the data depend on an algorithm and zero or more encryption keys.

Q. 8. *List some common information integrity functions.*

Ans. Identification, authorization, concurrence, liability, endorsement, validation, time of occurrence, registration

Q. 9. *Define Threat.*

Ans. A potential for violation of security, which exists when there is a circustances, capability, action or event that could breach security and cause harm. That is a threat is a possible danger that might exploit vulnerability.

Q. 10. *List some example of security attacks.*

Ans.
- Gain unauthorized access to information.
- Enlarge cheater's legitimate license.
- Pervert the function of software, typically by adding a convert function.

Review Questions

1. What is network?
2. Explain the network security concepts.
3. List out the elements of network security.
4. Explain briefly OSI security architecture.
5. What are all the security services available in network? Explain that.
6. Explain briefly network security services.
7. Explain briefly network security attacks.

❑❑❑

CHAPTER 2 CLASSICAL ENCRYPTION TECHNIQUES

2.1 INTRODUCTION

Symmetric encryption also referred to as conventional encryption or single-key encryption was the only type of encryption in use prior to the development of public-key encryption. It remains by far the most widely used of the two types of encryption. This Part examines a number of symmetric ciphers. In this chapter, we begin with a look at a general model for the symmetric encryption process; this will enable us to understand the context within which the algorithms are used. Next, we examine a variety of algorithms in use before the computer era. Finally, we look briefly at a different approach known as steganography.

Before beginning, we define some terms. An original message is known as the **plaintext**, while the coded message is called the **ciphertext**. The process of converting from plaintext to ciphertext is known as **enciphering** or **encryption**; restoring the plaintext from the ciphertext is **deciphering** or **decryption**. The many schemes used for enciphering constitute the area of study known as **cryptography**. Such a scheme is known as a **cryptographic system** or a **cipher**. Techniques used for deciphering a message without any knowledge of the enciphering details fall into the area of **cryptanalysis**. Cryptanalysis is what the layperson calls "breaking the code."

The areas of cryptography and cryptanalysis together are called **cryptology**.

2.2 SYMMETRIC CIPHER MODEL

Symmetric (conventional) encryption scheme has five ingredients (Fig. 2.1)

- **Plaintext** – original message
- **Ciphertext** – coded message
- **Enciphering, encryption** – process of converting from plaintext to ciphertext.
- **Deciphering, decryption** – restoring the plaintext from the ciphertext.

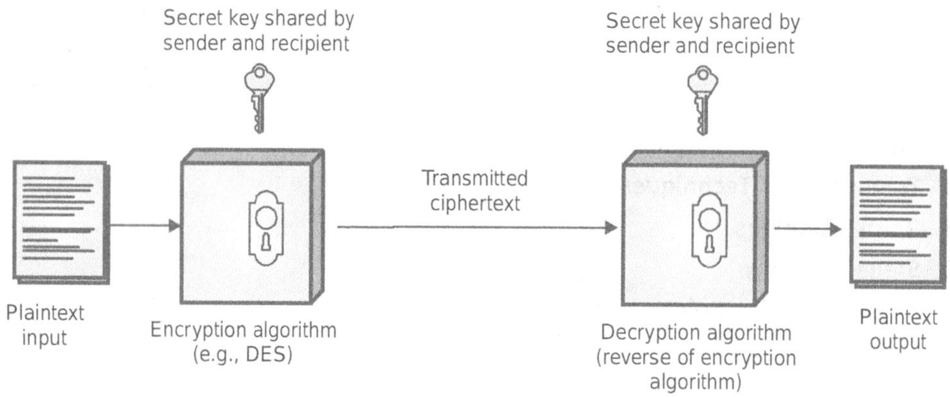

Fig. 2.1. *Simplified model of symmetric encryption.*

There are 2 requirements for secure use of conventional encryption:

1. We need a strong encryption algorithm – the opponent should be unable to decrypt ciphertext or to discover the key even if she/he is in the possession of a number of cipher texts together with the plaintext that produced each ciphertext
2. Sender and receiver must have obtained copies of the secret key in a secure fashion and must keep the key secure. If someone can discover the key and knows the algorithm, all communication using this key is readable

We assume that it is impractical to decrypt a message on the basis of the ciphertext plus knowledge of the encryption/decryption algorithm, *i.e.,* we do not need to keep the algorithm secret; we need to keep only the key secret.

Let's consider essential elements of a symmetric encryption scheme from the following Fig. 2.2.

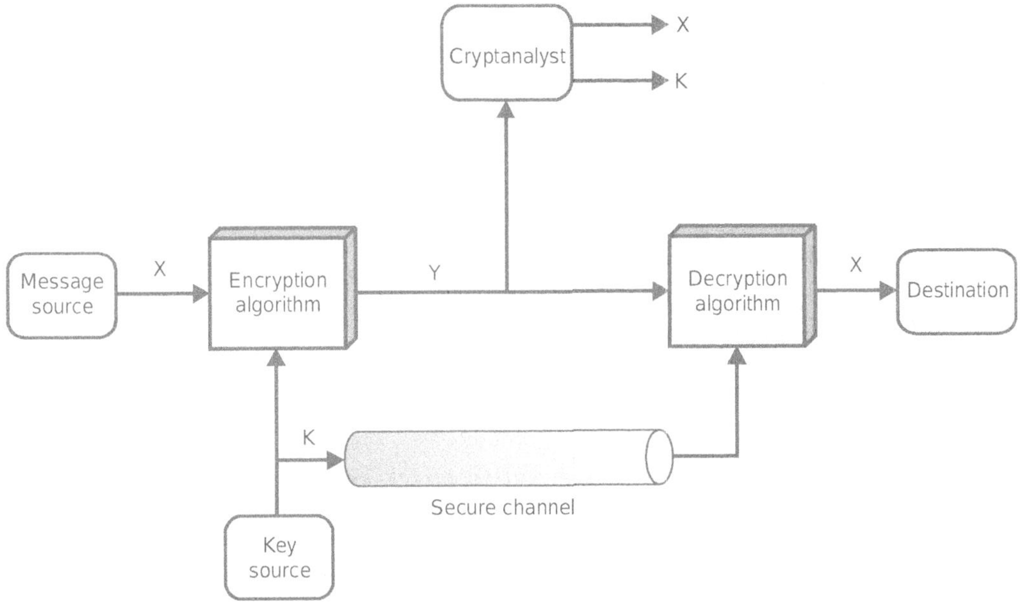

Fig. 2.2. *Model of conventional cryptosystem.*

Let us Consider a source produce a message in plaintext

$X = [X_1, X_2, \ldots, X_M]$, where M is the elements of X are letters in some finites alphabet. For encryption, a key of the form $K = [K_1, K_2, \ldots, K_j]$ is generated

We can write:

Encryption:

$$Y = E_K(X)$$

Decryption:

$$X = D_K(Y)$$

Opponent knows Y, E, D. He may be interested to recover X or/and K. Knowledge of K gives him opportunity to read future messages.

2.2.1 Cryptography

Cryptographic systems are characterized by

1. The type of operations used for transforming plaintext to ciphertext (substitution, transposition). Fundamental requirement – no information be lost
2. The number of keys used (1 key – symmetric, single-key, secret-key; 2 keys – asymmetric, 2 key, public-key)
3. The way in which the plaintext is processed (block cipher, stream cipher). Stream cipher may be viewed as a block cipher with block size equal to 1 element.

2.2.2 Cryptanalysis

There are two general approaches to attacking a conventional encryption scheme:

1. **Cryptanalysis:** Attempts to use characteristics of the plaintext or even some plaintext-ciphertext pairs to deduce a specific plaintext or key being used.
2. **Brute-force attack:** Every possible key is tried until an intelligible translation into plaintext is obtained. On average, half of all possible keys should be tried to achieve success.

Types of Cryptanalytic Attacks:

- **Ciphertext only**

  – only know algorithm/ciphertext, statistical, can identify plaintext
- **Known plaintext**

  – know/suspect plaintext and ciphertext to attack cipher
- **Chosen plaintext**

  – select plaintext and obtain ciphertext to attack cipher
- **Chosen ciphertext**

  – select ciphertext and obtain plaintext to attack cipher
- **Chosen text**

  – select either plaintext or ciphertext to en/decrypt to attack cipher

Unconditionally secure encryption scheme: Ciphertext generated by the scheme does not contain enough information to determine uniquely the corresponding plaintext, no matter how much ciphertext is available. Excepting a scheme known as one-time pad, there is no encryption algorithm that is unconditionally secure. Therefore, encryption algorithm should meet one or both of the following criteria:

– The cost of breaking the cipher exceeds the value of the encrypted information

– The time required to break the cipher exceeds the useful lifetime of the information.

Such algorithm is called **computationally secure.** The 56-bit key size is used with the DES (Data Encryption Standard), 168-bit – for triple DES, 128-bit – for AES (Advanced Encryption Standard). Results are also shown for substitution codes that use 26-character key, in which all possible permutations of the 26 characters serve as keys. It is assumed that it take 1 μs to perform a single decryption or encryption (in last column – 10^6 decryptions per 1 μs).

All forms of cryptanalysis for symmetric encryption try to exploit the fact that traces of structure or pattern in the plaintext may survive encryption and be discernible in the ciphertext. Cryptanalysis for public-key schemes tries to use mathematical properties of pair of keys to deduce one from the other.

2.3 SUBSTITUTION TECHNIQUE

A substitution technique is one in which the letters of plaintext are replaced by other letters or by numbers. If the plaintext is viewed as a sequence of bits, then substitution involves replacing plaintext bit patterns with ciphertext bit patterns

2.3.1 Caesar Cipher

It was used by Julius Caesar. The Caesar cipher involves replacing each letter of the alphabet with the letter standing three places further down the alphabet.

For example,

Plain:	*meet*	*me*	*after*	*the*	*toga*	*party*
Cipher:	*PHHW*	*PH*	*DIWHU*	*WKH*	*WRJD*	*SDUWB*

Transformation is made using the following mapping:

Plain: *a b c d e f g h i j k l m n o p q r s t u v w x y z*

Cipher: *D E F G H I J K L M N O P Q R S T U V W X Y Z A B C*

Let us assign a numerical equivalent to each letter from 0 to 25. Then the algorithm may be expressed as follows. For each plaintext letter p, substitute the ciphertext letter C:

$$C = E(p) = (p+3) \bmod 26$$

A shift may be of any amount, so that general Caesar algorithm is

$$C = E(p) = (p+k) \bmod 26,$$

where k takes on a value in the range 1 to 25. The decryption algorithm is simply

$$p = D(C) = (C-k) \bmod 26$$

If it is known that a given ciphertext is a Caesar cipher, then a brute-force cryptanalysis is easily performed: simply try all possible 25 keys.

Three important characteristics of this problem enable us to use brute-force cryptanalysis:

1. The encryption and decryption algorithms are known.
2. There are only 25 keys to try.
3. The language of the plaintext is known and easily recognizable.

In most networking situations algorithms are assumed to be known. Brute-force analysis is impractical when algorithm employs large of keys. The 3rd characteristic is also significant. If the language of the plaintext is not known, then the plaintext output may not be recognizable. The Brute – force crypt analysis of Caesar cipher from the following Fig. 2.3.

KEY	*PHHW*	*PH*	*DIWHU*	*WKH*	*WRJD*	*SDUWB*
1	oggv	og	chvgt	vjg	vqic	rctva
2	nffu	nf	bgufs	uif	uphb	qbsuz
3	meet	me	after	the	toga	party
4	ldds	ld	zesdq	sgd	snfz	ozqsx
5	kccr	kc	ydrcp	rfc	rmey	nyprw
6	jbbq	ia	wbpan	pda	pkcw	lwnpu
7	iaap	ia	wbpan	pda	pkcw	lwnpu
8	hzzo	hz	vaozm	ocz	ojbv	kvmot
9	gyyn	gy	uznyl	nby	niau	julns
10	fxxm	fx	tymxk	max	mhzt	itkmr
11	ewwl	ew	sxlwj	lzw	lgys	hsjlq
12	dvvk	dv	rwkvi	kyv	kfxr	grikp
13	cuuj	cu	qvjuh	jxu	jewq	fghjo
14	btti	bt	puitg	iwt	idvp	epgin
15	assh	as	othsf	hvs	hcuo	dofhm
16	zrrg	zr	nsgre	gur	gbtn	cnegl
17	yqqf	yq	mrfqd	ftq	fasm	bmdfk
18	xppe	xp	lqepc	esp	ezrl	alcej
19	wood	wo	kpdob	dro	dyqk	zkbdi
20	vnnc	vn	jocna	cqn	cxpj	yjach
21	ummb	um	inbmz	bpm	bwoi	xizbg
22	tlla	tl	hmaly	aol	avnh	whyaf
23	skkz	sk	glzkx	znk	zumg	vgxze
24	rjjy	rj	fkyjw	ymj	ytlf	ufwyd
25	qiix	qi	ejxiv	xli	xske	tevxc

Fig. 2.3. *Brute-force cryptanalysis of caesar cipher.*

Furthermore, if the input is compressed in some manner, again recognition is difficult. Below in example of compression by ZIP:

```
ˆ+Wμ"— Ω—O)≤4{∞‡ ë-Ω%ràu·¯Í ◊¯Z-
Ú≠2O#Åæ∂ œ«q7¸Ωn·®3N◊Ú Œz'Y-ƒ∞Ï[±Û_ èΩ,<NO¬±«ˇxâ Åä£èü3Å
x}ö§kºÂ
_yÍ ˆΔÉ] J⁄˚iTê&ı'c<uΩ-
ÄD(G WÄC~y_ıõÄW PÔı«ÎÜ†ç], ¡ˇÌ^üÑ
π˘≈ˇLˇ9Ogﬂ0¯&Œ≤¬≤ØÔ$˘: ˘Œ!SGqèvo^ ûError!
```

Fig. 2.4. *Sample of compressed text.*

If this file is then encrypted with a simple substitution cipher (expanded to include more than just 26 characters), then the plaintext may not be recognized.

2.3.2 Monoalphabetic Ciphers

With only 25 keys Caesar cipher is far from secure. A dramatic increase in the key space may be achieved by allowing an arbitrary substitution. If instead of

Plain: a b c d e f g h i j k l m n o p q r s t u v w x y z

Cipher: D E F G H I J K L M N O P Q R S T U V W X Y Z A B C

The cipher line can be any permutation of the 26 alphabetic symbols, and then there are 26! or greater than $4*10^{26}$ possible keys. There is however another line of attack. If the cryptanalyst knows the nature of the plaintext (*e.g.*, noncompressed English text), then the analyst can exploit the regularities of the language.

Let's consider example of ciphertext:

UZQSOVUOHXMOPVGPOZPEVSGZWSZOPFPESXUDBMETSXAIZ
VUEPHZHMDZSHZOWSFPAPPDTSVPQUZWYMXUZUHSX
EPYEPOPDZSZUFPOMBZWPFUPZHMDJUDTMOHMQ

As a first step, relative frequency of the letters can be determined and compared to a standard frequency distribution for English. It can show in following graph shown in Fig. 2.5.

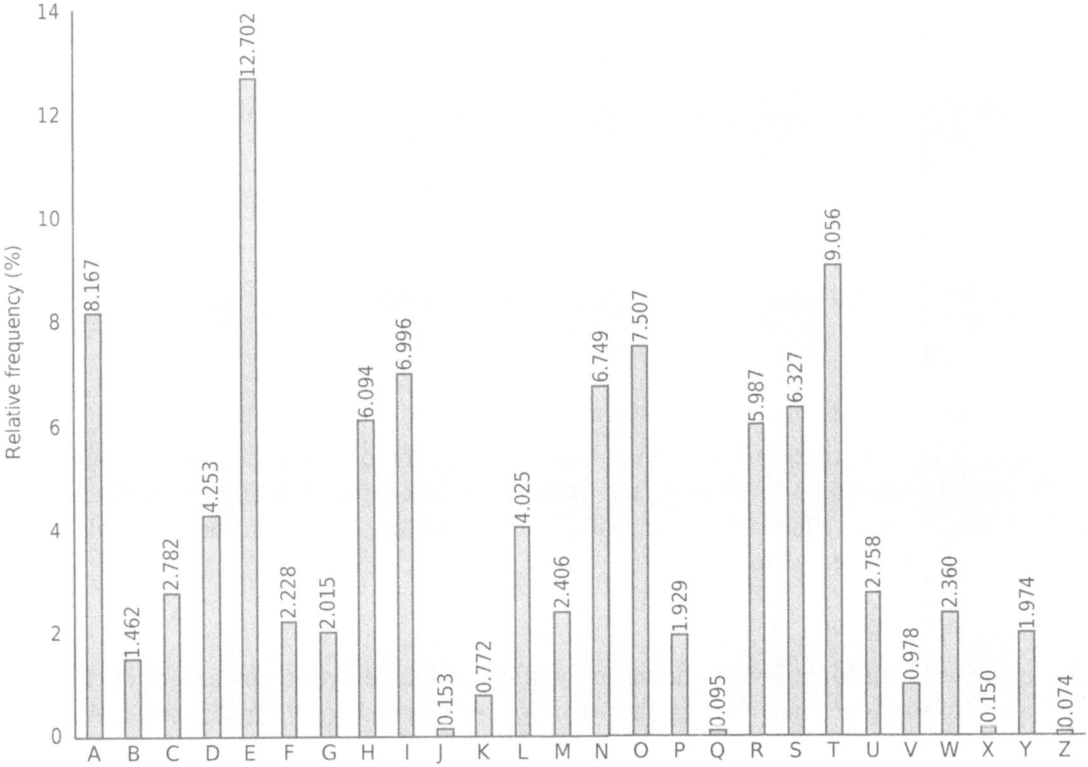

Fig. 2.5. *Relative frequency of letters in english text.*

The relative frequencies of the letters in the ciphertext (in percentages):

P 13.33	H 5.83	F 3.33	B 1.67	C 0.00
Z 11.67	D 5.00	W 3.33	G 1.67	K 0.00
S 8.33	E 5.00	Q 2.50	Y 1.67	L 0.00
U 8.33	V 4.17	T 2.50	I 0.83	N 0.00
O 7.50	X 4.17	A 1.67	J 0.83	R 0.00
M 6.67				

Comparing this with Fig. 2.4, it seems likely that cipher letters P and Z are the equivalents of plain letters e and t, but it is not certain which is which. The letters S, U, O, M, and H are all of the relatively high frequency and probably correspond to plain letters from the set {a, h, i, n, o, r, s}. The letters with the lowest frequencies (A, B, G, Y, I, J) are likely included in the set {b, j, k, q, v, x, z}. Now we could make some tentative assignments and start to fill plaintext to see if it looks like a reasonable "skeleton" of a message.

Another way, to consider frequency of two-letter combinations, is known as digrams. In our ciphertext, the most common digram is ZW, which appears 3 times. So, we make correspondence: Z – t, W – h. Then, P is equated with e. Now notice that sequence ZWP appears in the ciphertext, and we can translate it as "the". Next, notice ZWSZ in the first line. If they form a complete word, it will be th_t. If so, S equates with a. So far, then, we have

```
UZQSOVUOHXMOPVGPOZPEVSGZWSZOPFPESXUDBMETSXAIZ
 t a        e  e te  a that e e a       a
VUEPHZHMDZSHZOWSFPAPPDTSVPQUZWYMXUZUHSX
   e t   ta t ha e ee  a e  th    t  a
EPYEPOPDZSZUFPOMBZWPFUPZHMDJUDTMOHMQ
 e  e e tat  e   the  et
```

Continued analysis of frequencies plus trial and error may lead us to the solution

Two principal methods are used in substitution ciphers to lessen the extent to which the structure of the plaintext survives in the ciphertext: One approach is to encrypt multiple letters of the plaintext (Playfair Cipher, Hill Cipher), and the other is to use multiple cipher alphabets (Polyalphabetic Ciphers).

2.3.3 Playfair Cipher

The best-known multiple-letter encryption cipher is the Playfair (invented in 1854 by Sir Charles Wheatstone, but it bears the name of his friend Baron Playfair of St. Andrews, who championed the cipher at the British foreign office), which treats digrams in the plaintext as single units and translates these units into ciphertext digrams.

The Playfair algorithm is based on the use of a 5×5 matrix of letters constructed using a keyword. In the case of keyword *monarchy*, matrix is as follows:

M	O	N	A	R
C	H	Y	B	D
E	F	G	I/J	K
L	P	Q	S	T
U	V	W	X	Z

The matrix is constructed by filling in the letters of the keyword (minus duplicates) from left to right and from top to bottom, and then filling in the remainder of the matrix with the remaining letters in alphabetic order. The letters I and J count as one letter. Plaintext is encrypted two letters at a time, according to the following rules:

1. Repeating plaintext letters that would fall in the same pair are separated with a filler letter, such as *x*, so that *balloon* will be treated as *ba lx lo on*
2. Plaintext letters that would fall in the same row of matrix are each replaced with the letter to the right, with the first element of the row circularly following the last. For example, *ar* is encrypted as *RM*.
3. Plaintext letters that fall in the same column are each replaced by the letter beneath, with the top element of the row circularly following the last. For example, *mu* is encrypted as *CM*.
4. Otherwise, each plaintext letter is replaced by the letter that lies in its own row and the column occupied by the other plaintext letter. Thus, *hs* becomes *BP*, and *ea* becomes *IM* (or *JM*, as the encipherer wishes).

As far as number of digrams is $26 \times 26 = 676$ is significantly greater than number of letters, frequency analysis becomes much more difficult. For these reasons, Playfair cipher was for a long time considered unbreakable. It was used as standard field system by the British Army in World War I and still enjoyed considerable use by U.S. Army and other Allied forces during World War II.

Despite this level of confidence in its security, the Playfair cipher is relatively easy to break because it still leaves much of the structure of the plaintext language intact. A few hundred letters of ciphertext are generally sufficient.

2.3.4 Hill Cipher

It was developed by the mathematician Lester Hill in 1929. The encryption algorithm takes *m* successive plaintext letters and substitutes for them *m* ciphertext letters. The substitution is determined by *m* linear equations in which each character is assigned a numerical value:

a	b	c	D	e	f	g	h	i	j	k	l	m	n	o	P	q	r	s	t	u	v	w	x	y	z
0	1	2	3	4	5	6	7	8	9	10	11	12	13	14	15	16	17	18	19	20	21	22	23	24	25

For $m = 3$, the system can be described as follows:

$$C_1 = (K_{11}p_1 + K_{12}p_2 + K_{13}p_3) \bmod 26$$
$$C_2 = (K_{21}p_1 + K_{22}p_2 + K_{23}p_3) \bmod 26$$
$$C_3 = (K_{31}p_1 + K_{32}p_2 + K_{33}p_3) \bmod 26$$

This can be expressed in terms of column vectors and matrices:

$$C = KP \bmod 26,$$

where C and P are column vectors of length 3, representing the plaintext and ciphertext, and K is 3×3 matrix, representing the encryption key.

Operations are performed mod 26.

For example, consider the plaintext "payformoney", and use the encryption key

K =

17	17	5
21	18	21
2	2	19

The first 3 letters of the plaintext are represented by the vector (15 0 24). Then K(15 0 24) = (375 819 486) mod 26 = (11 13 18) = LNS. Continuing in this fashion, the ciphertext for the entire plaintext is LNSHDLEWMTRW.

Decryption requires using the inverse of the matrix K. The inverse K^{-1} of a matrix K is defined by $K K^{-1} = K^{-1} K = I$, where I is the unit matrix (1–s on the diagonal, other elements – zeroes). The inverse of the matrix does not always exist, but when it does, it satisfies the preceding equation. In this case, the inverse is

K^{-1} =

4	9	15
15	17	6
24	0	17

This is demonstrated as follows:

$K K^{-1}$ =

443	442	442
858	495	780
494	52	365

And after taking mod 26 of the elements above, unit matrix is obtained.

In general terms, the Hill system can be expressed as follows:

$$C = E_K(P) = KP \bmod 26$$
$$P = D_K(C) = K^{-1}C \bmod 26 = K^{-1}KP = P$$

As with Playfair, the strength of the Hill cipher is that it completely hides single-letter frequencies.

Although the Hill cipher is strong against a ciphertext-only attack (opponent has only ciphertext), it is easily broken with a known plaintext attack (opponent has pairs plaintext – ciphertext). For an $m \times m$ Hill cipher, suppose we have m plaintext-ciphertext pairs, each of length m. We label the pairs $P_j = (p_{1j}, p_{2j}, \ldots, p_{mj})$ and $C_j = (c_{1j}, c_{2j}, \ldots, c_{mj})$ such that $C_j = KP_j$ for $1 <= j <= m$ and for some unknown key matrix K. Now define two $m \times m$ matrices $X = (p_{ij})$ and $Y = (c_{ij})$.

Then we can form matrix equation Y = KX. If X has an inverse, then we can determine $K = YX^{-1}$. If X is not invertible, then a new version of X can be formed until an invertible X is obtained.

Suppose that the plaintext "friday" is encrypted using a 2×2 Hill cipher to yield the ciphertext PQCFKU. Thus, we know that

$$K(5\ 17) = (15\ 16);$$
$$K(8\ 3) = (2\ 5);$$
$$K(0\ 24) = (10\ 20).$$

Using the first 2 plaintext-ciphertext pairs, we have

$$\begin{pmatrix} 15 & 2 \\ 16 & 5 \end{pmatrix} = K\begin{pmatrix} 5 & 8 \\ 17 & 3 \end{pmatrix} \bmod 26$$

The inverse of X can be computed:

$$\begin{pmatrix} 5 & 8 \\ 17 & 3 \end{pmatrix}^{-1} = \begin{pmatrix} 9 & 2 \\ 1 & 15 \end{pmatrix}$$

$$K = \begin{pmatrix} 15 & 2 \\ 16 & 5 \end{pmatrix}\begin{pmatrix} 9 & 2 \\ 1 & 15 \end{pmatrix} = \begin{pmatrix} 137 & 60 \\ 149 & 107 \end{pmatrix} \bmod 26 = \begin{pmatrix} 7 & 8 \\ 19 & 3 \end{pmatrix}$$

Let's check now that this key matrix produces required transformation:

$$\begin{pmatrix} 7 & 8 \\ 19 & 3 \end{pmatrix}\begin{pmatrix} 5 \\ 17 \end{pmatrix} = \begin{pmatrix} 35 + 136 \\ 95 + 51 \end{pmatrix} = \begin{pmatrix} 171 \\ 146 \end{pmatrix} \bmod 26 = \begin{pmatrix} 15 \\ 16 \end{pmatrix}$$

$$\begin{pmatrix} 7 & 8 \\ 19 & 3 \end{pmatrix}\begin{pmatrix} 8 \\ 3 \end{pmatrix} = \begin{pmatrix} 56 + 24 \\ 152 + 9 \end{pmatrix} = \begin{pmatrix} 80 \\ 16 \end{pmatrix} \bmod 26 = \begin{pmatrix} 2 \\ 5 \end{pmatrix}$$

$$\begin{pmatrix} 7 & 8 \\ 19 & 3 \end{pmatrix}\begin{pmatrix} 0 \\ 24 \end{pmatrix} = \begin{pmatrix} 192 \\ 72 \end{pmatrix} \bmod 26 = \begin{pmatrix} 10 \\ 20 \end{pmatrix}$$

2.3.5 Polyalphabetic Ciphers

Another way to improve on the simple monoalphabetic technique is to use different monoalphabetic substitutions as one proceeds through the plaintext message. The general name for this approach is **polyalphabetic substitution cipher**. All these techniques have the following features in common:

1. A set of related monoalphabetic substitution rules is used.
2. A key determines which particular rule is chosen for a given transformation.

The best-known, and one of the simplest, such algorithms is referred to as the Vigenère cipher. In this scheme, the set of related monoalphabetic substitution rules consists of the 26 Caesar ciphers, with shifts of 0 through 25. Each cipher is denoted by a key letter, which is the ciphertext letter that substitutes for the plaintext letter a. Thus, a Caesar cipher with a shift of 3 is denoted by the key value d.

To aid in understanding the scheme and to aid in its use, a matrix known as the Vigenère table is constructed. Each of the 26 ciphers is laid out horizontally, with the key letter for each cipher to its left. A normal alphabet for the plaintext runs across the top. The process of encryption is simple: Given a key letter *x* and a plaintext letter y, the ciphertext letter is at the intersection of the row labelled *x* and the column labelled y; in this case the ciphertext is V.

To encrypt a message, a key is needed that is as long as the message. Usually, the key is a repeating keyword. For example, if the keyword is *deceptive*, the message "we are discovered save yourself" is encrypted as follows:

key: deceptivedeceptivedeceptive

plaintext: wearediscoveredsaveyourself

ciphertext: ZICVTWQNGRZGVTWAVZHCQYGLMGJ

Decryption is equally simple. The key letter again identifies the row. The position of the ciphertext letter in that row determines the column, and the plaintext letter is at the top of that column.

The strength of this cipher is that there are multiple ciphertext letters for each plaintext letter, one for each unique letter of the keyword. Thus, the letter frequency information is obscured. However, not all knowledge of the plaintext structure is lost.

It is instructive to sketch a method of breaking this cipher, because the method reveals some of the mathematical principles that apply in cryptanalysis.

First, suppose that the opponent believes that the ciphertext was encrypted using either monoalphabetic substitution or a Vigenère cipher. A simple test can be made to make a determination. If a monoalphabetic substitution is used, then the statistical properties of the ciphertext should be the same as that of the language of the plaintext. Thus, referring to Fig. 2.5, there should be one cipher letter with a relative frequency of occurrence of about 12.7%, one with about 9.25%, and so on. If only a single message is available for analysis, we would not expect an exact match of this small sample with the statistical profile of the plaintext language. Nevertheless, if the correspondence is close, we can assume a monoalphabetic substitution.

If, on the other hand, a Vigenère cipher is suspected, then progress depends on determining the length of the keyword, as will be seen in a moment. For now, let us concentrate on how the keyword length can be determined. The important insight that leads to a solution is the following: If two identical sequences of plaintext letters occur at a distance that is an integer multiple of the keyword length, they will generate identical ciphertext sequences. In the foregoing example, two instances of the sequence "red" are separated by nine character positions. Consequently, in both cases, r is encrypted using key letter e, e is encrypted using key letter p, and d is encrypted using key letter t. Thus, in both cases the ciphertext sequence is VTW.

An analyst looking at only the ciphertext would detect the repeated sequences VTW at a displacement of 9 and make the assumption that the keyword is either three or nine letters in length. The appearance of VTW twice could be by chance and not reflect identical plaintext letters encrypted with identical key letters. However, if the message is long enough, there will be a number of such repeated ciphertext sequences. By looking for common factors in the displacements of the various sequences, the analyst should be able to make a good guess of the keyword length.

Solution of the cipher now depends on an important insight. If the keyword length is N, then the cipher, in effect, consists of N monoalphabetic substitution ciphers. For example, with the keyword DECEPTIVE, the letters in positions 1, 10, 19, and so on are all encrypted with the same monoalphabetic cipher. Thus, we can use the known frequency characteristics of the plaintext language to attack each of the monoalphabetic ciphers separately.

The periodic nature of the keyword can be eliminated by using a nonrepeating keyword that is as long as the message itself. Vigenère proposed what is referred to as an auto key system, in which a keyword is concatenated with the plaintext itself to provide a running key. For our example:

key: deceptivewearediscoveredsav

plaintext: wearediscoveredsaveyourself

ciphertext: ZICVTWQNGKZEIIGASXSTSLVVWLA

Even this scheme is vulnerable to cryptanalysis. Because the key and the plaintext share the same frequency distribution of letters, a statistical technique can be applied. For example, *e* enciphered by *e*, by Fig. 2.5, can be expected to occur with a frequency of (0.127)2 [a] 0.016, whereas *t* enciphered by *t* would occur only about half as often. These regularities can be exploited to achieve successful cryptanalysis.

The ultimate defense against such a cryptanalysis is to choose a keyword that is as long as the plaintext and has no statistical relationship to it. Such a system was introduced by an AT&T engineer named Gilbert Vernam in 1918. His system works on binary data rather than letters. The system can be expressed succinctly as follows:

$$C_i = p_i \text{ “ } k_i$$

where p_i = ith binary digit of plaintext

k_i = ith binary digit of key

C_i = ith binary digit of ciphertext

“ = exclusive-or (XOR) operation

Thus, the ciphertext is generated by performing the bitwise XOR of the plaintext and the key. Because of the properties of the XOR, decryption simply involves the same bitwise operation:

$$p_i = C_i \text{ “ } k_i$$

The essence of this technique is the means of construction of the key. Vernam proposed the use of a running loop of tape that eventually repeated the key, so that in fact the system worked with a very long but repeating keyword. Although such a scheme, with a long key, presents formidable cryptanalytic difficulties, it can be broken with sufficient ciphertext, the use of known or probable plaintext sequences, or both.

2.4 TRANSPOSITION TECHNIQUES

All the techniques examined so far involve the substitution of a ciphertext symbol for a plaintext symbol. A very different kind of mapping is achieved by performing some sort of permutation on the plaintext letters. This technique is referred to as a transposition cipher.

The simplest such cipher is the rail fence technique, in which the plaintext is written down as a sequence of diagonals and then read off as a sequence of rows. For example, to encipher the message "meet me after the toga party" with a rail fence of depth 2, we write the following:

m e m a t r h t g p r y

e t e f e t e o a a t

The encrypted message is:

MEMATRHTGPRYETEFETEOAAT

This sort of thing would be trivial to cryptanalysis. A more complex scheme is to write the message in a rectangle, row by row, and read the message off, column by column, but permute the order of the columns. The order of the columns then becomes the key to the algorithm. For example:

Key : 3 4 2 1 5 6 7

Plaintext : a t t a c k p

o s t p o n e

d u n t i l t

w o a m x y z

Ciphertext : TTNAAPTMTSUOAODWCOIXKNLYPETZ

A pure transposition cipher is easily recognized because it has the same letter frequencies as the original plaintext. For the type of columnar transposition just shown, cryptanalysis is fairly straightforward and involves laying out the ciphertext in a matrix and playing around with column positions. Digram and trigram frequency tables can be useful.

The transposition cipher can be made significantly more secure by performing more than one stage of transposition. The result is a more complex permutation that is not easily reconstructed. Thus, if the foregoing message is re-encrypted using the same algorithm:

Key : 3 4 2 1 5 6 7
Input : t t n a a p t
m t s u o a o
d w c o i x k
n l y p e t z
Output : NSCYAUOPTTWLTMDNAOIEPAXTTOKZ

To visualize the result of this double transposition, designate the letters in the original plaintext message by the numbers designating their position. Thus, with 28 letters in the message, the original sequence of letters is:

01 02 03 04 05 06 07 08 09 10 11 12 13 14
15 16 17 18 19 20 21 22 23 24 25 26 27 28

After the first transposition we have:

03 10 17 24 04 11 18 25 02 09 16 23 01 08
15 22 05 12 19 26 06 13 20 27 07 14 21 28

which has a somewhat regular structure. But after the second transposition, we have:

17 09 05 27 24 16 12 07 10 02 22 20 03 25
15 13 04 23 19 14 11 01 26 21 18 08 06 28

This is a much less structured permutation and is much more difficult to cryptanalyze.

2.5 ROTOR MACHINES

Cryptography is the science of conducting secure communication. Cryptanalysis is the study of recovering communications by those other than the intended receiver. Cryptology is the umbrella term for cryptography and cryptanalysis, although cryptography is often used to mean cryptology. Cryptography has attracted much interest in recent years. While historically, cryptography was thought of as of interest to hobbyists and spies only, the increasing need for the secure transmission of large quantities of information and the advances made in public key cryptography have made cryptography an attractive subject. Statistics forms the basis of much cryptanalysis, and is also important in testing cryptographic systems for possible weaknesses.

Rotor machines: Rotor machines are cryptographic devices that became popular in the early part of this century. They formed the basis for most military and commercial cryptography until the late 1950s. The German Enigma, the Hebern machine and the Converter M-325 are variations on the basic machine we use.

The mechanisation of cryptography was seen as a great advance, and most at the time felt these new systems were practically unbreakable. A rotor is a small disk with electrical contacts on either side, one for every letter of the alphabet, which form a permutation on the set of all letters. A rotor machine is formed by concatinating rotors to form a new permutation. Rotors rotate after the encipherment of each letter to yield a new permutation. (See Fig. 2.6)

Fig. 2.6. *Rotor machine.*

Most famous of all rotor machines was the enigma. The enigma had three or four rotors and a reflector, whiched passed the signal back through the rotors. The enigma was famously broken by Alan Turing and the others at Bletchley Park. They had a huge advantage over our method of attack: they had a copy of the machine. We assumed no such advantage, and aimed to recover a copy of the machine and the plaintext.

Working Mechanisms

In the early part of the 20th century a solution to the problem was found. Both the problem of providing a complex algorithm and the task of encoding and decoding it could be solved mechanically.

Imagine an electrical system with 26 switches attached to 26 light bulbs. When you turn on any one of the switches, the corresponding light bulb lights up. Now replace the switches with the keys on a typewriter attached to those switches, and label the bulbs with letters. Typing the letter "A" makes the bulb labelled "A" light up, and typing a message makes the bulbs light up in turn as the keys are pressed.

To turn this system into an encryption system, all one has to do is change the wiring. Instead of the typewriter key for "A" running to the bulb labelled "A", run it to X for instance. Now typing in a message encrypts it, with zero effort on the operator's part.

The system just described is identical to the original single-alphabet substitution system, and just as insecure. The new idea in these machines was to place this scrambled wiring on the rotor, and then rotate it with a gear every time a letter was pressed. So while pressing "A" the first time would generate an "X", the next time it would generate a "J". Every letter pressed on the keyboard would spin the rotor and get a new substitution.

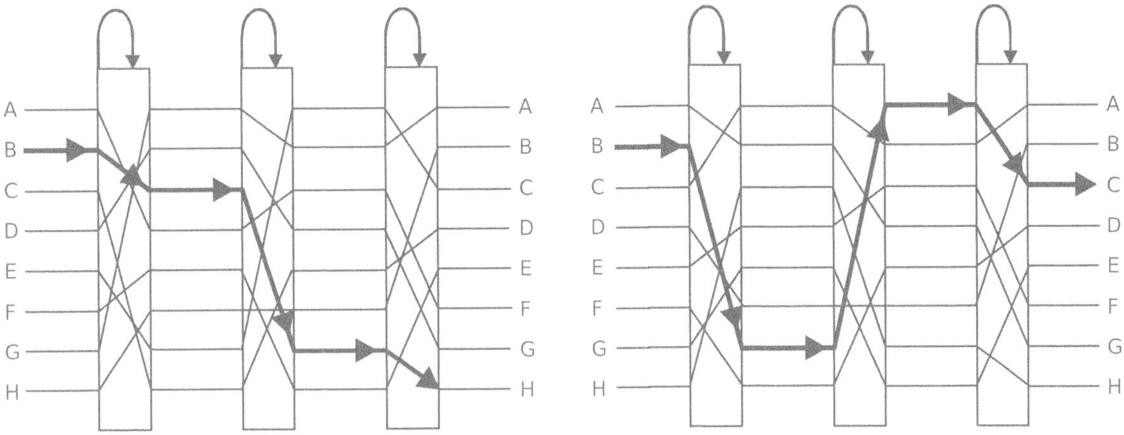

Fig. 2.7. *A three rotor machine for an eight letter alphabet before and after the first rotor has moved once.*

In effect, the rotors are generating a key from a simple algorithm, "use the next alphabet with every key press". Most of the key is hidden in the wiring of the disk. All that is needed to communicate the key between two parties is to say where to set the rotor before pressing the first key. A single letter (or number) now generates a huge key mechanically – the problem is solved.

Well almost. Depending on the size of the rotor, this may or may not be more secure than hand cyphers. If the rotor has only 26 positions on it, one for each letter, then all messages will have a (repeating) key 26 letters long. Although the key itself (mostly hidden in the wiring of the rotor) might not be known the systems for attacking these types of codes don't need that information. So while such a *single rotor* machine is certainly easy to use, it's less secure than most other polyalphabetic systems.

But this too is easy to correct. Simply stack more rotors next to each other, and gear them together. After the first rotor spins "all the way", make the rotor beside it spin one position. Now you would have to type 26 × 26 = 676 letters (for English) before the key repeats, and yet it still only requires you to communicate a key of two letters to set things up. A key of 676 length is not enough? Add another rotor, now you have a key 17,576 letters long. And so forth.

In order to be as easy to decipher as encypher, rotor machines were *symmetrical*. This makes sense if you consider how they work, if the current is sent from the battery (eventually) to the lamp, putting the current back in at the lamp end would reverse the circuit. Of course one cannot cause a typewriter key to "light up" (at least until recently), and in practice the rotors had to be reversed instead, thereby reversing the scrambling. Note that modern cryptography uses 'symmetrical' to mean that both cypher users must use the same key, not that the encyphering algorithm is run backwards to decrypt.

2.6 STEGANOGRAPHY

Steganography is the science of hiding information. Whereas the goal of cryptography is to make data unreadable by a third party, the goal of steganography is to hide the data from a third party. In this article, I will discuss what steganography is, what purposes it serves, and will provide an example using available software.

There are a large number of steganographic methods that most of us are familiar with (especially if you watch a lot of spy movies!), ranging from invisible ink and microdots to secreting a hidden message in the second letter of each word of a large body of text and spread spectrum radio communication. With computers and networks, there are many other ways of hiding information, such as:

- Covert channels (*e.g.,* Loki and some distributed denial-of-service tools use the Internet Control Message Protocol, or ICMP, as the communications channel between the "bad guy" and a compromised system).
- Hidden text within Web pages.
- Hiding files in "plain sight" (*e.g.,* what better place to "hide" a file than with an important sounding name in the *c:\winnt\system32* directory?).
- Null ciphers (*e.g.,* using the first letter of each word to form a hidden message in an otherwise innocuous text).

Steganography today, however, is significantly more sophisticated than the examples above suggest, allowing a user to hide large amounts of information within image and audio files. These forms of steganography often are used in conjunction with cryptography so that the information is doubly protected; first it is encrypted and then hidden so that an adversary has to first find the information (an often difficult task in and of itself) and then decrypt it.

There are a number of uses for steganography besides the mere novelty. One of the most widely used applications is for so-called digital watermarking. A watermark, historically, is the replication of an image, logo, or text on paper stock so that the source of the document can be at least partially authenticated. A digital watermark can accomplish the same function; a graphic artist, for example, might post sample images on her Web site complete with an embedded signature so that she can later prove her ownership in case others attempt to portray her work as their own.

Stego can also be used to allow communication within an underground community. There are several reports, for example, of persecuted religious minorities using steganography to embed messages for the group within images that are posted to known Web sites.

2.6.1 Steganographic Methods

The following formula provides a very generic description of the pieces of the steganographic process:

cover_medium + hidden_data + stego_key = stego_medium

In this context, the *cover_medium* is the file in which we will hide the *hidden_data*, which may also be encrypted using the *stego_key*. The resultant file is the *stego_medium* (which will, of course. be the same type of file as the cover_medium). The cover_medium (and, thus, the stego_medium) are typically image or audio files. In this article, I will focus on image files and will, therefore, refer to the cover_image and stego_image.

Before discussing how information is hidden in an image file, it is worth a fast review of how images are stored in the first place. An image file is merely a binary file containing a binary representation of the color or light intensity of each picture element (pixel) comprising the image.

Images typically use either 8-bit or 24-bit color. When using 8-bit color, there is a definition of up to 256 colors forming a palette for this image, each color denoted by an 8-bit value. A 24-bit color scheme, as the term suggests, uses 24-bits per pixel and provides a much better set of colors. In this case, each pix is represented by three bytes, each byte representing the intensity of the three primary colors red, green, and blue (RGB), respectively. The Hypertext Markup Language (HTML) format for indicating colors in a Web page often uses a 24-bit format employing six hexadecimal digits, each pair representing the amount of red, blue, and green, respectively. The color orange, for example, would be displayed with red set to 100% (decimal 255, hex FF), green set to 50% (decimal 127, hex 7F), and no blue (0), so we would use "#FF7F00" in the HTML code.

The size of an image file, then, is directly related to the number of pixels and the granularity of the color definition. A typical 640 × 480 pix image using a palette of 256 colors would require a file about 307 KB in size (640 • 480 bytes), whereas a 1024×768 pix high-resolution 24-bit color image would result in a 2.36 MB file (1024 • 768 • 3 bytes).

To avoid sending files of this enormous size, a number of compression schemes have been developed over time, notably Bitmap (BMP), Graphic Interchange Format (GIF), and Joint Photographic Experts Group (JPEG) file types. Not all are equally suited to steganography, however.

GIF and 8-bit BMP files employ what is known as lossless compression, a scheme that allows the software to exactly reconstruct the original image. JPEG, on the other hand, uses lossy compression, which means that the expanded image is very nearly the same as the original but not an exact duplicate. While both methods allow computers to save storage space, lossless compression is much better suited to applications where the integrity of the original information must be maintained, such as steganography. While JPEG can be used for stego applications, it is more common to embed data in GIF or BMP files.

The simplest approach to hiding data within an image file is called least significant bit (LSB) insertion. In this method, we can take the binary representation of the hidden data and overwrite the LSB of each byte within the cover image. If we are using 24-bit color, the amount of change will be minimal and indiscernible to the human eye. As an example, suppose that we have three adjacent pixels (nine bytes) with the following RGB encoding:

10010101 00001101 11001001
10010110 00001111 11001010
10011111 00010000 11001011

Now suppose we want to "hide" the following 9-bits of data (the hidden data is usually compressed prior to being hidden): 101101101. If we overlay these 9-bits over the LSB of the 9 bytes above, we get the following (where bits in bold have been changed):

10010101 00001100 11001001
10010111 00001110 11001011
10011111 00010000 11001011

Note that we have successfully hidden 9-bits but at a cost of only changing 4, or roughly 50%, of the LSBs.

This description is meant only as a high-level overview. Similar methods can be applied to 8-bit color but the changes, as the reader might imagine, are more dramatic. Gray-scale images, too, are very useful for steganographic purposes. One potential problem with any of these methods is that they can be found by an adversary who is looking. In addition, there are other methods besides LSB insertion with which to insert hidden information.

Without going into any detail, it is worth mentioning steganalysis, the art of detecting and breaking steganography. One form of this analysis is to examine the color palette of a graphical image. In most images, there will be a unique binary encoding of each individual color. If the image contains hidden data, however, many colors in the palette will have duplicate binary encodings since, for all practical purposes, we can't count the LSB. If the analysis of the color palette of a given file yields many duplicates, we might safely conclude that the file has hidden information.

2.7 KEY TERMS, KEY POINTS AND REVIEW QUESTIONS

Key Terms

Block Cipher	**Cryptology**	**Rotor Machine**
Brute-Force Attack	**Deciphering**	**Plain Text**
Caesar Cipher	**Enciphering**	**Single-Key Encryption**
Ciphertext	**Encryption**	**Steganography**
Computionally Secure	**Hill Cipher**	**Stream Cipher**
Cryptography	**One-Time Pad**	**Symmetric Encryption**
		Unconditionally Secure

Key Points

- Symmetric encryption also referred to as conventional encryption or single-key encryption was the only type of encryption in use prior to the development of public-key encryption.
- The areas of cryptography and cryptanalysis together are called cryptology.
- Cryptanalysis is the study of recovering communications by those other than the intended reciever.
- Cryptanalysis is attempts to use characteristics of the plaintext or even some plaintext-ciphertext pairs to deduce a specific plaintext or key being used

- ➢ Brute-force attack is every possible key is tried until an intelligible translation into plaintext is obtained. On average, half of all possible keys should be tried to achieve success.
- ➢ A substitution technique is one in which the letters of plaintext are replaced by other letters or by numbers.
- ➢ The Caesar cipher involves replacing each letter of the alphabet with the letter standing three places further down the alphabet.
- ➢ The best-known multiple-letter encryption cipher is the Playfair
- ➢ A Rotor machine used for encrypting and decrypting secret messages.
- ➢ Steganography is the science of hiding information.

Question with Answers *(2 Marks)*

Q. 1. *What are the essential ingradients of a symmetric cipher?*

Ans. A symmetric encryption scheme has five ingradients: Plaintext, Encryption algorithm, Secret Key, Cipher text, Decryption algorithm.

Q. 2. *What are the two basic functions used in the encryption algorithm?*

Ans. All the encryption algorithms are based on two general principles:

- **Substitution:** In which elements in the plaintext is mapped into another element.
- **Transposition:** In which elements in the plaintext are rearranged. The fundamental requirement is that no information be lost.

Q. 3. *How many keys are required for two people to communicate via a cipher?*

Ans. If both sender and receiver use the same key, the system is referred as symmetric, single key, secret-key or conventional encryption. If both sender and receiver use a different key, the system is referred as asymmetric, two-key or public key encryption.

Q. 4. *What are the two general approaches to attacking a cipher?*

Ans. The general two approaches

- **Cryptanalysis:** Cryptanalysis attacks rely on the nature of the algorithm plus perhaps some knowledge of the general characteritics of the plaintext or even some samples plaintext-cipher text pairs.
- **Brute-force attack:** The attacker tries every possible key on piece of cipher text untill an intelligible translation into plaintext is obtained.

Q. 5. *Define Caesar cipher.*

Ans. The caesar cipher involves replacing each letter of the alphabet with letter standing three places down the alphabet. The alphabet is wrapped around.

Q. 6. *Define Monoalphabetic cipher.*

Ans. A dramatic increase in the key space is achieved by allowing an arbitrary substitution. There are 26! Possible keys. It is referred to as monoalphabetic substitution cipher, because a single cipher alphabet is used per message.

Q. 7. *Define the playfair cipher.*

Ans. The playfair cipher treats the diagrams in the plaintext as single units and translates these units into cipher text diagrams. This algorithm is based on the use of a 5 × 5 matrix of letters constructed using keyword.

Q. 8. *What is the difference between a Monoalphabetic cipher and Polyalphabetic cipher?*

Ans. In monoalphabetic cipher single cipher alphabet is used per message. But in polyalphabetic cipher there are multiple cipher text letters for each plaintext letter, one for each unique letter of keyword.

Review Questions

1. What are the essential ingredients of a symmetric cipher?
2. How many keys are required for two people to communicate through a cipher?
3. State the difference between a block cipher and a stream cipher.
4. What are the two general approaches to attacking a cipher?
5. List and briefly define types of cryptanalytic attacks.
6. Briefly define the Caeaser cipher.
7. Briefly explain the playfair cipher.
8. Briefly define the monoalphabetic cipher.
9. State the difference between monoalphabetic cipher and playfair cipher.
10. What is a transposition cipher?
11. Explain about Rotor Machine with diagram.
12. What is steganography?

❑❑❑

CHAPTER 3

BLOCK CIPHERS AND THE DATA ENCRYPTION STANDARD

3.1 DATA ENCRYPTION STANDARD

Introduction

The Data Encryption Standard (DES) is a cipher (a method for encrypting information) selected as an official Federal Information Processing Standard (FIPS) for the United States in 1976, and which has subsequently enjoyed widespread use internationally. The algorithm was initially controversial, with classified design elements, a relatively short key length, and suspicions about a National Security Agency (NSA) backdoor. DES consequently came under intense academic scrutiny, and motivated the modern understanding of block ciphers and their cryptanalysis.

DES is now considered to be insecure for many applications. This is chiefly due to the 56-bit key size being too small; DES keys have been broken in less than 24 hours. There are also some analytical results which demonstrate theoretical weaknesses in the cipher, although they are infeasible to mount in practice. The algorithm is believed to be practically secure in the form of Triple DES, although there are theoretical attacks. In recent years, the cipher has been superseded by the Advanced Encryption Standard (AES).

It was adopted in 1977 by the National Bureau of Standards (NBS), now National Institute of Standards and Technology (NIST), as Federal Information Processing Standard 46 (FIPS PUB 46). In 1971, IBM's team under Horst Feistel leadership developed algorithm LUCIFER, operating on 64-bit blocks with 128-bit key. Further, IBM's team leaded by Walter Tuchman and Carl Meyer revised LUCIFER to make it more resistant to cryptanalysis, but they reduced key size to 56-bits. In 1973, NBS issued a request for proposals for a national cipher standard. IBM submitted results of its Tuchman-Meyer project. This was by far the best algorithm proposed and was adopted in 1977 as Data Encryption Standard. In 1994, NIST reaffirmed DES for federal use for another 5 years. In 1999, NIST issued a new version of its standard (FIPS PUB 46-3) that indicated that DES should only be used for legacy systems and that triple DES be used.

Fundamentally DES performs only two operations on its input, bit shifting, and bit substitution. The key controls exactly how this process works. By doing these operations repeatedly and in a non-linear manner you end up with a result which can not be used to retrieve the original without the key. Those familiar with chaos theory should see a great deal of similarity to what DES does. By applying relatively simple operations repeatedly a system can achieve a state of near total randomness.

DES works on 64-bits of data at a time. Each 64-bits of data is iterated on from 1 to 16 times (16 is the DES standard). For each iteration a 48-bit subset of the 56-bit key is fed into the encryption block represented by the dashed rectangle above. Decryption is the inverse of the encryption process. The "F" module shown in the diagram is the heart of DES. It actually consists of several different transforms and non-linear substitutions. Consult one of the references in the bibliography for details.

3.2 DES ENCRYPTION

The overall scheme for DES encryption is illustrated in chapter 2. As with any encryption scheme, there are two inputs to the encryption function:

The algorithm is designed to encipher and decipher blocks of data consisting of 64-bits under control of a 64-bit key. Deciphering must be accomplished by using the same key as for enciphering, but with the schedule of addressing the key bits altered so that the deciphering process is the reverse of the enciphering process. A block to be enciphered is subjected to an initial permutation **IP**, then to a complex key-dependent computation and finally to a permutation which is the inverse of the initial permutation $\mathbf{IP^{-1}}$. The key-dependent computation can be simply defined in terms of a function ***f***, called the cipher function, and a function **KS**, called the key schedule. A description of the computation is given first, along with details as to how the algorithm is used for encipherment. Next, the use of the algorithm for decipherment is described. Finally, a definition of the cipher function ***f*** is given in terms of primitive functions which are called the selection functions $\mathbf{S_i}$ and the permutation function **P**.

The following notation is convenient: Given two blocks **L** and **R** of bits, **LR** denotes the block consisting of the bits of **L** followed by the bits of **R**. Since concatenation is associative, B_1, B_2, ..., B_8, for example, denotes the block consisting of the bits of B_1 followed by the bits of B_2...followed by the bits of B_8.

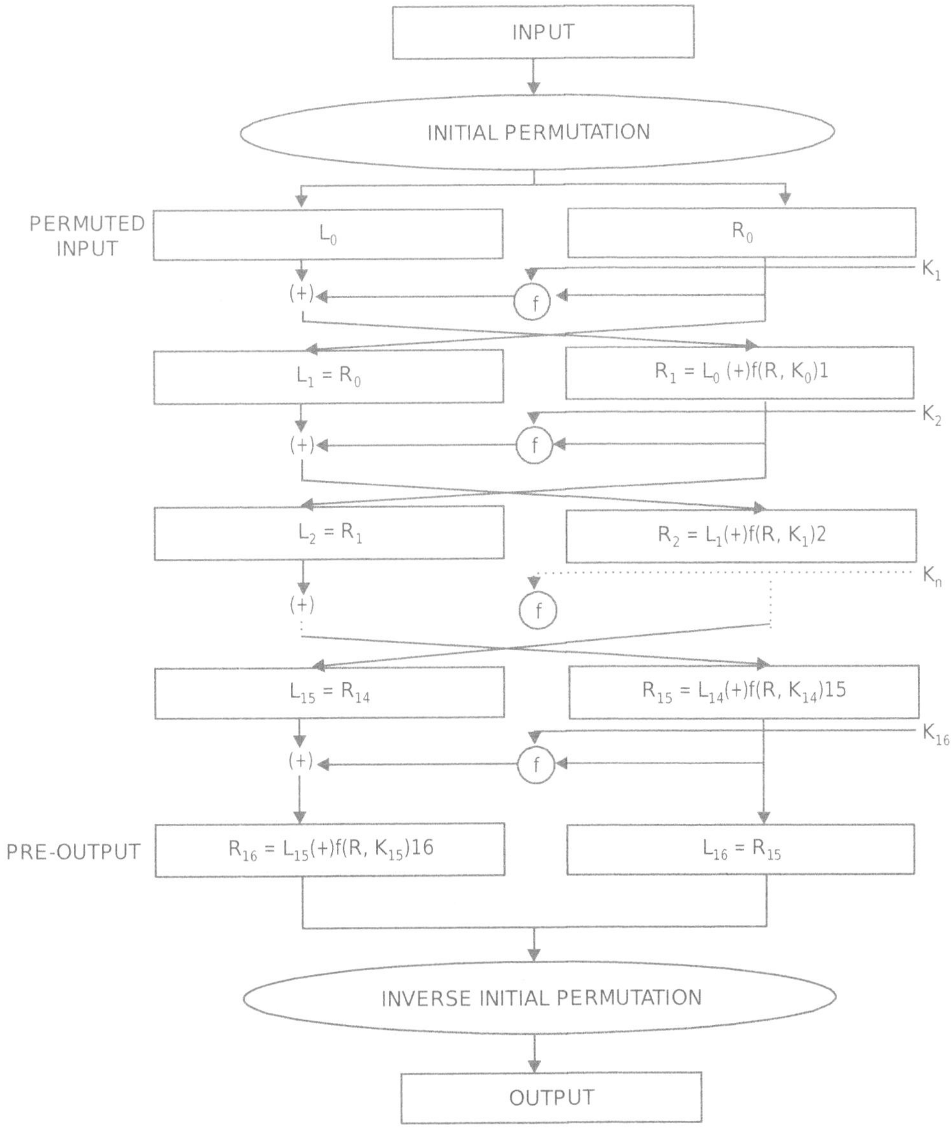

Fig. 3.1. *Enciphering computation.*

3.2.1 Enciphering

A sketch of the enciphering computation is given in Fig. 3.1.

The 64-bits of the input block to be enciphered are first subjected to the following permutation, called the initial permutation **IP**:

IP^{-1}

58	50	42	34	26	18	10	2
60	52	44	36	28	20	12	4
62	54	46	38	30	22	14	6
64	56	48	40	32	24	16	8
57	49	41	33	25	17	9	1
59	51	43	35	27	19	11	3
61	53	45	37	29	21	13	5
63	55	47	39	31	23	15	7

That is the permuted input has bit 58 of the input as its first bit, bit 50 as its second bit, and so on with bit 7 as its last bit. The permuted input block is then the input to a complex key-dependent computation described below. The output of that computation, called the pre output, is then subjected to the following permutation which is the inverse of the initial permutation:

IP^{-1}

40	8	48	16	56	24	64	32
39	7	47	15	55	23	63	31
38	6	46	14	54	22	62	30
37	5	45	13	53	21	61	29
36	4	44	12	52	20	60	28
35	3	43	11	51	19	59	27
34	2	42	10	50	18	58	26
33	1	41	9	49	17	57	25

That is, the output of the algorithm has bit 40 of the pre output block as its first bit, bit 8 as its second bit, and so on, until bit 25 of the pre output block is the last bit of the output.

The computation which uses the permuted input block as its input to produce the pre output block consists, but for a final interchange of blocks, of 16 iterations of a calculation that is described below in terms of the cipher function ***f*** which operates on two blocks, one of 32-bits and one of 48-bits, and produces a block of 32-bits.

Let the 64-bits of the input block to an iteration consist of a 32-bit block **L** followed by a 32-bit block **R**. Using the notation defined in the introduction, the input block is then **LR**.

Let **K** be a block of 48-bits chosen from the 64-bit key. Then the output L′R′ of an iteration with input **LR** is defined by:

$$\begin{aligned} L' &= R \\ R' &= L(+)f(R,K) \end{aligned} \quad \text{...(1)}$$

where (+) denotes bit-by-bit addition modulo 2.

As remarked before, the input of the first iteration of the calculation is the permuted input block. If **L′R′** is the output of the 16th iteration then R′L′ is the preoutput block. At each iteration a different block **K** of key bits is chosen from the 64-bit key designated by **KEY**.

With more notation we can describe the iterations of the computation in more detail. Let **KS** be a function which takes an integer n in the range from 1 to 16 and a 64-bit block **KEY** as input and yields as output a 48-bit block $\mathbf{K_n}$ which is a permuted selection of bits from **KEY**. That is

$$K_n = KS(n, KEY) \qquad ...(2)$$

with $\mathbf{K_n}$ determined by the bits in 48 distinct bit positions of **KEY. KS** is called the key schedule because the block K used in the nth iteration of (1) is the block $\mathbf{K_n}$ determined by (2).

As before, let the permuted input block be **LR**. Finally, let $\mathbf{L_0}$ and $\mathbf{R_0}$ be respectively **L** and **R** and let L_n and R_n be respectively L′ and R′ of (1) when L and R are respectively $\mathbf{L_{n-1}}$ and $\mathbf{R_{n-1}}$ and **K** is $\mathbf{K_n}$; that is, when n is in the range from 1 to 16,

$$\begin{aligned} L_n &= R_{n-1} \\ R_n n &= L_{n-1} (+) f(R_{n-1}, K_n) \end{aligned} \qquad ...(3)$$

The pre output block is then RL.

The key schedule **KS** of the algorithm is described in detail in the Appendix. The key schedule produces the 16 $\mathbf{K_n}$ which are required for the algorithm.

3.2.2 Deciphering

The permutation $\mathbf{IP^{-1}}$ applied to the pre output block is the inverse of the initial permutation **IP** applied to the input. Further, from (1) it follows that:

$$\begin{aligned} R &= L' \\ L &= R' \quad (+) \quad f(L', K) \end{aligned} \qquad ...(4)$$

Consequently, to **decipher** it is only necessary to apply the **very same algorithm to an enciphered message block,** taking care that at each iteration of the computation **the same block of key bits K is used** during decipherment as was used during the encipherment of the block. Using the notation of the previous section, this can be expressed by the equations:

$$\begin{aligned} R_{n-1} &= L_n \\ L_{n-1} &= R_n \quad (+) \quad f(L_n, K_n) \end{aligned} \qquad ...(5)$$

where now $\mathbf{R_{16}L_{16}}$ is the permuted input block for the deciphering calculation and $\mathbf{L_0}$ and $\mathbf{R_0}$ is the preoutput block. That is, for the decipherment calculation with $\mathbf{R_{16}L_{16}}$ as the permuted input, $\mathbf{K_{16}}$ is used in the first iteration, $\mathbf{K_{15}}$ in the second, and so on, with $\mathbf{K_1}$ used in the 16th iteration.

3.2.3 The Cipher Function *f*

A sketch of the calculation of ***f*(R, K)** is given in **Fig. 3.2.**

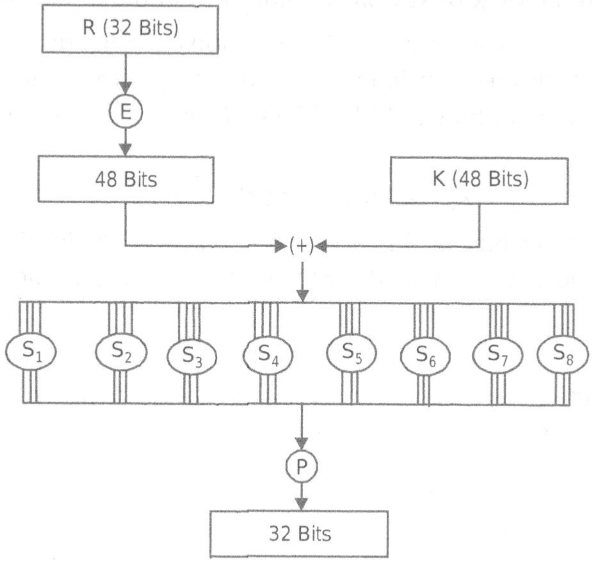

Fig. 3.2. *Calculation of f(R, K).*

Let **E** denote a function which takes a block of 32-bits as input and yields a block of 48-bits as output. Let **E** be such that the 48-bits of its output, written as 8 blocks of 6-bits each, are obtained by selecting the bits in its inputs in order according to the following table:

Table: ***E*** **BIT-SELECTION**

32	1	2	3	4	5
4	5	6	7	8	9
8	9	10	11	12	13
12	13	14	15	16	17
16	17	18	19	20	21
20	21	22	23	24	25
24	25	26	27	28	29
28	29	30	31	32	1

Thus the first three bits of **E(R)** are the bits in positions 32, 1 and 2 of **R** while the last 2 bits of **E(R)** are the bits in positions 32 and 1. Each of the unique selection functions $\mathbf{S_1}$, $\mathbf{S_2}$, ..., $\mathbf{S_8}$, takes a 6-bit block as input and yields a 4-bit block as output and is illustrated by using a table containing the recommended $\mathbf{S_1}$:

S_1

Row No.	Column Number															
	0	1	2	3	4	5	6	7	8	9	10	11	12	13	14	15
0	14	4	13	1	2	15	11	8	3	10	6	12	5	9	0	7
1	0	15	7	4	14	2	13	1	10	6	12	11	9	5	3	8
2	4	1	14	8	13	6	2	11	15	12	9	7	3	10	5	0
3	15	12	8	2	4	9	1	7	5	11	3	14	10	0	6	13

If $\mathbf{S_1}$ is the function defined in this table and **B** is a block of 6-bits, then $\mathbf{S_1(B)}$ is determined as follows: The first and last bits of **B** represent in base 2 a number in the range 0 to 3. Let that number be *i*. The middle 4-bits of **B** represent in base 2 a number in the range 0 to 15. Let that number be *j*. Look up in the table the number in the *i*th row and *j*th column. It is a number in the range 0 to 15 and is uniquely represented by a 4-bit block. That block is the output $\mathbf{S_1(B)}$ of $\mathbf{S_1}$ for the input **B.** For example, for input 011011 the row is 01, that is row 1, and the column is determined by 1101, that is column 13. In row 1 column 13 appears 5 so that the output is 0101.

The permutation function P yields a 32-bit output from a 32-bit input by permuting the bits of the input block. Such a function is defined by the following table:

P

16	7	20	21
29	12	28	17
1	15	23	26
5	18	31	10
2	8	24	14
32	27	3	9
19	13	30	6
22	11	4	25

The output **P(L)** for the function **P** defined by this table is obtained from the input **L** by taking the 16th bit of **L** as the first bit of **P(L),** the 7th bit as the second bit of **P(L),** and so on until the 25th bit of **L** is taken as the 32nd bit of **P(L).** The permutation function P of the algorithm is repeated in the Appendix.

Now let $\mathbf{S_1, ..., S_8}$ be eight distinct selection functions, let **P** be the permutation function and let E be the function defined above.

To define ***f*(R, K)** we first define $\mathbf{B_1, ..., B_8}$ to be blocks of 6-bits each for which

$$B_1, B_2, ..., B_8 = K(+)E(R) \qquad ...(6)$$

The block *f*(R, K) **is then defined to be**

$$P(S_1(B_1)S_2(B_2)...S_8(B_8)) \qquad ...(7)$$

Thus **K(+)E(R)** is first divided into the 8 blocks as indicated in (6). Then each $\mathbf{B_i}$ is taken as an input to $\mathbf{S_i}$ and the 8 blocks $\mathbf{(S_1(B_1)S_2(B_2)...S_8(B_8)}$ of 4 bits each are consolidated into a single block of 32 bits which forms the input to **P.** The output (7) is then the output of the function ***f*** for the inputs **R** and **K.**

3.2.4. Primitive Functions for the Data Encryption Algorithm

The choice of the primitive functions **KS,** $\mathbf{S_1,...,S_8}$ and **P** is critical to the strength of an encipherment resulting from the algorithm. Specified below is the recommended set of functions, describing $\mathbf{S_1,...,S_8}$ and **P** in the same way they are described in the algorithm. For the interpretation of the tables describing these functions, see the discussion in the body of the algorithm.

The primitive functions $\mathbf{S_1,...,S_8}$ are:

S_1

14	4	13	1	2	15	11	8	3	10	5	12	5	9	0	7
0	15	7	4	14	2	13	1	10	6	12	11	9	5	3	8
4	1	14	8	13	6	2	11	15	12	9	7	3	10	5	0
15	12	8	2	4	9	1	7	5	11	3	14	10	0	6	13

S_2

15	1	8	14	6	11	3	4	9	7	2	13	12	0	5	10
3	13	4	7	15	2	8	14	12	0	1	10	6	9	11	5
0	14	7	11	10	4	13	1	5	8	12	6	9	3	2	15
13	8	10	1	3	15	4	2	11	6	7	12	0	5	14	9

S_3

10	0	9	14	6	3	15	5	1	13	12	7	11	4	2	8
13	7	0	9	3	4	6	10	2	8	5	14	12	11	15	1
13	6	4	9	8	15	3	0	11	1	2	12	5	10	14	7
1	10	13	0	6	9	8	7	4	15	14	3	11	5	2	12

S_4

7	13	14	3	0	6	9	10	1	2	8	5	11	12	4	15
13	8	11	5	6	15	0	3	4	7	2	12	1	10	14	9
10	6	9	0	12	11	7	13	15	1	3	14	5	2	8	4
3	15	0	6	10	1	13	8	9	4	5	11	12	7	2	14

S_5

2	12	4	1	7	10	11	6	8	5	3	15	13	0	14	9
14	11	2	12	4	7	13	1	5	0	15	10	3	9	8	6
4	2	1	11	10	13	7	8	15	9	12	5	6	3	0	14
11	8	12	7	1	14	2	13	6	15	0	9	10	4	5	3

S_6

12	1	10	15	9	2	6	8	0	13	3	4	14	7	5	11
10	15	4	2	7	12	9	5	6	1	13	14	0	11	3	8
9	14	15	5	2	8	12	3	7	0	4	10	1	13	11	6
4	3	2	12	9	5	15	10	11	14	1	7	6	0	8	13

S_7

4	11	2	14	15	0	8	13	3	12	9	7	5	10	6	1
13	0	11	7	4	9	1	10	14	3	5	12	2	15	8	6
1	4	11	13	12	3	7	14	10	15	6	8	0	5	9	2
6	11	13	8	1	4	10	7	9	5	0	15	14	2	3	12

S_8

13	2	8	4	6	15	11	1	10	9	3	14	5	0	12	7
1	15	13	8	10	3	7	4	12	5	6	11	0	14	9	2
7	11	4	1	9	12	14	2	0	6	10	13	15	3	5	8
2	1	14	7	4	10	8	13	15	12	9	0	3	5	6	11

The primitive function P **is:**

16	7	20	21
29	12	28	17
1	15	23	26
5	18	31	10
2	8	24	14
32	27	3	9
19	13	30	6
22	11	4	25

Recall that $\mathbf{K_n}$, for $1 <= n <= 16$, is the block of 48-bits in (2) of the algorithm.

Hence, to describe **KS,** it is sufficient to describe the calculation of $\mathbf{K_n}$ from **KEY** for $n = 1, 2, \ldots, 16$. That calculation is illustrated in **Fig. 3.3.** To complete the definition of **KS** it is therefore sufficient to describe the two permuted choices, as well as the schedule of left shifts. One bit in each 8-bit byte of the **KEY** may be utilized for error detection in key generation, distribution and storage. Bits 8, 16,..., 64 are for use in assuring that each byte is of odd parity. Permuted choice 1 is determined by the following table:

PC-1

57	49	41	33	25	17	9
1	58	50	42	34	26	18
10	2	59	51	43	35	27
19	11	3	60	52	44	36
63	55	47	39	31	23	15
7	62	54	46	38	30	22
14	6	61	53	45	37	29
21	13	5	28	20	12	4

The table has been divided into two parts, with the first part determining how the bits of $\mathbf{C_0}$ are chosen, and the second part determining how the bits of $\mathbf{D_0}$ are chosen. The bits of **KEY** are numbered 1 through 64. The bits of $\mathbf{C_0}$ are respectively bits 57, 49, 41,..., 44 and 36 of **KEY,** with the bits of $\mathbf{D_0}$ being bits 63, 55, 47,..., 12 and 4 of **KEY.**

With $\mathbf{C_0}$ and $\mathbf{D_0}$ defined, we now define how the blocks $\mathbf{C_n}$ and $\mathbf{D_n}$ are obtained from the blocks $\mathbf{C_{n-1}}$ and $\mathbf{D_{n-1}}$, respectively, for $n = 1, 2,..., 16$. That is accomplished by adhering to the following schedule of left shifts of the individual blocks:

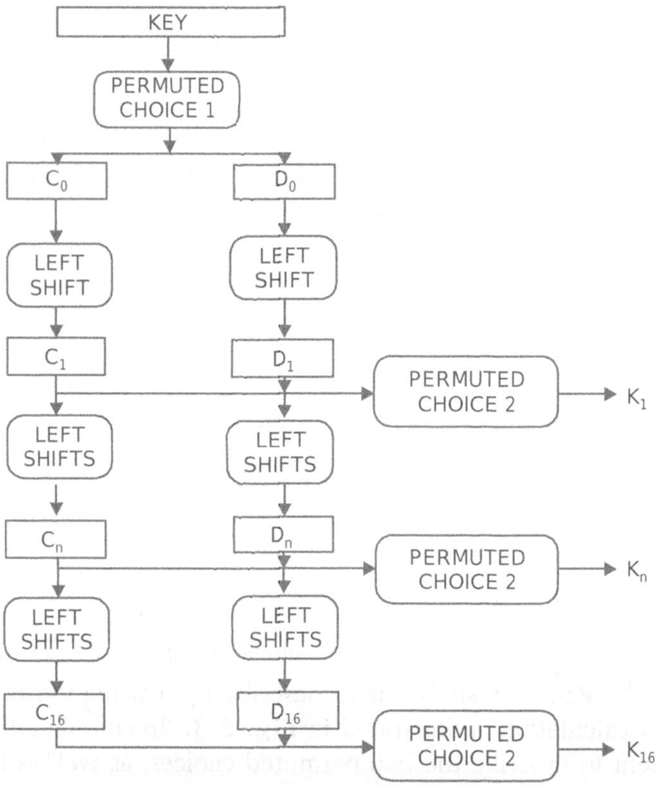

Fig. 3.3. *Key schedule calculation.*

Iteration Number	Number of Left Shifts
1	1
2	1
3	2
4	2
5	2
6	2
7	2
8	2
9	1
10	2
11	2
12	2
13	2
14	2
15	2
16	1

For example, $\mathbf{C}_3$ and $\mathbf{D}_3$ are obtained from $\mathbf{C}_2$ and $\mathbf{D}_2$, respectively, by two left shifts, and $\mathbf{C}_{16}$ and $\mathbf{D}_{16}$ are obtained from $\mathbf{C}_{15}$ and $\mathbf{D}_{15}$, respectively, by one left shift. In all cases, by a single left shift is meant a rotation of the bits one place to the left, so that after one left shift the bits in the 28 positions are the bits that were previously in positions 2, 3, ..., 28, 1.

Permuted choice 2 is determined by the following table:

PC-2

14	17	11	24	1	5
3	28	15	6	21	10
23	19	12	4	26	8
16	7	27	20	13	2
41	52	31	37	47	55
30	40	51	45	33	48
44	49	39	56	34	53
46	42	50	36	29	32

Therefore, the first bit of $\mathbf{K}_n$ is the 14th bit of $\mathbf{C}_n\mathbf{D}_n$, the second bit the 17th, and so on with the 47th bit the 29th, and the 48th bit the 32nd.

The Avalance Effect in DES

1 bit change in the plaintext leads to 34-bit difference in the ciphertext. 1 bit change in the key leads to 35-bit difference in the ciphertext.

3.3 THE STRENGTH OF DES

DES proved insecure in July 1998, when the Electronic Frontier Foundation (EFF) announced that it had broken a DES encryption using a special-purpose "DES cracker" machine that was built for less than \$250 000. The attack took less than 3 days.

Design criteria for S-boxes were not made public, so there was a concern that cryptanalysis is possible for an opponent who knows the weaknesses in S-boxes. Up to now, there are no published results about such weaknesses in S-boxes.

DES also appears to be resistant to timing attack but suggest some avenues to explore. Timing attack tries to understand essence of algorithm by analysis of time of its work on different inputs. One of such approaches yields a Hamming weight (number of bits equal to 1) of the secret key.

3.4 DIFFERENTIAL AND LINEAR CRYPTANALYSIS

Differential cryptanalysis attack is first published attack that is capable of breaking DES in less than 2^{55} complexity. The scheme can successfully cryptanalyze DES with an effort of the order of 2^{47}, requiring 2^{47} chosen plaintexts. Idea is to follow differences in 2 plaintexts in the rounds of DES transformations, and to estimate probability of the output difference depending on the used key. The first open publication on the differential cryptanalysis was in 1990.

Linear cryptanalysis was described in 1993. Idea is to find linear equation (with XOR operations) between bits of plaintext, ciphertext and key that holds with probability greater than 0.5.

3.5 BLOCK CIPHER DESIGN PRINCIPLES

As block cipher have different modes of operation (we will discuss this topic later in this lecture) and of applications than stream cipher.

A block cipher transform a plaintext block of n letters into an encrypted block. For the alphabet with 26 letters, there are $26n$ possible different plaintext blocks. The most general way of encrypting a n-letter block is to take each of the plaintext blocks and map it to a cipher block (arbitrary n-letter substitution cipher). For decryption to be possible, such mapping needs to be one-to-one (*i.e.*, each plaintext block must be mapped to a unique ciphertext block). The number of different one-to-one mappings among n-letter blocks is $(26n)!$.

The length of block n cannot be too short in order to secure the cryptographic scheme. For example, $n = 1$ gives a monoalphabetic cipher. Such schemes, as we have seen, are vulnerable to frequency analysis and brute-force attacks. However, an arbitrary reversible substitution cipher for a large block size n is not practical. Let's consider the problem of specifying a mapping of all possible n-letter blocks. In a cipher, each key specifies such a mapping. Let's assume the key consists of a block of k letters. Then the number of all possible keys is 26*k*. Then for a *n*-letter arbitrary substitution block cipher, the key size needs to satisfy 26*k* _ (26*n*)!, *i.e.*, *k* _ *n* × 26*n*!.

So the major challenge to design a symmetric key cryptographic scheme is to provide enough security (*e.g.*, using a reasonable large block size) with a reasonable small size key.

However, how do we know that a cryptographic system is secure enough? To answer this question, Claude Shannon theoretically deduced the following principles that should be followed to design secure cryptographic systems. These principles aim at thwarting cryptanalysis based on known statistical properties of the plaintext.

Confusion. In Shannon's original definitions, confusion makes the relation between the key and the ciphertext as complex as possible. Ideally, every letter in the key influences every letter of the ciphertext block. Replacing every letter with the one next to it on the typewriter keyboard is a simple example of confusion by substitution. However, good confusion can only be achieved when each character of the ciphertext depends on several parts of the key, and this dependence appears to be random to the observer. Ciphers that do not offer much confusion (such as Vigen'ere cipher) are vulnerable to frequency analysis.

Diffusion. Diffusion refers to the property that the statistics structure of the plaintext is dissipated into long range statistics of the ciphertext. In contrast to confusion, diffusion spreads the influence of a single plaintext letter over many ciphertext letters. In terms of the frequency statistics of letters, digrams, etc in the plaintext, diffusion randomly spreads them across several characters in the ciphertext. This means that much more ciphertexts are needed to do a meaningful statistical attack on the cipher.

3.6 DES DESIGN CRITERIA

1. No output of any S-box should be too close a linear function of the input bits.
2. Each row of an S-box should include all 16 possible output combinations
3. If two inputs to an S-box differ in exactly 1 bit, the outputs must differ in at least 2 bits.
4. If 2 inputs to an S-box differ in the 2 middle bits exactly, the outputs must differ in at least 2 bits.
5. If 2 inputs to an S-box differ in their first 2 bits and are identical in their last 2 bits, the 2 outputs must not be the same
6. For any nonzero 6-bit difference between inputs, no more than 8 of the 32 pairs of inputs exhibiting that difference may result in the same output difference.

These criteria are intended to increase confusion properties.

The criteria for the permutation P are as follows:

The 4 output bits from each S-box at round I are distributed so that 2 of them affect (provide input for) "middle bits" of round (I+1) and the other 2 affect end bits. The 2 middle bits of input to an S-box are not shared by adjacent S-boxes. The end bits are the 2 left-hand bits and the 2 right-hand bits which are shared with adjacent S-boxes (for example, bits 1, 2, 3, 4 – outputs of S_1, affect on bits 9, 17 (end-bits) and 23, 31 (middle-bits) respectively.

1. The 4 output bits from each S-box affect 6 different S-boxes on the next round, and no 2 affect the same S-box (for example, bits 1, 2, 3, 4 – outputs of S_1, affect (S_2, S_3) – bit 1, (S_4, S_5) – bit 2, S_6 – bit 3, S_8 – bit 4.
2. For 2 S-boxes *j, k,* if an output bit from S_j affects a middle bit of S_k on the next round, then an output bit from S_k cannot affect a middle bit of S_j. This implies that for $j = k$, an output bit from S_j must not affect a middle bit of S_j. For example, output bit 3 of S_1 affects middle bit of S_6. Then we are to have that output bits of S_6 are not to affect middle bits of S_1. Output bits of S_6 are 21, 22, 23, 24. Bit 21 affects bit 4 – end bit of S_1, S_2; bit 22 affects bit 29 – end bit of S_7, S_8; bit 23 affects bit 11 – middle bit of S_3; bit 24 affects bit 19 – middle bit of S_5. So, middle bits of S_1 are not affected by output bits of S_6.

These criteria are intended to increase diffusion properties.

Number of rounds: The greater this number, the more difficult is cryptanalysis. If DES had 15 or less rounds, differential cryptanalysis would require less effort than brute-force attack.

Function F should be nonlinear, provide avalanche effect. Also, bit independence criterion is used: output bits j and k should change independently when any single bit I is inverted, for all *i, j, k.*

Size of S-boxes: Larger size – more resistant to differential and linear cryptanalysis. S-boxes may be made randomly or according to mathematical rules automatically. Contents of S-boxes may depend on the key.

Key schedule algorithm: No general principles for this have yet been promulgated. Key schedule (production of subkeys) should guarantee key/ciphertext avalanche criterion and bit independence criterion.

3.6.1 Block Cipher Modes of Operation

Four DES modes of operations have been defined:

Mode	*Description*	*Typical application*
Electronic Codebook (ECB)	Each block of 64 plaintext bits is encoded independently using the same key.	Secure transmission of single values (*e.g.*, an encryption key).
Cipher Block Chaining (CBC)	The input to the encryption algorithm is the XOR of the next 64 bits of the plaintext and the preceding 64-bits of the ciphertext.	General-purpose block-oriented transmission Authentication
Cipher Feedback (CFB)	Input is processed s bits at a time. Preceding ciphertext is used as input to the encryption algorithm to produce pseudorandom output, which is XORed with plaintext to produce next unit of ciphertext.	General-purpose stream-oriented transmission Authentication

Output Feedback (OFB)	Similar to CFB, except that the input to the encryption algorithm is the preceding DES output.	Stream-oriented transmission over noisy channel (*e.g.*, satellite communication)
Counter (CTR)	Each block of plaintext is XORed with an encrypted counter. The counter is incremented for each subsequent block.	General-purpose block-oriented transmission. Useful for high-speed requirements

3.6.2 Electronic Codebook Mode

It may be considered that each 64-bit plaintext is mapped to respective 64-bit ciphertext, and each such possible pair represents 1 page of the codebook.

For lengthy messages ECB mode may be not secure. If the message has repetitive elements with a period of repetition a multiple of 64-bits, then these elements can be identified by the analyst.

3.6.3 Cipher Block Chaining Code

We need that same plaintext block, if repeated, produces different ciphertext blocks. The simple way is CBC mode:

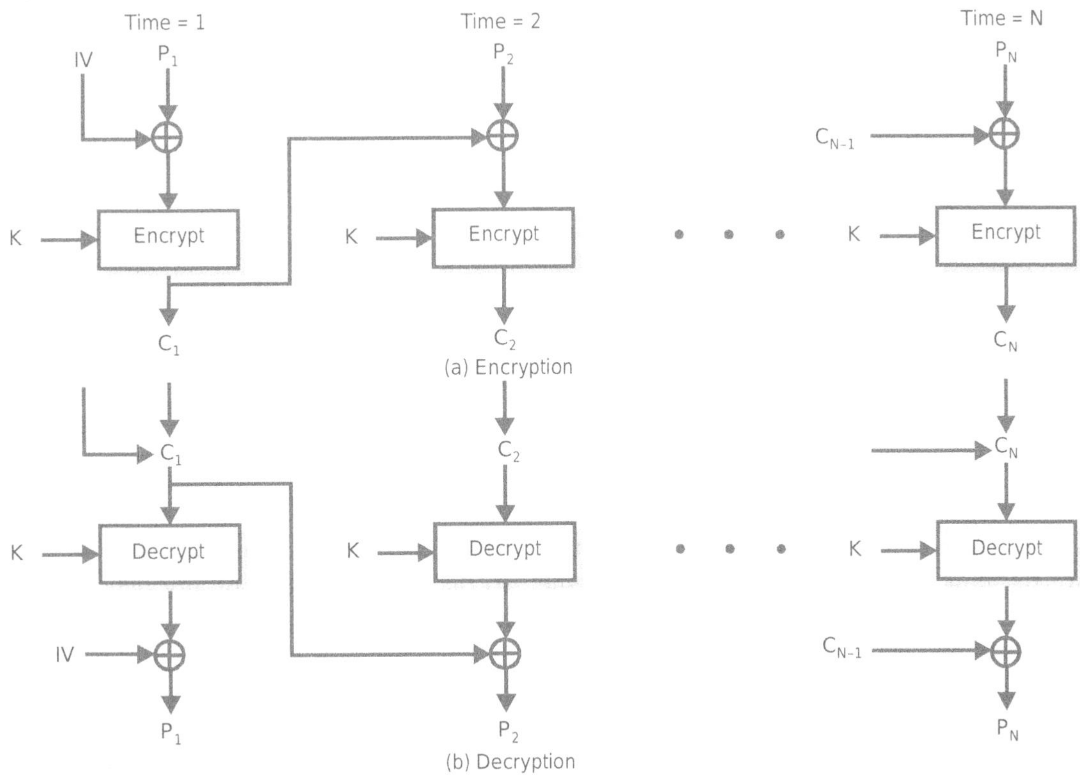

Fig. 3.4. *Figure cipher block chaining (CBC) mode.*

Here IV- Initialization Vector – must be known to both sender and receiver.

3.6.4 Cipher Feedback Mode

DES is a block cipher, but it may be used as a stream cipher if to use the Cipher Feedback (CFB) Mode or the Output Feedback (OFB) Mode. A stream cipher eliminates the need to pad a message to be an integral number of blocks. It also can operate in real time. Thus, if a character stream is being transmitted, each character can be encrypted and transmitted immediately using a character-oriented stream cipher.

CFB scheme follows:

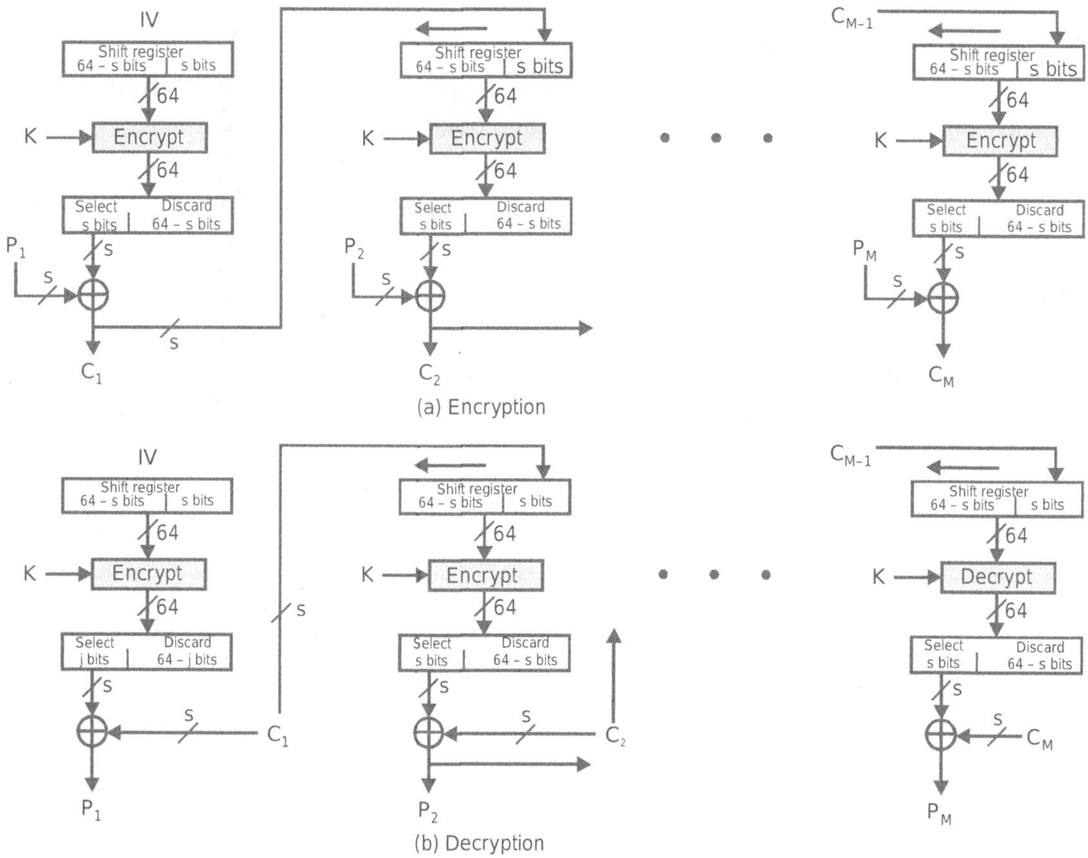

Fig. 3.5. *s-bit cipher feedback (CFB) mode.*

In Fig. 3.5. It is assumed that the unit of transmission is s bits; usually, s=8. As with CBC, the units of plaintext are chained together, so that the ciphertext of any plaintext unit is a function of all the preceding plaintext. In this case, rather than units of 64 bits, the plaintext is divided into segments of s bits.

Consider encryption, the input to the encryption function is a 64-bit shift register that is initially set to some initialization vector (IV). The leftmost (most significant) s bits of the output of the encryption function are XORed with the first segment of plaintext P_1 to produce the first unit of ciphertext C_1, which is then transmitted. In addition, the contents of the shift register are shifted left by s bits and C_1 is placed in the rightmost (least significant) s bits of the shift register. This process continues until all plaintext units have been encrypted.

For decryption, the same scheme is used except that the received ciphertext unit is XORed with the output of the encryption function to produce the plaintext unit.

3.6.5 Output Feedback Mode

The Output Feedback (OFB) Mode is similar in structure to that of CFB:

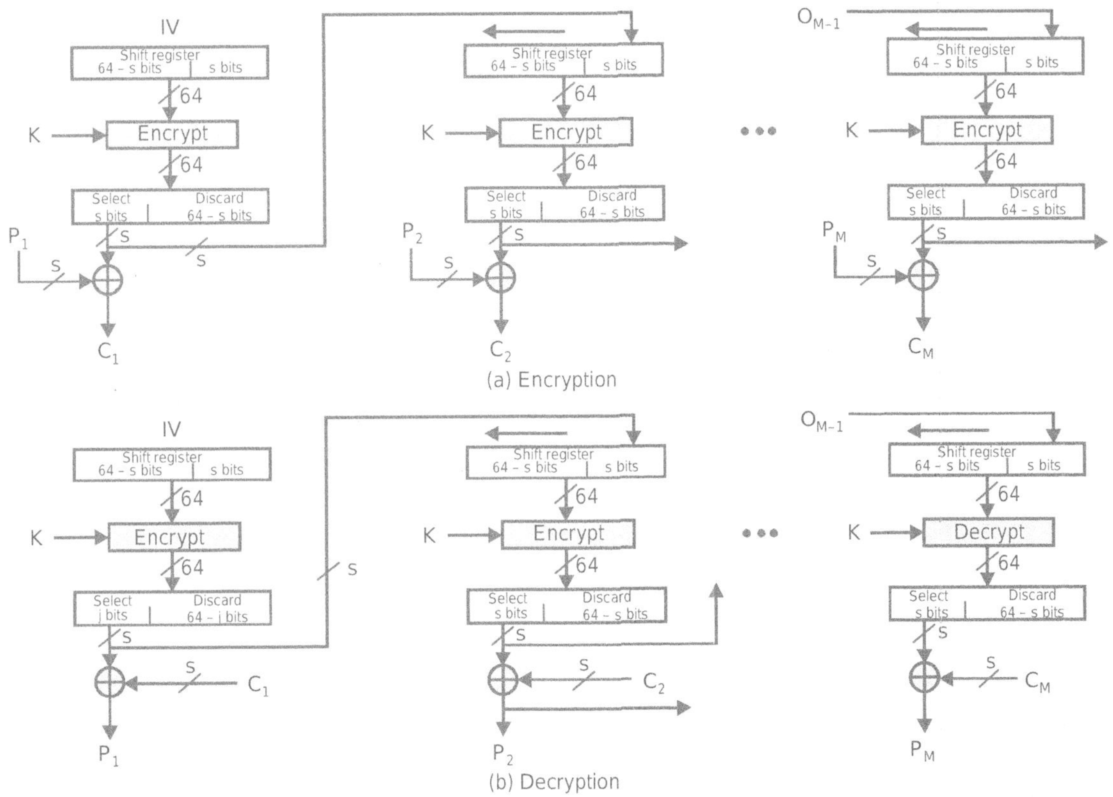

Fig. 3.6. *s-bit output feedback (OFB) mode.*

As can be seen, it is the output of the encryption function that is feedback to the shift register in OFB, whereas in CFB the ciphertext unit is feedback to the shift register. One advantage of the OFB method is that bit errors in transmission do not propagate.

3.6.6 Counter Mode

A counter, equal to the plaintext block size is used. The only requirement stated in SP 800–38 A NIST Special Publication 800–38 A, 2001 Edition, Morris Dworkin, Recommendations (for Block Cipher Modes of Operation) is that the counter value must be different for each plaintext block that is encrypted. This mode is with applications to ATM (asynchronous transfer mode) and IPsec (IP security) now-a-days, but it was proposed in 1979.

Counter Mode works as follows:

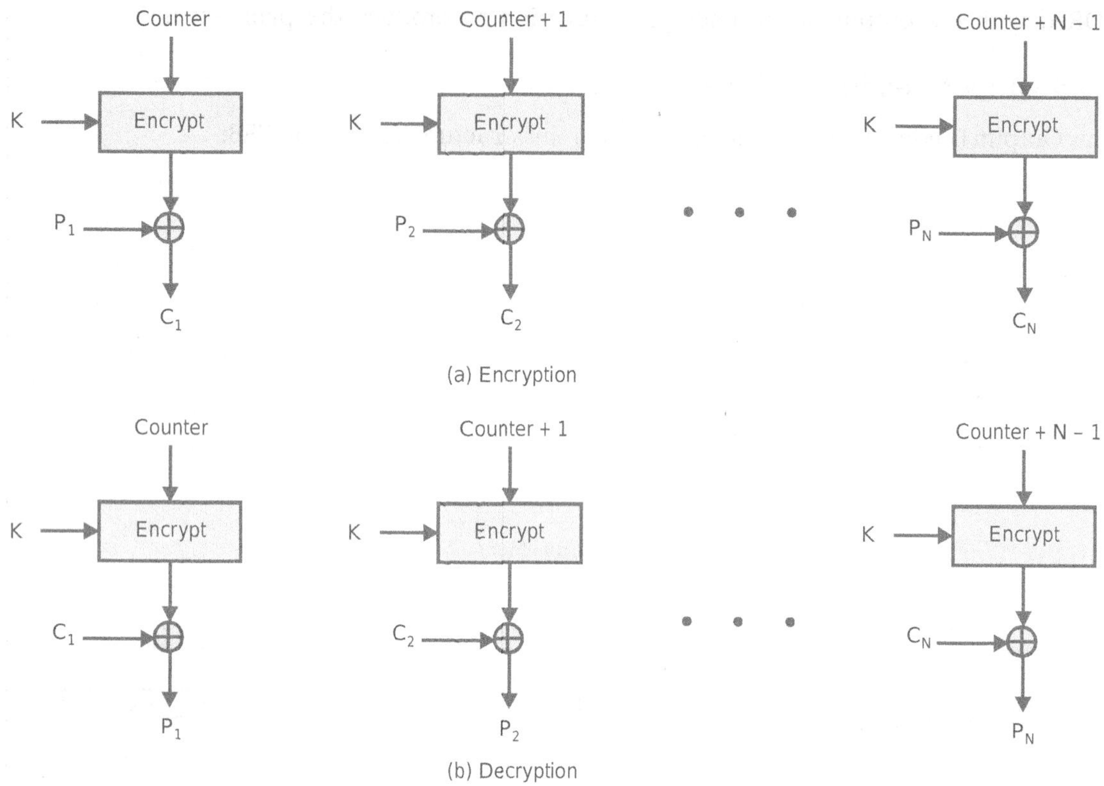

Fig. 3.7. *Counter (CTR) mode.*

Addition is made modulo 2^b, where b is a block size. CTR mode is effective because blocks may be processed in parallel; encryption of keys may be made in advance, and only XOR will be made on-line; only necessary blocks may be decrypted; provides not less security than chaining modes but significantly simpler.

3.7 KEY TERMS, KEY POINTS AND REVIEW QUESTIONS

Key Terms

Avalanche Effect **Block Cipher** **Cipher Block Chaining (CBC) Mode** **Counter Mode (CTR)** **Data Encryption Standard (DES)**	**Differential Cryptanalysis** **Diffusion** **Electronic Code Book (ECB) Mode** **Feistel Ciphering** **Linear Cryptanalysis**	**Permutations** **Product Cipher** **Round** **Round Function** **Sream Cipher** **Subkey**

Key Points

- ➢ The Data Encryption Standard (DES) is a cipher (a method for encrypting information) selected as an official Federal Information Processing Standard (FIPS) for the United States in 1976.
- ➢ Any encryption scheme, there are two inputs to the encryption function 1. Enciphering 2. Deciphering
- ➢ Differential cryptanalysis attack is first published attack that is capable of breaking DES in less than 2^{55} complexity.
- ➢ Diffusion refers to the property that the statistics structure of the plaintext is dissipated into long range statistics of the ciphertext.
- ➢ Confusion makes the relation between the key and the ciphertext as complex as possible.
- ➢ Electronic CodeBook Mode has each 64-bit plaintext is mapped to respective 64-bit ciphertext, and each such possible pair represents 1 page of the codebook.
- ➢ A stream cipher eliminates the need to pad a message to be an integral number of blocks.

Question with Answers *(2 Marks)*

Q. 1. *What is difference between diffusion and confusion?*

Ans. **Diffusion:** The statistical structure of the plaintext is dissipated into long range statistics of the cipher text.

Confusion: Seeks to make a relationship between the statistics of the ciphertext and value of the encryption key as complex as possible.

Q. 2. *What is avalanche effect?*

Ans. The property of any encryption algorithm is that a small change in either the plaintext or the key should produce a significant change in the ciphertext.

Q. 3. *What is a brute force attack?*

Ans. A brute force attack consists of trying every possible code, combination, or password until you find the right one.

Q. 4. *What is DES?*

Ans. The **Data Encryption Standard (DES)** is a cipher (a method for encrypting information) selected as an official Federal Information Processing Standard (FIPS) for the United States in 1976, and which has subsequently enjoyed widespread use internationally. DES utilizes a 56-bit key. This key size is vulnerable to a brute force attack using current technology.

Q. 5. *What are ECB and CBC modes?*

Ans. When we use a block cipher to encrypt a message of arbitrary length, we use techniques that are known as modes of operation for the block cipher.

ECB: Each plaintext block is encrypted independently with the block cipher.

CBC: Each plaintext block is exclusive-Ored with previous ciphertext block, then encrypted.

Q. 6. *Which parameters and design choices determine the actual algorithm of a feistel cipher?*

Ans.
- Block size
- Key size
- Number of rounds
- Sub key generation algorithm
- Round functions.

Review Questions

1. What is enciphering and deciphering is DES?
2. Why is it important to study the Feistel cipher?
3. What is the difference between a block cipher and a stream cipher?
4. What is a product cipher?
5. What is the purpose of the S-boxes in DES?
6. Explain avalanche effect.
7. What is the difference between differential and linear cryptanalysis?
8. Explain in detail the DES?
9. What are the Block Cipher Principles? Explain.

❑❑❑

CHAPTER 4

ADVANCED ENCRYPTION STANDARD

4.1 THE ORIGINS OF AES

The principal drawback of 3DES (which was recommended in 1999, Federal Information Processing Standard FIPS PUB 46-3 as new standard with 168-bit key) is that the algorithm is relatively sluggish in software. A secondary drawback is the use of 64-bit block size. For reasons of both efficiency and security, a larger block size is desirable.

In 1997, National Institute of Standards and Technology NIST issued a call for proposals for a new Advanced Encryption Standard (AES), which should have security strength equal to or better than 3DES, and significantly improved efficiency. In addition, NIST also specified that AES must be a symmetric block cipher with a block length of 128-bits and support for key lengths of 128, 192, and 256-bits.

In a first round of evaluation, 15 proposed algorithms were accepted. A 2nd round narrowed to 5 algorithms. NIST completed its evaluation process and published a final standard (FIPS PUB 197) in November, 2001. NIST selected Rijndael as the proposed AES algorithm. The 2 researches of AES are Dr. Joan Daemon and Dr. Vincent Rijmen from Belgium.

4.1.1 AES Evaluation

Security – 128 minimal key size provides enough security

Cost – AES should have high computational efficiency

4.1.2 AES Evaluation Criteria

- Initial criteria:
  - security – effort for practical cryptanalysis
  - cost – in terms of computational efficiency
  - algorithm and implementation characteristics
- Final criteria
  - general security
  - ease of software and hardware implementation
  - implementation attacks
  - flexibility (in en/decrypt, keying, other factors)

The Origins of AES (Cont 1)

Table 4.1. NIST Evaluation Criteria for AES

SECURITY
• **Actual security:** Compared to other submitted algorithms (at the same key and block size).
• **Randomness:** The extent to which the algorithm output is indistinguishable from a random permutation on the input block.
• **Soundness:** Soundness of the mathematical basis for the algorithm's security.
• **Other security factors:** Raised by the public during the evaluation process, including any attacks which demonstrate that the actual security of the algorithm is less than the strength claimed by the submitter.
COST
• **Licensing requirements:** NIST intends that when the AES is issued, the algorithm(s) specified in the AES shall be available on a worldwide, non-exclusive, royalty-free basis.
• **Computational efficiency:** The evaluation of computational efficiency will be applicable to both hardware and software implementations. Round q analysis by NIST will focus primarily on software implementations and specifically on one key block size combination (128–128); more attention will be paid to hardware implementations and other supported key-block size combinations during Round 2 analysis. Computational efficiency essentially refers to the speed of the algorithm. Public comments on each algorithm's efficiency (particularly for various platforms and applications) will also be taken into consideration by NIST.

- **Memory requirements:** The memory required to implement a candidate algorithm—for both hardware and software implementations of the algorithm—will also be considered during the evaluation process. Round 1 analysis by NIST will focus primarily on software implementations; more attention will be paid to hardware implementations during Round 2. Memory requirements will include such factors as gate counts for hardware implementations, and code size and RAM requirements for software implementations.

Algorithm and implementation characteristics: This includes variety of considerations, including flexibility, suitability for hardware and software implementations, simplicity.

The Origins of AES (Cont 2)

Table 4.2. NIST Algorithm and implementation characteristics

ALGORITHM AND IMPLEMENTATION CHARACTERISTICS

- **Flexibility:** Candidate algorithms with greater flexibility will meet the needs of more users than less flexible ones, and therefore, inter alia, are preferable. However, some extremes of functionality are of little practical application (*e.g.*, extremely short key lengths); for those cases, preference will not be given. Some examples of flexibility may include (but are not limited to) the following:
  (*a*) The algorithm can accommodate additional key—and block-sizes (*e.g.*, 64-bit block sizes, key sizes other than those specified in the Minimum Acceptability Requirements section), (*e.g.*, keys between 128 and 256 that are multiples of 32-bits, etc.)
  (*b*) The algorithm can be implemented securely and efficiently in a wide variety of platforms and applications (*e.g.*, 8-bit processors, ATM networks, voice and satellite communications, HDTV, B-ISDN, etc.).
  (*c*) The algorithm can be implemented as a stream cipher, message authentication code (MAC) generator, pseudorandom number generator, hashing algorithm, etc.
- **Hardware and software suitability:** A candidate algorithm shall not be restrictive in the sense that it can only be implemented in hardware. If one can also implement the algorithm efficiently in firmware, then this will be an advantage in the area of flexibility.
- **Simplicity:** A candidate algorithm shall be judged according to relative simplicity of design.

Additional criteria include: general security, software implementations, restricted-space environments, hardware implementations, attacks on implementation (timing attacks), encryption versus decryption, key agility, flexibility, potential for instruction-level parallelism.

The Origins of AES (Cont 3)

General Security

Rijndael has no known security attacks. Rijndael uses S-boxes as nonlinear components. Rijndael appears to have an adequate security margin, but has received some criticism suggesting that its mathematical structure may lead to attacks. On the other hand, the simple structure may have facilitated its security analysis during the timeframe of the AES development process.

Software Implementations

Rijndael performs encryption and decryption very well across a variety of platforms, including 8-bit and 64-bit platforms, and DSPs. However, there is a decrease in performance with the higher key sizes because of the increased number of rounds that are performed. Rijndael's high inherent parallelism facilitates the efficient use of processor resources, resulting in very good software performance even when implemented in a mode not capable of interleaving, Rijndael's key setup time is fast.

Restricted-Space Environments

In general, Rijndael is very well suited for restricted-space environments where either encryption or decryption is implemented (but not both). It has very low RAM and ROM requirements. A drawback is that ROM requirements will increase if both encryption and decryption are implemented simultaneously, although it appears to remain suitable for these environments. The key schedule for decryption is separate from encryption.

Hardware Implementations

Rijndael has the highest throughout of any of the finalists for feedback modes and second highest for non-feedback modes. For the 192 and 256-bit key sizes, throughput falls in standard and unrolled implementations because of the additional number of rounds. For fully piplined implementations, the area requirement increases, but the throughput is unaffected.

The Origins of AES (Cont 4)

Attacks on Implementations

The operations used by Rijndael are among the easiest to defend against power and timing attacks. The use of masking techniques to provide Rijndael with some defense against these attacks does not cause significant performance degradation relative to the other finalists, and its RAM requirement remains reasonable. Rijndael appears to gain a major speed advantage over its competitors when such protections are considered.

Encryption vs Decryption

The encryption and decryption functions in Rijndael differ. One FPGA study reports that the implementation of both encryption and decryption takes about 60% more space than the implementation of encryption alone. Rijndael's speed does not vary significantly between encryption and decryption, although the key setup performance is slower for decryption than for encryption.

Key Agility

Rijndael supports on-the-fly subkey computation for encryption. Rijndael requires a one-time execution of the key schedule to generate all subkeys prior to the first decryption with a specific key. This places a slight resource burden on the key agility of Rijndael.

Other Versatility and Flexibility

Rijndael fully supports block sizes and key sizes of 128-bits, 192-bits and 256-bits, in any combination. In principle, the Rijndael structure can accommodate any block sizes and key sizes that are multiples of 32, as well as changes in the number of rounds that are specified.

Potential for Instruction-Level Parallelism

Rijndael has an excellent potential for parallelism for a single block encryption.

4.2 OVERALL AES STRUCTURE

The following Fig. 4.1 shows the overall structure of AES.

Several comments about the overall AES Structure:

- data block of 4 columns of 4 bytes is state
- key is expanded to array of words
- has 9/11/13 rounds in which state undergoes:
  - byte substitution (1 S-box used on every byte)
  - shift rows (permute bytes between groups/columns)
  - mix columns (subs using matrix multipy of groups)
  - add round key (XOR state with key material)
  - view as alternating XOR key and scramble data bytes
- initial XOR key material and incomplete last round
- with fast XOR and table lookup implementation

Overall Structure of AES

The input to the encryption and decryption algorithm is a single 128-bit block, this block, in FIPS PUB 197, is depicted as a square matrix of bytes. This block is copied into the State array, which is modified at each stage of encryption or decryption. After the final stage, State is copied to an output matrix. These operations are depicted in Fig. 4.1(*a*).

Similarly, the 128-bit is depicted as a square matrix of bytes. This key is expanded into an array of key schedule words; each word is 4 bytes and the total key schedule is 44 words for the 128-bit key [Fig. 4.1 (*b*)]. Ordering of bytes within a matrix is by column.

Before delving into details, we can make several comments about overall AES structure:

1. This cipher is not a Feistel structure.
2. The key that is provided as input is expanded into an array of 44 words (32-bits each), w[i]. 4 distinct words (128-bits) serve as a round key for each round; these are indicated in Fig. 4.1.
3. 4 different stages are used, 1 permutation and 3 of substitution:
   - Substitute bytes – Uses an S-box to perform a byte-to-byte substitution of the block
   - Shift rows – A simple permutation
   - Mix columns – A substitution that makes use of arithmetic over GF(2^8).
   - Add round key – A simple bitwise XOR of the current block with the portion of the expanded key
4. The structure is quite simple. Fig. 4.2 depicts the structure of a full encryption round.

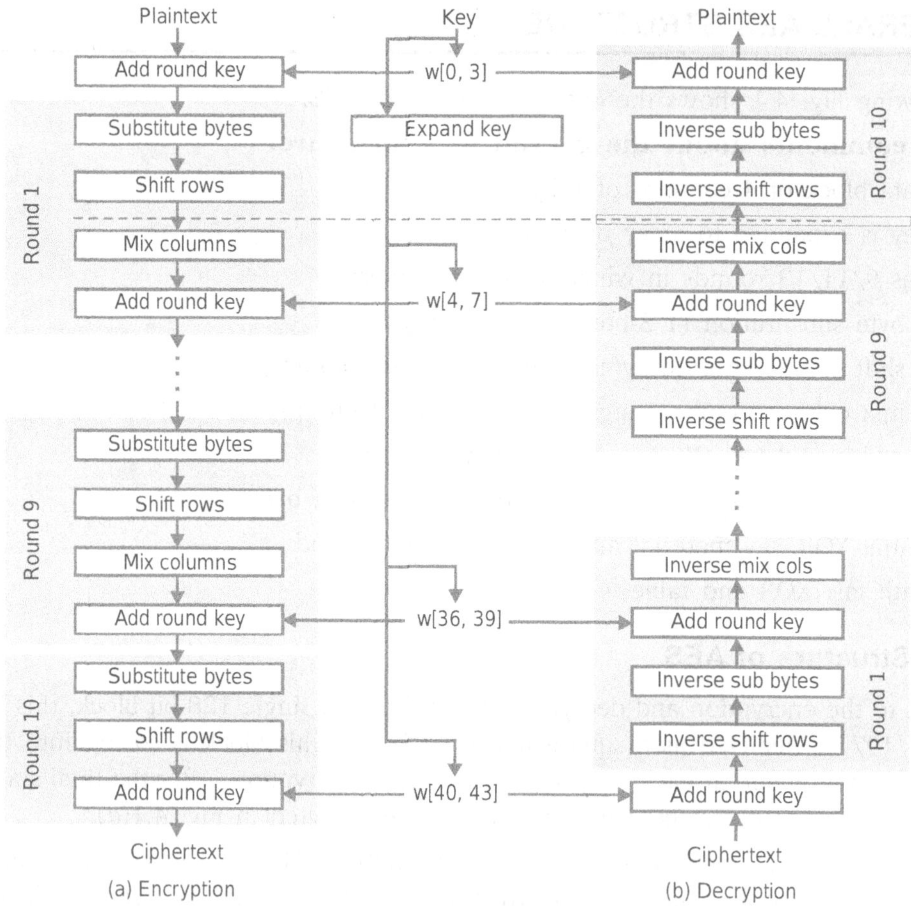

Fig. 4.1. *Overall structure of AES.*

Overall Structure of AES (Cont 1)

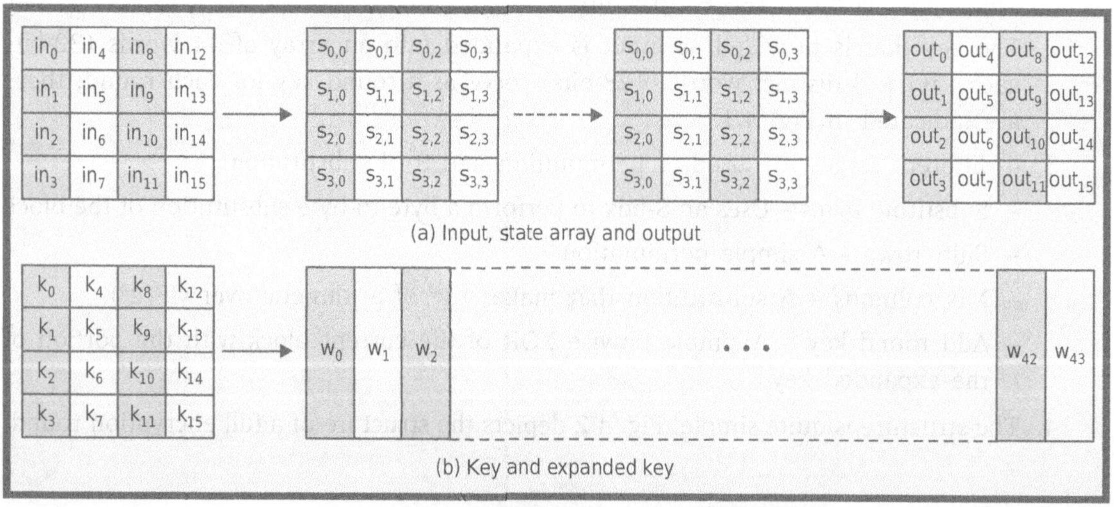

Fig. 4.2 *AES Data structures.*

Overall Structure of AES (Cont 2)

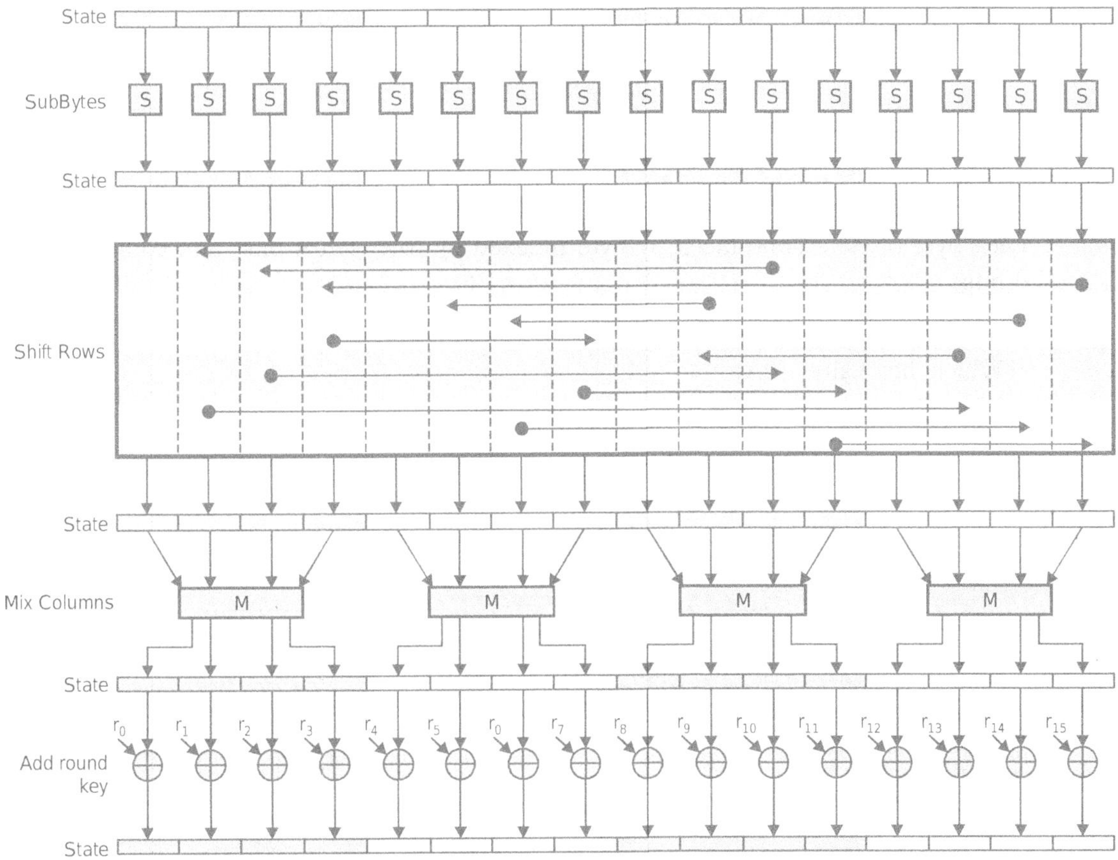

Fig. 4.3. *AES encryption round.*

5. Only the Add Round Key stage uses the key. Any other stage is reversible without knowledge of the key.
6. The Add Round Key is a form of Vernam cipher and by itself would not be formidable. The other 3 stages together provide confusion, diffusion, and nonlinearity, but by themselves would provide no security because they do not use the key. We can view the cipher as alternating operations of XOR encryption (Add Round Key), followed by scrambling of the block.
7. Each stage is easily reversible.
8. Decryption uses the same keys but in the reverse order. Decryption is not identical to encryption.
9. At each horizontal point (*e.g.*, the dashed line) in Fig. 4.2. State is the same for both encryption and decryption.
10. The final round of both encryption and decryption consists of only 3 stages; it is the consequence of the particular structure of AES.

4.2.1 Substitute Byte Transformation

Forward and Inverse Transformation

The forward substitute byte transformation, called SubBytes, is a simple table lookup [Fig. 4.4 (*a*)].

- A simple substitution of each byte
- Uses one table of 16×16 bytes containing a permutation of all 256 8-bit values
- Each byte of state is replaced by byte indexed by row (left 4-bits) and column (right 4-bits)
  - Ex: Byte {95} is replaced by byte in row 9, column 5
  - Which has value {2A}
- S-box constructed using defined transformation of values in GF(28)
- Designed to be resistant to all known attacks

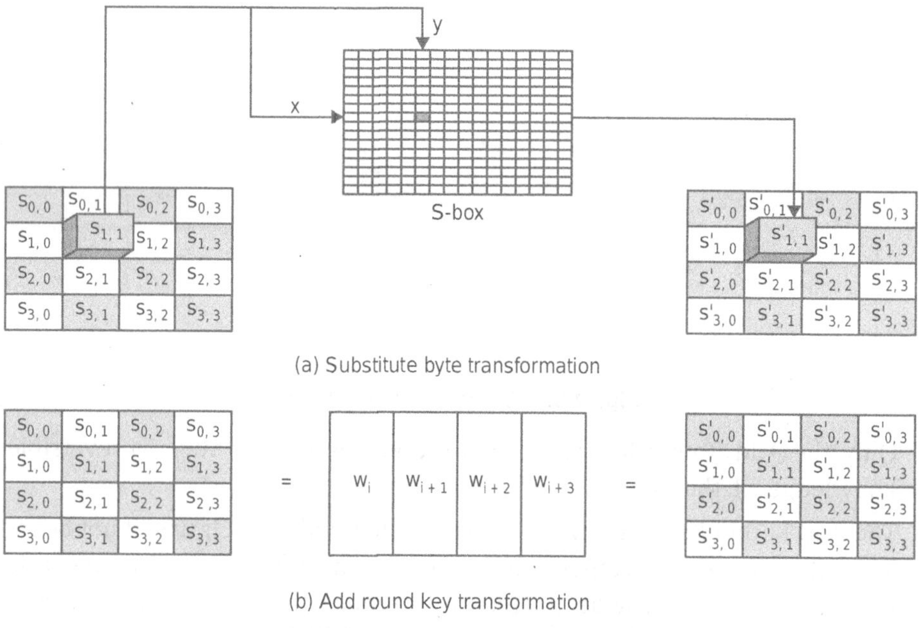

Fig. 4.4. *Substitute byte transformation.*

AES defines a 16×16 matrix of byte values, called an S-box [Table 4.3 (*a*)], that contains a permutation of all possible 256 8-bit values. Each individual byte of State is mapped into a new byte in the following way: The leftmost 4-bits are used as a row value and the rightmost 4-bits are used as a column value. These row and column values serve as indexes into the S-box to select a unique 8-bit output value. For example, the hexadecimal value {95} references row 9, column 5 of the S-box, which contains the value {2*a*}.

Table 4.3. AES S-Boxes

(a) S-box

		y															
		0	1	2	3	4	5	6	7	8	9	A	B	C	D	E	F
x	0	63	7C	77	7B	F2	6B	6F	C5	30	01	67	2B	EF	D7	AB	76
	1	CA	82	C9	7D	FA	59	47	F0	AD	D4	A2	AF	9C	A4	72	C0
	2	B7	FD	93	26	36	3F	F7	CC	34	A5	E5	F1	71	D8	31	15
	3	04	C7	23	C3	18	96	05	9A	07	12	80	E2	EB	27	B2	75
	4	09	83	2C	1A	1B	6E	5A	A0	52	3B	D6	B3	29	E3	2F	84
	5	53	D1	00	ED	20	FC	B1	5B	6A	CB	BE	39	4A	4C	58	CF
	6	D0	EF	AA	FB	43	4D	33	85	45	F9	02	7F	50	3C	9F	A8
	7	51	A3	40	8F	92	9D	38	F5	BC	B6	DA	21	10	FF	F3	D2
	8	CD	0C	13	EC	5F	97	44	17	C4	A7	7E	3D	64	5D	19	73
	9	60	81	4F	DC	22	2A	90	88	46	EE	B8	14	DE	5E	0B	DB
	A	E0	32	3A	0A	49	06	24	5C	C2	D3	AC	62	91	95	E4	79
	B	E7	C8	37	6D	8D	D5	4E	A9	6C	56	F4	EA	65	7A	AE	08
	C	BA	78	25	2E	1C	A6	B4	C6	E8	DD	74	1F	4B	BD	8B	8A
	D	70	3E	B5	66	48	03	F6	03	61	35	57	B9	86	C1	1D	9E
	E	E1	F8	98	11	69	D9	8E	94	9B	1E	87	E9	CE	55	28	DF
	F	8C	A1	89	0D	BF	E6	42	68	41	99	2D	0F	B0	54	BB	16

(b) Inverse S-box

		y															
		0	1	2	3	4	5	6	7	8	9	A	B	C	D	E	F
x	0	52	09	6A	D5	30	36	A5	38	BF	40	A3	9E	81	F3	D7	FB
	1	7C	E3	39	82	9B	2F	FF	87	34	8E	43	44	C4	DE	E9	CB
	2	54	7B	94	32	A6	C2	23	3D	EE	4C	95	0B	42	FA	C3	4E
	3	08	2E	A1	66	28	D9	24	B2	76	5B	A2	49	6D	8B	D1	25
	4	72	F8	F6	64	86	68	98	16	D4	A4	5C	CC	5D	65	B6	92
	5	6C	70	48	50	FD	ED	B9	DA	5E	15	46	57	A7	8D	9D	84
	6	90	D8	AB	00	8C	BC	D3	0A	F7	E4	58	05	B8	B3	45	06
	7	D0	2C	1E	8F	CA	3F	0F	02	C1	AF	BD	03	01	13	8A	6B
	8	3A	91	11	41	4F	67	DC	EA	97	F2	CF	CE	F0	B4	E6	73
	9	96	AC	74	22	E7	AD	35	85	E2	F9	37	E8	1C	75	DF	6E
	A	47	F1	1A	71	1D	29	C5	89	6F	B7	62	0E	AA	18	BE	1B
	B	FC	56	3E	4B	C6	D2	79	20	9A	DB	C0	FE	78	CD	5A	F4
	C	1F	DD	A8	33	88	07	C7	31	B1	12	10	59	27	80	EC	5F
	D	60	51	7F	A9	19	B5	4A	0D	2D	E5	7A	9F	93	C9	9C	EF
	E	A0	E0	3B	4D	AE	2A	F5	B0	C8	EB	BB	3C	83	53	99	61
	F	17	2B	04	7E	BA	77	D6	26	E1	69	14	63	55	21	0C	7D

The S-box is constructed in the following fashion:

1. Initialize the S-box with the byte values in ascending order row-by-row. Thus, the value of the byte at row x, column y is $\{xy\}$.

2. Map each byte in the S-box to its multiplicative inverse in the finite field GF(2^8); the value {00} is mapped to itself.
3. Consider that each byte in the S-box consists of 8-bits labelled ($b7$, $b6$, $b5$, $b4$, $b3$, $b2$, $b1$, $b0$). Apply the following transformation to each bit of each byte in the S-box:

$$b_i' = b_i \oplus b_{(i+4) \bmod 8} \oplus b_{(i+5) \bmod 8} \oplus b_{(i+6) \bmod 8} \oplus b_{(i+7) \bmod 8} \oplus c_i \qquad \text{...(1)}$$

where c_i is the ith bit of byte c with the value {63}, that is ($c7c7c5c4c3c2c1c0$) = (01100011). The prime (′) indicates that the variable is to be updated by the value on the right. The AES standard depicts this transformation in matrix form as follows:

$$\begin{bmatrix} B_0' \\ B_1' \\ B_2' \\ B_3' \\ B_4' \\ B_5' \\ B_6' \\ B_7' \end{bmatrix} = \begin{bmatrix} 1 & 0 & 0 & 0 & 1 & 1 & 1 & 1 \\ 1 & 1 & 0 & 0 & 0 & 1 & 1 & 1 \\ 1 & 1 & 1 & 0 & 0 & 0 & 1 & 1 \\ 1 & 1 & 1 & 1 & 0 & 0 & 0 & 1 \\ 1 & 1 & 1 & 1 & 1 & 0 & 0 & 0 \\ 0 & 1 & 1 & 1 & 1 & 1 & 0 & 0 \\ 0 & 0 & 1 & 1 & 1 & 1 & 1 & 0 \\ 0 & 0 & 0 & 1 & 1 & 1 & 1 & 1 \end{bmatrix} \times \begin{bmatrix} B_0 \\ B_1 \\ B_2 \\ B_3 \\ B_4' \\ B_5 \\ B_6' \\ B_7 \end{bmatrix} + \begin{bmatrix} 1 \\ 1 \\ 0 \\ 0 \\ 0 \\ 1 \\ 1 \\ 0 \end{bmatrix} \qquad \text{...(2)}$$

Each element in the product matrix is the bitwise XOR of elements of one row and one column. Further, the final addition.

$$\begin{bmatrix} 1 & 0 & 0 & 0 & 1 & 1 & 1 & 1 \\ 1 & 1 & 0 & 0 & 0 & 1 & 1 & 1 \\ 1 & 1 & 1 & 0 & 0 & 0 & 1 & 1 \\ 1 & 1 & 1 & 1 & 0 & 0 & 0 & 1 \\ 1 & 1 & 1 & 1 & 1 & 0 & 0 & 0 \\ 0 & 1 & 1 & 1 & 1 & 1 & 0 & 0 \\ 0 & 0 & 1 & 1 & 1 & 1 & 1 & 0 \\ 0 & 0 & 0 & 1 & 1 & 1 & 1 & 1 \end{bmatrix} \times \begin{bmatrix} 0 \\ 1 \\ 0 \\ 1 \\ 0 \\ 0 \\ 0 \\ 1 \end{bmatrix} + \begin{bmatrix} 1 \\ 1 \\ 0 \\ 0 \\ 0 \\ 1 \\ 1 \\ 0 \end{bmatrix} = \begin{bmatrix} 1 \\ 0 \\ 0 \\ 1 \\ 0 \\ 0 \\ 1 \\ 1 \end{bmatrix} + \begin{bmatrix} 1 \\ 1 \\ 0 \\ 0 \\ 0 \\ 1 \\ 1 \\ 0 \end{bmatrix} = \begin{bmatrix} 0 \\ 1 \\ 0 \\ 1 \\ 0 \\ 1 \\ 0 \\ 0 \end{bmatrix}$$

As an example, consider the input value {95}. The multiplicative inverse in GF(2^8) is $\{95\}^{-1}$ ={8a}, which is 10001010 in binary. Using equation (2).

The result is {2a}, which should appear in row {09}, column {05} of the S-box.

4.2.2 The Inverse Substitute Byte Transformation

Inverse substitute byte transformation, called InvSubBytes, makes use of the inverse of S-box shown in below table. Note, for example, that the input $\{2a\}$ produces the output $\{95\}$, and the input $\{95\}$ to the S-box produces $\{2a\}$. The inverse S-box is constructed by applying the inverse of the transformation followed by taking the multiplicative inverse in GF(2^8).

The inverse transformation is

$$b_i' = b_{(i+2) \bmod 8} \oplus b_{(i+5) \bmod 8} \oplus b_{(i+7) \bmod 8} \oplus d_i$$

where $d = \{05\}$, or 0000 0101. We can depict this transformation as follows:

$$\begin{bmatrix} B_0' \\ B_1' \\ B_2' \\ B_3' \\ B_4' \\ B_5' \\ B_6' \\ B_7' \end{bmatrix} = \begin{bmatrix} 0 & 0 & 1 & 0 & 0 & 1 & 0 & 1 \\ 1 & 0 & 0 & 1 & 0 & 0 & 1 & 0 \\ 0 & 1 & 0 & 0 & 1 & 0 & 0 & 1 \\ 1 & 0 & 1 & 0 & 0 & 1 & 0 & 0 \\ 0 & 1 & 0 & 1 & 0 & 0 & 1 & 0 \\ 0 & 0 & 1 & 0 & 1 & 0 & 0 & 1 \\ 1 & 0 & 0 & 1 & 0 & 1 & 0 & 0 \\ 0 & 1 & 0 & 0 & 1 & 0 & 1 & 0 \end{bmatrix} \times \begin{bmatrix} B_0 \\ B_1 \\ B_2 \\ B_3 \\ B_4 \\ B_5 \\ B_6 \\ B_7 \end{bmatrix} + \begin{bmatrix} 1 \\ 0 \\ 1 \\ 0 \\ 0 \\ 0 \\ 0 \\ 0 \end{bmatrix}$$

To see that InvSubBytes is the inverse of SubBytes, label the matrices in SubBytes and InvSubBytes as X and Y, respectively, and the vector versions of constants c and d as C and D, respectively. For some 8-bit vector B, equation (2) becomes

$$B' = XB \oplus C \quad (*)$$

Assume that

$$Y = X^{-1} : YX = E$$

where E is the unity matrix.

Multiplying both parts of (*) by Y, we have

$$YB' = YXB \oplus YC = B + YC$$
$$B = YB' \oplus YC = YB' \oplus D$$

Let's check partially that Y is the inverse of X: diagonal elements of product should be 1's, other elements – 0's. For example, let's calculate 2nd diagonal element (multiply 2nd row of Y by 2nd column of X, start numbering from 0):

$$0*0+1*0+0*0+0*1+1*1+0*1+0*1+1*0 = 1$$

If we multiply 2nd row of Y by 1st of X, then

$$0*0+1*1+0*1+0*1+1*1+0*1+0*0+1*0 = 1+1 = 0.$$

So, we got 1 on the diagonal, and 0 outside of diagonal.

The S-box is designed to be resistant to known cryptanalytic attacks. It provides low correlation between input bits and output bits, output cannot be expressed as simple mathematical function of the input, it has not fixed points (S-box(a) = a).

4.2.3 Shift Row Transformation

Forward and Inverse Transformation

- A circular byte shift in each
  - 1st row is unchanged
  - 2nd row does 1 byte circular shift to left
  - 3rd row does 2 byte circular shift to left
  - 4th row does 3 byte circular shift to left
- Decrypt inverts using shifts to right.
- Since state is processed by columns, this step permutes bytes between the columns.

The forward shift row transformation, called ShiftRows, is depicted in Fig. 4.5.

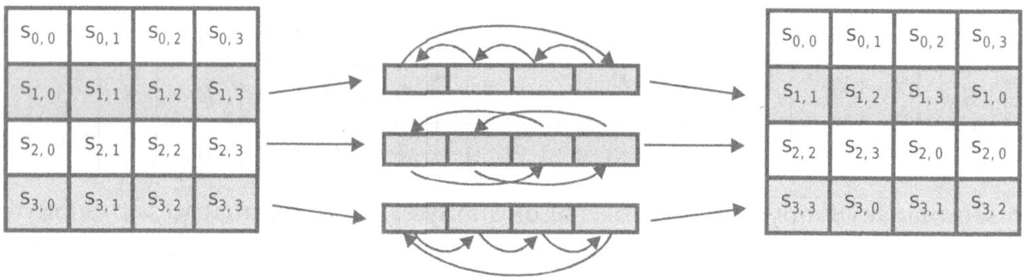

(a) Shift row transformation

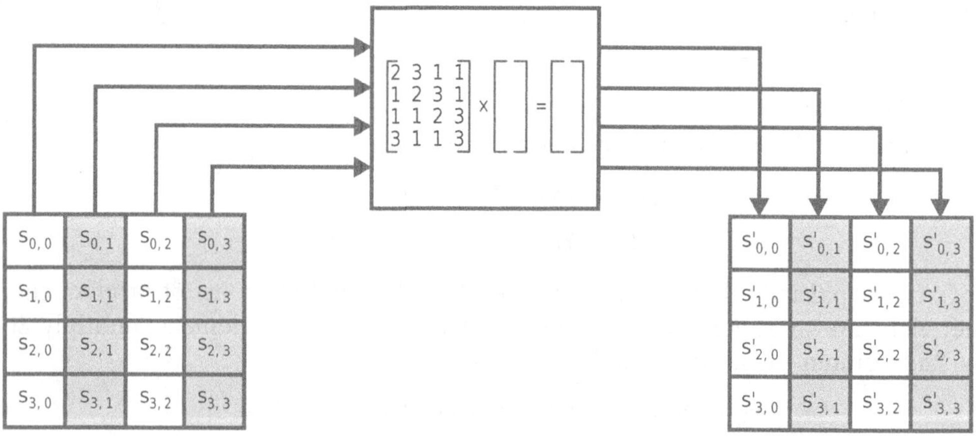

(b) Mix column transformation

Fig. 4.5. *AES row and column operations.*

The 1st row (number 0) is not altered, row number i is shifted left by i-byte circular left shift, i=1, 2, 3. The following is the example of such shift:

87	F2	4D	97
EC	6E	4C	90
4A	C3	46	E7
8C	D8	95	A6

$\Rightarrow$

87	F2	4D	97
6E	4C	90	EC
46	E7	4A	C3
A6	8C	D8	95

The inverse shift row transformation, called InvShiftRows, performs the right circular shift of ith row by i bytes, $i = 0, 1, 2, 3$. Shift row transformation ensures that the 4-bytes of one column are spread out to four different columns.

4.2.4 Mix Column Transformation

Forward and Inverse Transformation

The forward mix column transformation, called MixColumns, operates on each column individually. Each byte is mapped into a new value that is a function of all four bytes in the column.

- each column is processed separately
- each byte is replaced by a value dependent on all 4-bytes in the column
- effectively a matrix multiplication in GF(28) using prime poly $m(x) = x8+x4+x3+x+1$

The transformation can be defined as the following matrix multiplication on State.

02	03	01	01
01	02	03	01
01	01	02	03
03	01	01	02

$\times$

S00	S01	S02	S03
S10	S11	S12	S13
S20	S21	S22	S23
S30	S31	S32	S33

$=$

S00′	S01′	S02′	S03′
S10′	S11′	S12′	S13′
S20′	S21′	S22′	S23′
S30′	S31′	S32′	S33′

...(3)

Each element in the product matrix is the sum of products of elements of one row and one column. In this case, multiplications and additions are performed in $GF(2^8)$.

The following is the example of MixColumns:

87	F2	4D	97
6E	4C	90	EC
46	E7	4A	C3
A6	8C	D8	95

$\Rightarrow$

47	40	A3	4C
37	D4	70	9F
94	E4	3A	42
ED	A5	A6	BC

...(4)

1st column of the result is obtained by:

{02){87}+{03}{6E}+{46}+{A6} = {47}

{87}+{02}{6E}+{03}{46}+{A6} = {37}

{87}+{6E}+{02}{46}+{03}{A6} = {94}

{03}{87}+{6E}+{46}+{02}{A6} = {ED}

For the 1st equation, we have {02}{87}=(0000 0010)(1000 0111)=

$x(x^7 + x^2 + x + 1) = (x^8 + x^3 + x^2 + x) \bmod (x^8 + x^4 + x^3 + x + 1)$

$= x^4 + x^2 + 1 =$ (0001 0101) = {15}

{03}{6E} = (0000 0011)(0110 1110) = $(x + 1)(x^6 + x^5 + x^3 + x^2 + x)$

$= x^7 + x^5 + x^4 + x =$ (1011 0010) = {B2}

{02){87} + {03}{6E} + {46} + {A6} = {15} + {B2} + {46} + {A6}

= (0001 0101) + (1011 0010) + (0100 0110) + (1010 0110)

= (0100 0111) = {47}

The inverse mix column transformation, called InvMixColumns, is defined by the following matrix multiplication:

0E	0B	0D	09		S00	S01	S02	S03		S00′	S01′	S02′	S03′	
09	0E	0B	0D	×	S10	S11	S12	S13	=	S10′	S11′	S12′	S13′	...(5)
0D	09	0E	0B		S20	S21	S22	S23		S20′	S21′	S22′	S23′	
0B	0D	09	0E		S30	S31	S32	S33		S30′	S31′	S32′	S33′	

To show that matrix in (5) is inverse of matrix in (3), we are to check that their product in GF(2^8) is a unity matrix. Let's make such partial check for S00′ (product of 0th row by 0th column):

S00′=(0E}{02}+{0B}{01}+{0D}{01}+{09}{03}=(0E}{02}+{0B}+{0D}+{09}{03}

{0E}{02}=(0000 1110)(0000 0010)=$(x^3 + x^2 + x)\, x = x^4 + x^3 + x^2$

=(0001 1100)={1C}

{09}{03}=(0000 1001)(0000 0011)=$(x^3 + 1)(x + 1) = x^4 + x + x^3 + 1$

=(0001 1011)={1B}

(0E}{02}+{0B}+{0D}+{09}{03}={1C}+{0B}+{0D}+{1B}=

(0001 1100)+

(0000 1011)+

(0000 1101)+

(0001 1011)=

(0000 0001)={01}

The other elements are verified similarly.

The AES document describes MixColumns in terms of polynomial arithmetic. In the standard, MixColumns is defined by considering each column of State to be a four-term polynomial with coefficients in GF(2^8). Each column is multiplied modulo ($x^4 + 1$) by the fixed polynomial $a(x)$, given by

$$a(x) = \{03\}x^3 + \{01\}x^2 + \{01\}x + \{02\} \quad ...(6)$$

Let's show that such multiplication by polynomial is equivalent to matrix multiplication, represented by (3). Each column of State matrix is viewed as set of coefficients of respective polynomial, *e.g.*, 1st column of State corresponds to the polynomial:

$$S_0(x) = S_{30}x^3 + S_{20}x^2 + S_{10}x + S_{00}$$

Then

$$\begin{aligned}
a(x)S_0(x) &= (\{03\}x^3 + \{01\}x^2 + \{01\}x + \{02\})(S_{30}x^3 + S_{20}x^2 + S_{10}x + S_{00}) \\
&= (\{03\}S_{30}x^6 + (\{03\}S_{20} + S_{30})x^5 + (\{03\}S_{10} + S_{20} + S_{30})x^4 + (\{02\}S_{30} \\
&\quad + S_{20} + S_{10} + \{03\}S_{00})x^3 + (\{02\}S_{20} + S_{10} + S_{00})x^2 + (\{02\}S_{10} + S_{00})x \\
&\quad + \{02\}S_{00})\text{mod}(x^4 + 1) \\
&= (\{03\}S_{30}x^6 \text{ mod}(x^4 + 1) + (\{03\}S_{20} + S_{30})x^5 \text{ mod}(x^4 + 1) + (\{03\}S_{10} \\
&\quad + S_{20} + S_{30})x^4 \text{ mod}(x^4 + 1) + (\{02\}S_{30} + S_{20} + S_{10} + \{03\}S_{00})x^3 \\
&\quad + (\{02\}S_{20} + S_{10} + S_{00})x^2 + (\{02\}S_{10} + S_{00})x + \{02\}S_{00}) \\
&= (\{03\}S_{30}x^2 + (\{03S_{20} + S_{30})x + (\{03\}S_{10} + S_{20} + S_{30}) + (\{02\}S_{30} \\
&\quad + S_{20} + S_{10} + \{03\}S_{00})x^3 + (\{02\}S_{20} + S_{10} + S_{00})x^2 + (\{02\}S_{10} + S_{00})x \\
&\quad + \{02\}S_{00}) \\
&= (\{02\}S_{30} + S_{20} + S_{10} + \{03\}S_{00})x^3 + (\{03\}S_{30} + \{02\}S_{20} + S_{10} + S_{00})x^2 \\
&\quad + (S_{30} + \{03\}S_{20} + \{02\}S_{10} + S_{00})x + (S_{30} + S_{20} + \{03\}S_{10} + \{02\}S_{00}) \\
&= (\{02\}S_{00} + \{03\}S_{10} + S_{20} + S_{30}) + (S_{00} + \{02\}S_{10} + \{03\}S_{20} + S_{30})x \\
&\quad + (S_{00} + S_{10} + \{02\}S_{20} + \{03\}S_{30})x^2 + (\{03\}S_{00} + S_{10} + S_{20} + \{02\}S_{30})x^3
\end{aligned}$$

In the last polynomial, coefficients are just same as used in matrix multiplication according to (3). Actually, 1st column of the result in (3) may be written as follows:

$$\begin{aligned}
S00' &= \{02\}S00+\{03\}S10+S20+S30 \\
S10' &= S00+\{02)S10+\{03\}S20+S30 \\
S20' &= S00+S10+\{02\}S20+\{03\}S30 \quad ...(7) \\
S30' &= \{03\}S00+S10+S20+\{02\}S30
\end{aligned}$$

Similarly, it may be shown that the transformation in the (5) corresponds to treating each column as a 4-term polynomial and multiplying each column by $b(x)$, given by

$$b(x) = \{0b\}x^3 + \{0d\}x^2 + \{09\}x + \{0e\} \quad ...(8)$$

It can be shown that $b(x) = a^{-1}(x) \text{ mod } (x^4 + 1)$

The mix column transformation combined with the shift row transformation ensures that after a few rounds, all output bits depend on all input bits.

4.3 ADD ROUND KEY FUNCTIONS

Add Round Key Transformation

Forward and Inverse Transformation

In the forward add round key transformation, called Add Round Key, the 128-bits of State are bitwise XORed with the 128-bits of the round key. The Add Round Key transformation is as simple as possible and affects every bit of State. The complexity of the round key expansion together with the complexity of other stages of AES, ensures security.

- XOR state with 128-bits of the round key
- again processed by column (though effectively a series of byte operations)
- inverse for decryption identical
  - since XOR own inverse, with reversed keys
- designed to be as simple as possible
  - a form of Vernam cipher on expanded key
  - requires other stages for complexity/security

4.4 AES KEY EXPANSION

The AES key expansion algorithm takes as input a 4-word (16-byte) key and produces a linear array of 44 words (156 bytes).

- takes 128-bit (16-byte) key and expands into array of 44/52/60 32-bit words
- start by copying key into first 4 words
- then loop creating words that depend on values in previous and 4 places back
  - in 3 of 4 cases just XOR these together.
  - 1st word in 4 has rotate + S-box + XOR round constant on previous, before XOR 4th back.

The following pseudo code describes the expansion:

```
KeyExpansion(byte key[16], word w[44]){
Word temp;
For(i=0;i<4;i++) w[i]=(key[4*i], key[4*i+1], key[4*i+2], key[4*i+3]);
For(i=4;i<44;i++){
  Temp=w[i-1];
  If(I mod 4 = 0) temp = SubWord(RotWord(temp)) XOR Rcon[i/4];
  W[i]=w[i-4] XOR temp;
  }
}
```

The key is copied into the 1st four words of the expanded key. The remainder of the expanded key is filled in four words at a time. Each added word w[i] depends on the immediately preceding word, w[i-1], and the word four positions back, w[i-4]. In three out of four cases, a simple XOR is used. For a word whose position in the array w is a multiple of 4, a more complex function is used. Fig. 4.5 illustrates the generation of the one to eight words of the expanded key, using the symbol *g* to represent the complex function. The function *g* consists of the following subfunctions:

1. RotWord performs a 1-byte circular left shift on a word. This means that an input word $[b_0, b_1, b_2, b_3]$ is transformed into $[b_1, b_2, b_3, b_0]$.
2. SubWord performs a byte substitution on each byte of its input word, using the S-box.
3. The result of steps 1 and 2 is XORed with a round constant, Rcon[j]

4.4.1 Key Expansion Rationale

- Designed to resist known attacks
- Design criteria included
  - Knowing part key insufficient to find many more
  - Invertible transformation
  - Fast on wide range of CPU's
  - Use round constants to break symmetry
  - Diffuse key bits into round keys
  - Enough non-linearity to hinder analysis
  - Simplicity of description

4.5 TRIPLE DES ENCRYPTION

Overview

The Data Encryption Standard (DES) was developed by an IBM team around 1974 and adopted as a national standard in 1977. Triple DES is a minor variation of this standard. It is three times slower than regular DES but can be billions of times more secure if used properly. Triple DES enjoys much wider use than DES because DES is so easy to break with today's rapidly advancing technology. In 1998 the Electronic Frontier Foundation, using a specially developed computer called the DES Cracker, managed to break DES in less than 3 days. And this was done for under $250,000. The encryption chip that powered the DES Cracker was capable of processing 88 billion keys per second. In addition, it has been shown that for a cost of one million dollars a dedicated hardware device can be built that can search all possible DES keys in about 3.5 hours. This just serves to illustrate that any organization with moderate resources can break through DES with very little effort these days. No same security expert would consider using DES to protect data.

Triple DES was the answer to many of the shortcomings of DES. Since it is based on the DES algorithm, it is very easy to modify existing software to use Triple DES. It also has the advantage of proven reliability and a longer key length that eliminates many of the shortcut attacks that can be used to reduce the amount of time it takes to break DES. However, even this more powerful version of DES may not be strong enough to protect data for very much longer. The DES algorithm itself has become obsolete and is in need of replacement. To this end the National Institute of Standards and Technology (NIST) is holding a competition to develop the Advanced Encryption Standard (AES) as a replacement for DES. Triple DES has been endorsed by NIST as a temporary standard to be used until the AES is finished sometime in 2001.

The AES will be at least as strong as Triple DES and probably much faster. Many security systems will probably use both Triple DES and AES for at least the next five years. After that, AES may supplant Triple DES as the default algorithm on most systems if it lives up to its expectations. But Triple DES will be kept around for compatibility reasons for many years after that. So the useful lifetime of Triple DES is far from over, even with the AES near completion. For the foreseeable future Triple DES is an excellent and reliable choice for the security needs of highly sensitive information.

4.5.1 Triple DES with Two-Keys

An obvious counter to the meet in the middle attack is to use three stages of encryption with three different keys. This raises the cost of the known plaintext attack, which is beyond what is practical now. However, it has the drawback of requiring a key length of $56 \times 3 =$ 168-bits. The following point carried out of triple DES.

- With triple DES, each block of plain text is processed three times
- pros: two key version of DES is estimated to be $10^{13} \times$ stronger
  - the triple DES even stronger
    - o triple DES uses two keys, K1 used, K2 used, then K1 used again
- cons: if key1, key2 are the same triple DES collapses to single DES
  - key management is harder
- hence must use 3 encryptions
  - would seem to need 3 distinct keys
- but can use 2 keys with E-D-E sequence
  - C = EK1(DK2(EK1(P)))
  - nb encrypt and decrypt equivalent in security
  - if K1=K2 then can work with single DES
- standardized in ANSI X9.17 and ISO8732
- no current known practical attacks

4.5.2 Triple DES with Three-Keys

The following points to be explain about Triple-DES with Three-Keys

- Although are no practical attacks on two-key Triple-DES have some indications
- Can use Triple-DES with Three-Keys to avoid even these
  - C = EK3(DK2(EK1(P)))
- Has been adopted by some Internet applications, *e.g.*, PGP, S/MIME

4.6 PLACEMENT OF ENCRYPTION

There are two fundamental encryption placement alternatives: link encryption and end-to-end encryption.

With link encryption, each vulnerable communications link is equipped on both ends with an encryption device. But all the potential links in a path from source to destination must use link encryption. Each pair of nodes that share a link should share a unique key, with a different key used on each link. Thus, many keys must be provided.

With end-to-end encryption, the encryption process is carried out at the two end systems. Thus end-to-end encryption relieves the end user of concerns about the degree of security of networks and links that support the communication. The user data is secure, but the traffic pattern is not because packet headers are transmitted in the clear.

See Fig. 4.6 for more detailed comparison between these alternatives.

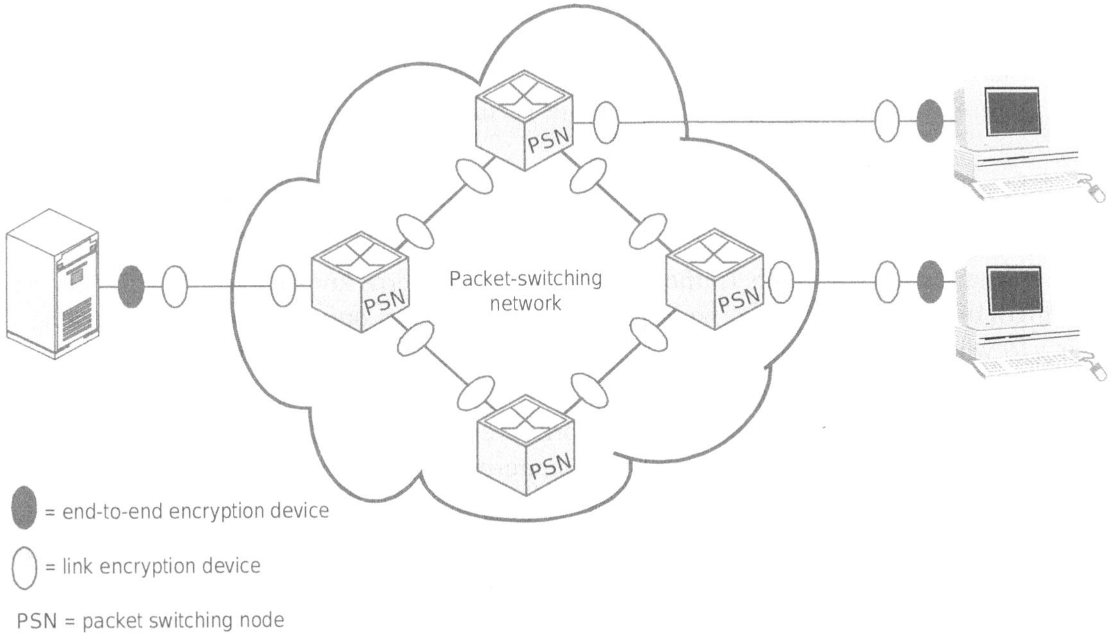

Fig. 4.6. *Packet switching network.*

- when using end-to-end encryption must leave headers in clear
  - so network can correctly route information
- hence although contents protected, traffic pattern flows are not
- ideally want both at once
  - end-to-end protects data contents over entire path and provides authentication
  - link protects traffic flows from monitoring.

  With end-to-end encryption, user data are secure, but the traffic pattern is not because packet headers are transmitted in the clear. However end-to-end encryption does provide a degree of authentication, since a recipient is assured that any message that it receives comes from the alleged sender, because only that sender shares the relevant key. Such authentication is not inherent in a link encryption scheme. To achieve greater security, both link and end-to-end encryption are needed, as is shown in figure an place encryption function at various layers in OSI Reference Model.

- ink encryption occurs at layers 1 or 2
- end-to-end can occur at layers 3, 4, 6, 7
- as move higher less information is encrypted but it is more secure though more complex with more entities and keys.

- Can place encryption at any of a number of layers in the OSI Reference Model. Link encryption can occur at either the physical or link layers.
- End-to-end encryption could be performed at the network layer (for all processes on a system, perhaps in a Front End Processor), at the Transport layer (now possibly per process), or at the Presentation/Application layer.
- Can view alternatives noting that as you move up the communications hierarchy, less information is encrypted but it is more secure.

4.7 TRAFFIC ANALYSIS

Some users are concerned with Traffic Analysis, which concerns knowledge about the number and length of messages between nodes which may enable an opponent to determine who is talking to whom, and hence suggest when important information is being exchanged, or to correlate with observed events.

With the use of link encryption, network-layer headers are encrypted, reducing the opportunity for traffic analysis. An effective countermeasure to this attack is traffic padding.

If only end-to-end encryption is employed, then the measures available to the defender are more limited since various protocol headers are visible. Padding of application data and null messages can be used.

4.7.1 Application of Traffic Analysis

- is monitoring of communications flows between parties
  - useful both in military and commercial spheres
  - can also be used to create a covert channel
- link encryption obscures header details
  - but overall traffic volumes in networks and at end-points is still visible
- traffic padding can further obscure flows
  - but at cost of continuous traffic

4.8. KEY TERMS, KEY POINTS AND REVIEW QUESTIONS

Key Terms

Advanced Encryption Standard (AES)	**MixColumns**	**SubBytes**
Add Round Key	**Power Analysis**	**S-Box**
Link encryption	**Rijndael**	

Key Points

- Advanced Encryption Standard (AES), which should have security strength equal to or better than DES, and significantly improved efficiency.
- AES must be a symmetric block cipher with a block length of 128-bits and support for key lengths of 128, 192, and 256-bits.
- AES Cipher Designed by Rijmen-Daemon in Belgium.
- The Forward substitute byte transformation, called SubBytes, is a simple table lookup.
- The Add Round Key is a form of Vernam cipher and by itself would not be formidable.
- Inverse substitute byte transformation, called InvSubBytes, makes use of the inverse of S-box.
- The forward mix column transformation, called MixColumns, operates on each column individually.
- The Add Round Key transformation is as simple as possible and affects every bit of State.
- The AES key expansion algorithm takes as input a 4-word (16-byte) key and produces a linear array of 44 words (156 bytes).
- The Data Encryption Standard (DES) was developed by an IBM team around 1974 and adopted as a national standard in 1977.
- With link encryption, each vulnerable communications link is equipped on both ends with an encryption device.

Question with Answers *(2 Marks)*

Q. 1. *How many keys are required for two people to communicate via a cipher?*

Ans. If both sender and receiver use the same key, the system is referred a s symmetric, single key, secret-key or conventional encryption. If both sender and receiver use a different key, the system is referred as asymmetric, two-key or public key encryption.

Q. 2. *What are the two general approaches to attacking a cipher?*

Ans. The general two approaches

- **Cryptanalysis:** Cryptanalysis attacks rely on the nature of the algorithm plus perhaps some knowledge of the general characteritics of the plaintext or even some samples plaintext-cipher text pairs.
- **Brute-force attack:** The attacker tries every possible key on piece of cipher text untill an intelligible translation into plaintext is obtained.

Q. 3. *Define Caesar cipher.*

Ans. The caesar cipher involves replacing each letter of the alphabet with letter standing three places down the alphabet. The alphabet is wrapped around.

Q. 4. *Define Monoalphabetic cipher.*

Ans. A dramatic increase in the key space is achieved by allowing an arbitrary substitution. There are 26! Possible keys. It is referred to as monoalphabetic substitution cipher, because a single cipher alphabet is used per message.

Q. 5. *Define the playfair cipher.*

Ans. The playfair cipher treats the diagrams in the plaintext as single units and translates these units into cipher text diagrams. This algorithm is based on the use of a 5×5 matrix of letters constructed using keyword.

Q. 6. *What is the difference between a Monoalphabetic cipher and Polyalphabetic cipher?*

Ans. In monoalphabetic cipher single cipher alphabet is used per message. But in polyalphabetic cipher there are multiple cipher text letters for each plaintext letter, one for each unique letter of keyword.

Q. 7. *What is the difference between Rijndael and AES?*

Ans. AES was developed by NIST. AES is a symmetric block cipher that is intended to replace DES. NIST selected Rijndael as the proposed AES algorithm. The two reseachers who developed and submitted Rijndael for the AES are the both cryptographers from Belgium.

Q. 8. *List out the Encryption Placement Alternatives.*

Ans. There are two fundamental encryption placement alternatives: link encryption and end-to-end encryption.

Q. 9. *What is traffic analysis?*

Ans. Traffic Analysis, which concerns knowledge about the number and length of messages between nodes which may enable an opponent to determine who is talking to whom.

Q. 10. *List out the applications of traffic analysis.*

Ans. It is monitoring of communications flows between parties

Link encryption obscures header details

Traffic padding can further obscure flows.

Review Questions

1. Briefly Explain AES Evaluation Criteria.
2. Explain briefly AES Structure.
3. How is the S-Box constructed?
4. Briefly describe SubBytes
5. Briefly describe ShiftRows.
6. How many bytes in state are affected by ShiftRows?
7. Briefly describe MixColumns.
8. Briefly describe Add Round Key.
9. Briefly describe the key expansion algorithm.
10. What is the difference between ShiftBytes and SubWord?

❑❑❑

PART 2
ASYMMETRIC CIPHERS

Chapters

CHAPTER 5

NUMBER THEORY

5.1 INTRODUCTION

Number theory is the branch of pure mathematics concerned with the properties of numbers in general, and integers in particular, as well as the wider classes of problems that arise from their study. A number of concepts from number theory are essential in the design of public key cryptographic algorithms.

5.2 PRIME NUMBERS

In mathematics, a prime number (or a prime) is a natural number which has exactly two distinct natural number divisors: 1 and itself. Infinitude of prime numbers exists, as demonstrated by Euclid in about 300 BC. The first thirty prime numbers are:

2, 3, 5, 7, 11, 13, 17, 19, 23, 29, 31, 37, 41, 43, 47, 53, 59, 61, 67, 71, 73, 79, 83, 89, 97, 101, 103, 107, 109, 113

(sequence A000040 in OEIS)

See the list of prime numbers for a longer list. The number one is by definition not a prime number; see the discussion below under Primality of one.

The property of being a prime is called Primality, and the word prime is also used as an adjective. Since two is the only even prime number, the term odd prime refers to all prime numbers greater than two.

The study of prime numbers is part of number theory, the branch of mathematics which encompasses the study of natural numbers. Prime numbers have been the subject of intense research, yet some fundamental questions, such as the Riemann hypothesis and the Goldbach conjecture, have been unresolved for more than a century. The problem of modelling the distribution of prime numbers is a popular subject of investigation for number theorists: when looking at individual numbers, the primes seem to be randomly distributed, but the "global" distribution of primes follows well-defined laws.

The notion of prime number has been generalized in many different branches of mathematics. In ring theory, a branch of abstract algebra, the term "prime element" has a specific meaning. Here, a non-zero, non-unit ring element a is defined to be prime if whenever a divides bc for ring elements b and c, then a divides at least one of b or c. With this meaning, the additive inverse of any prime number is also prime. In other words, when considering the set of integers as a ring, –7 is a prime element. Without further specification, however, "prime number" always means a positive integer prime. Among rings of complex algebraic integers, Eisenstein primes, and Gaussian primes may also be of interest.

In knot theory, a prime knot is a knot which can not be written as the knot sum of two lesser nontrivial knots.

Prime Factorisation

- to **factor** a number n is to write it as a product of other numbers: $n = a \times b \times c$.
- note that factoring a number is relatively hard compared to multiplying the factors together to generate the number.
- the **prime factorisation** of a number n is when its written as a product of primes: *e.g.,* $91 = 7 \times 13$; $3600 = 24 \times 32 \times 52$.

Relatively Prime Numbers and GCD

- Two numbers a, b are **relatively prime** if have **no common divisors** apart from 1.
  - *e.g.,* 8 and 15 are relatively prime since factors of 8 are 1, 2, 4, 8 and of 15 are 1, 3, 5, 15 and 1 is the only common factor.
- Conversely can determine the greatest common divisor by comparing their prime factorisations and using least powers.
  - *e.g.,* $300 = 21 \times 31 \times 52$ $18 = 21 \times 32$, hence GCD (18,300) $= 21 \times 31 \times 50 = 6$.

5.3 FERMAT'S AND EULER THEOREMS

5.3.1 Fermat's Theorem

Although not as widely known as Fermat's Last Theorem, this Theorem (also known as Fermat's Little Theorem) is probably the most widely used. It forms the basis of most simple primality tests, which is why it is of interest to cryptographers.

If p is prime and p does not divide a, then $a^{p-1} \equiv 1 \pmod p$

Note that if p|a, then $a^p \equiv 0 \equiv a$, so the above is equivalent to:

If p is prime, then $a^p \equiv a \pmod p$

This gives a necessary, but not sufficient condition for primality.

To test a number x for primality, calculate $a^x \pmod x$ for some small number a (note that modular exponentiations can be done very quickly).

If you do not have that $a^x \equiv a \pmod x$, then x is a composite number. Otherwise x is a pseudo prime to the base a. It is not necessarily a prime, as some composites will pass this test. However, if it passes for several different values of a, then it is very likely to be prime. Unless, of course, you happened to choose a *Carmichael number...*

Fermat claimed to have a proof, but unfortunately it was too long, so he didn't write it down (similar to a certain other theorem he claimed to prove...). The first published proof was given by Euler in 1749.

Unfortunately the only proofs I can think of at the moment can't be conveniently expressed in HTML! So it is left as an exercise for the reader—it is quite easy if you know a bit of number theory.

5.3.2 Euler's Totient Function

The Euler totient function, also called the Euler phi function and written as

if gcd(x, n) = 1, then

x^phi(n) mod n = 1 or x^phi(n) ð 1 mod n

phi(n), is the number of positive integers less than n that are relatively prime to n. For example, the reduced set of residues mod 12 is {1, 5, 7, 11}. Unlike Fermat's little theorem, n does not have to be prime. For this reason, Euler's Totient Function is referred to as Euler's generalization of Fermat's little theorem.

Euler's totient function is multiplicative. If

phi(12) = 4 and phi(10) = 4,

then phi(12 * 10) = 4 * 4 = 16

If n is prime, then phi(n) = n – 1, since all numbers less than a prime are not divisors of a prime. Euler's function is multiplicative, so if n = p * q, where p and q are prime, then

phi(n) = (p – 1) * (q – 1). This will allow d to open c, as we will see in the section on the inner workings.

Now taking the inverse of Euler's totient function,

y ð x^phi(n)–1 mod n

and putting this equation into the form for e and d in the RSA algorithm,

d ð e^phi(p–1)*(q–1)–1 (mod (p – 1) * (q – 1))

Remember that this is equivalent to the definition of the private key

d ð e^–1 (mod (p – 1) * (q – 1))

and we will later use the fact that this is in turn equivalent to the Diophantine equation we have already seen to determine d * e, that is

d * e = (p – 1) * (q – 1) * k + 1

Choosing two primes, p and q, and choosing e at random and relatively prime to (p – 1) * (q – 1), we can now easily find d.

Setting p = 2, q = 17, e = 5

d ð e^phi(n)–1 (mod (p – 1) * (q – 1))

d ð 5^phi(2–1)*(17–1)–1 (mod (2 – 1) * (17 – 1))

d ð 5^phi(16)–1 mod 16

There are 8 elements relatively prime to 16: 1, 3, 5, 7, 9, 11, 13, 15, therefore phi(16) = 8.

d ð 5^8–1 mod 16 ð 5^7 mod 16 ð 78125 mod 16 = 13

We have now used both the extended Euclid's algorithm and Euler's totient function to calculate inverses to solve for d. Euclid's algorithm is generally faster for calculating large inverses.

THE INNER WORKINGS

Why does d decrypt c? Since

c^d mod n = (m^e)^d mod n = m^e*d mod n

and remembering the Diophantine equation above for e * d, our exponent in m^e*d becomes

m^(p–1)*(q–1)*k+1 mod n

and since n = p * q, and remembering that Euler's totient theorem is multiplicative,

phi(n) = phi(p * q) = (p – 1) * (q – 1)

Therefore,

c^d mod n = m^phi(n)*k+1 mod n

and according to Euler,

m^phi(n) mod n = 1

and of course, m^1 = m. Therefore

c^d mod n = (1^k * m) CHECK!

Example: If our message m = 6, and e = 5, d = 13, p = 2, q = 17,

c = m^e mod n = 6^5 mod 34 = 7776 mod 34 = 24

Now if cyphertext c = 24, to restore the original message we take

c^d mod n = 24^13 mod 34

= ((24^3 mod 34) * (24^5 mod 34) * (24^5 mod 34) mod 34

= (20 * 28 * 28) mod 34 = 15680 mod 34 = 6 CHECK!

Overview of Euler's Totient Function

- When doing arithmetic modulo n
- **complete set of residues** is: 0...n–1
- **reduced set of residues** is those numbers (residues) which are relatively prime to n
  - *e.g.,* for n=10,
  - complete set of residues is {0, 1, 2, 3, 4, 5, 6, 7, 8, 9}
  - reduced set of residues is {1, 3, 7, 9}
- number of elements in reduced set of residues is called the **Euler Totient Function ø(n)**
- to compute ø(n) need to count number of elements to be excluded
- in general need prime factorization, but
  - for p (p prime) ø(p) = p–1
  - for p.q (p,q prime) ø(p.q) = (p–1)(q–1)
- *e.g.,*
  - ø(37) = 36
  - ø(21) = (3–1)×(7–1) = 2×6 = 12

5.3.3 Euler's Theorem

Let n be the product of two primes p and q. Let e and d be two numbers whose product ed leaves a remainder of 1 when divided by (p–1)(q–1). Let m be any positive number 85 smaller than both p and q. Then the power m^(ed) = (m^e)^d, when divided by n leaves a remainder of m.

(The above is actually a special case of Euler's theorem, but sufficient to understand the RSA algorithm.)

Example 1. Let p = 3, q = 5. Then n = 15. Let e = 11 and d = 3. Then ed = 33, which when divided by (p–1)(q–1) = 2*4 = 8 gives a quotient of 4 and a remainder of 1. Now take m = 2. Then 2^33 = 8589934592. When divided by 15 this gives a quotient of 572662306 and a remainder of 2, as predicted by Euler's theorem.

To apply Euler's theorem to cryptography we need another fact from /elementary algebra: when computing the remainder of an expression involving powers, products, sums and differences, one can compute the remainders at each intermediate stage. For example to compute the remainder of 14*32*12*17 when divided by 15, instead of multiplying out all four numbers to obtain 91392, then dividing by 15 to obtain the remainder of 12, one can proceed as follows:

14*32 = 448 which leaves a remainder of 13 when divided by 15

12*17 = 204 which leaves a remainder of 9 when divided by 15

Now multiply together the remainders obtained in the preceding steps: 13*9 = 102 and divide by 15. We obtain the same remainder of 12. Noting that m ^ (ed) = (m ^ e) ^ d, the remainder of m ^ (ed) by n in Euler's theorem can be computed first taking the remainder of the expression m ^ e , then taking this remainder and raising it to the dth power, then taking the remainder again. In Example 1 we would compute as follows: 2 ^ 33 = (2 ^ 11) ^ 3. Now 2 ^ 11 = 2048, which leaves a quotient of 136 and a remainder of 8 when divided by 15, and 8 ^ 3 = 512, which leaves a quotient of 34 and a remainder of 2.

5.4 TESTING FOR PRIMALITY

A **primality test** is an algorithm for determining whether an input number is prime. It is important to note the difference between primality testing and integer factorisation. As of 2007, factorisation is a computationally hard problem, whereas primality testing is comparatively easy.

5.4.1 Miller-Rabin Primality Test

The **Miller-Rabin primality test** or **Rabin-Miller primality test** is a primality test: an algorithm which determines whether a given number is prime, similar to the Fermat primality test and the Solovay-Strassen primality test. Its original version, due to Gary L. Miller, is deterministic, but it relies on the unproven generalised Riemann hypothesis; Michael O. Rabin modified it to obtain an unconditional probabilistic algorithm.

The Miller-Rabin prime test is a probabilistic test based on the following:

Theorem 1: *Let $N \geq 3$ be an odd number and $N - 1 = 2^t n$, n odd. If and only if for every $a \in \mathbb{Z}$ with gcd(a, N) = 1 we have*

$$a^n \equiv 1 \bmod N \qquad \ldots 1(a)$$

or

$$a^{2^* n} \equiv -1 \bmod N \qquad \ldots 1(b)$$

for some $s \in \{0, \ldots, t - 1\}$, then N is prime. If N is not prime, then let A be the set of all a satisfying the above conditions. We have

$$Card\ (A) \leq \frac{1}{4}\varphi(N),$$

where φ is Euler's Phi-function.

A composite number N satisfying conditions (1) for some $a \in \mathbb{Z}$ is called a strong pseudo prime in the basis *a*. Note that this theorem states that there are no such things as Carmichael numbers for strong pseudo primes (*i.e.*, composite numbers that are strong pseudo primes for all values of *a*). From this theorem we can construct the following algorithm:

1. Choose a random $2 \leq a \leq N - 1$.
2. If gcd(*a*, *N*) ≠ 1, we have a non-trivial divisor of *N*, so *N* is not prime.

3. If $\gcd(a, N) = 1$, check if the conditions (1) are satisfied. If not, N is not prime, otherwise the probability that N is not prime is less than $\frac{1}{4}$.

In general the probability, that the test falsely reports N as a prime is far less than $\frac{1}{4}$. Of course the algorithm can be applied several times in order to reduce the probability, that N is not a prime but reported as one.

When comparing this test with the related Solovay-Strassen test one sees that this test is superior is several ways:

- There is no need to calculate the Jacobi symbol.
- The amount of false witnesses, *i.e.*, numbers a that report N as a prime when it is not, is at most $\frac{N}{4}$ instead of $\frac{N}{2}$.
- One can even show that N which passes Miller-Rabin for some a also passes Solovay-Strassen for that a, so Miller-Rabin is always better.

Note that when the test returns that N is composite, then this is indeed the case, so it is really a compositeness test rather than a test for primality.

Probabilistic Considerations

- If Miller-Rabin returns "composite" the number is definitely not prime
- Otherwise is a prime or a pseudo-prime
- Chance it detects a pseudo-prime is < 1/4.
- Hence if repeat test with different random a then chance n is prime after t tests is:
  - Pr(n prime after t tests) = 1 – 4 – t
  - *e.g.*, for $t = 10$ this probability is > 0.99999

Prime Distribution

- Prime number theorem states that primes occur roughly every ($\ln n$) integers
- Since can immediately ignore evens and multiples of 5, in practice only need test 0.4 $\ln(n)$ numbers of size n before locate a prime
  - Note this is only the "average" sometimes primes are close together, at other times are quite far apart

5.5 THE CHINESE REMAINDER THEOREM

Let r and s be positive integers which are relatively prime and let a and b be any two integers. Then there is an integer N such that

$$N \equiv a \pmod{r} \qquad \text{...(1)}$$

and

$$N \equiv b \pmod{s} \qquad \text{...(2)}$$

Moreover, N is uniquely determined modulo rs. An equivalent statement is that if $(r, s) = 1$, then every pair of residue classes modulo r and s corresponds to a simple residue class modulo rs.

The Chinese remainder theorem is implemented in *Mathematics* as Chinese Remainder $[\{a_1, a_2, ...\}\{m_1, m_2, ...\}]$. The Chinese remainder theorem is also implemented indirectly using Reduce in with a domain specification of Integers.

The theorem can also be generalized as follows. Given a set of simultaneous congruences

$$x \equiv a_i (\text{mod } m_i) \quad ...(3)$$

for $i = 1, ..., r$ and for which the m_i are pairwise relatively prime, the solution of the set of congruences is

$$x = a_1 b_1 \frac{M}{m_1} + ... + a_r b_r \frac{M}{m_r} (\text{mod } M) \quad ...(4)$$

where $M \equiv m_1, m_2, ..., m_r$ ...(5)

and the b_i are determined from

$$b_i \frac{M}{m_i} \equiv 1 \ (\text{mod } m_i). \quad ...(6)$$

5.5.1 Computational Efficiency and the Chinese Remainder Theorem (CRT)

Key generation is only carried out occasionally and so computational efficiency is less of an issue. The calculation $a = b\hat{}e$ mod n is known as *modular exponentiation* and one efficient method to carry this out on a computer is the *binary left-to-right method.* To solve **y = x^e mod n** let e be represented in base 2 as

$$e = e_{(k-1)} e_{(k-2)} \cdots e_{(1)} e_{(0)}$$

where $e_{(k-1)}$ is the most significant non-zero bit and bit $e_{(0)}$ the least.

```
set y = x
for bit j = k - 2 downto 0
begin
  y = y * y mod n /* square */
  if e(j) = 1 then
    y = y * x mod n /* multiply */
end
return y
```

The time to carry out modular exponentiation increases with the number of bits set to one in the exponent e. For encryption, an appropriate choice of e can reduce the computational effort required to carry out the computation of $c = m\hat{}e$ mod n. Popular choices like 3, 17 and 65537 are all primes with only two bits set: 3 = 0011'B, 17 = 0×11, 65537 = 0×10001.

The bits in the decryption exponent d, however, will not be so convenient and so decryption using the standard method of modular exponentiation will take longer than encryption. An alternative method of representing the private key uses the *Chinese Remainder*

Theorem (CRT). The private key is represented as a quintuple (p, q, dP, dQ, and qInv), where p and q are prime factors of n, dP and dQ are known as the *CRT exponents*, and qInv is the *CRT coefficient*. The CRT method of decryption is four times faster overall than calculating $m = c^{\wedge d} \bmod n$. The extra values for the private key are:

$dP = (1/e) \bmod (p-1)$

$dQ = (1/e) \bmod (q-1)$

$\text{qInv} = (1/q) \bmod p$, where $p > q$

These are pre-computed and saved along with p and q as the private key. To compute the message m given c do the following:

$m_1 = c \wedge dP \bmod p$

$m_2 = c \wedge dQ \bmod q$

$h = \text{qInv}(m_1 - m_2) \bmod p$

$m = m_2 + hq$

Even though there are more steps in this procedure, the modular exponentiations to be carried out uses much shorter exponents and so it is less expensive overall.

5.6 DISCRETE LOGARITHM

In mathematics, specifically in abstract algebra and its applications, **discrete logarithms** are group-theoretic analogues of ordinary logarithms. The problem of computing discrete logarithms is a sort of sibling to the problem of integer factorisation, in that both problems are difficult (no efficient algorithms are known for non-quantum computers), algorithms from one problem are often adapted to the other, and the difficulty of both problems has been exploited to construct various cryptographic (code) systems.

Discrete logarithm are fundamental to a number of public key algorithms, including Diffie-Hellman key exchange and the Digital signature algorithms.

5.7 KEY TERMS, KEY POINTS AND REVIEW QUESTIONS

Key Terms

Bijection **Composite** **Chinese Remainder Theorem** **Discrete Logarithm**	**Euler's Theorem** **Euler's Totient Function** **Fermat's Theorem**	**Order** **Prime Number** **Primitive Root**

Key Points

- Number theory is the branch of pure mathematics concerned with the properties of numbers in general.
- A number of concepts from number theory are essential in the design of public key cryptographic algorithms.
- A prime number is an integer that can only be divided without remainder by positive and negative values of itself and 1.
- In knot theory, a prime knot is a knot which can not be written as the knot sum of two lesser nontrivial knots
- Cryptanalysis is the science of making encrypted data unencrypted.
- A Primarily test is an algorithm for determining whether an input number is prime.
- Fermat's theorem states that, if **p** is prime number and a postive integer not divisible by p then $a^{p-1} = 1 \pmod{p}$.
- Discrete logarithms are group-theoretic analogues of ordinary logarithms.
- Trapdoor one-way function is a one-way function for which the inverse direction is easy given a certain piece of information, but difficult otherwise.

Question with Answers *(2 Marks)*

Q. 1. *What is Number Theory?*

Ans. Number theory is the branch of pure mathematics concerned with the properties of numbers in general.

Q. 2. *What is cryptanalysis?*

Ans. Cryptanalysis is the science of making encrypted data unencrypted.

Q. 3. *What is knot theory?*

Ans. In knot theory, a prime knot is a knot which can not be written as the knot sum of two lesser nontrivial knots

Q. 4. *Define Primarily test.*

Ans. A Primarily test is an algorithm for determining whether an input number is prime.

Q. 5. *What is prime number?*

Ans. A prime number is an integer than can only be divided without remainder by positive and negative values of itself and 1.

Q. 6. *Define Fermat's theorem.*

Ans. Fermat's theorem states that if p is prime number and **a** is positive integer not divisible by p, then $a^{p-1} = 1 \pmod{p}$.

Q. 7. *Define Discrete Logarithms.*

Ans. **Discrete Logarithms** are group-theoretic analogues of ordinary logarithms. The problem of computing discrete logarithms is a sort of sibling to the problem of integer factorisation.

Q. 8. *What is trapdoor one-way function?*

Ans. Trapdoor one-way function is a one-way function for which the inverse direction is easy given a certain piece of information, but difficult otherwise.

Review Questions

1. Explain Number Theory
2. What is prime Number? Explain briefly.
3. Explain Fermat's theorem briefly.
4. Explain Euler's theorem.
5. What is Primality test?
6. Explain Miller-Rabin prime test briefly.
7. Explain the Chinese Remainder Theorem.

❑❑❑

CHAPTER 6 PUBLIC-KEY, CRYPTOGRAPHY AND RSA

6.1 PUBLIC-KEY CRYPTOGRAPHY

Introduction

- Public-key cryptography, also known as asymmetric cryptography, is a form of cryptography in which a user has a pair of cryptographic keys—a public key and a private key. The private key is kept secret, while the public key may be widely distributed. The keys are related mathematically, but the private key cannot be practically derived from the public key. A message encrypted with the public key can be decrypted only with the corresponding private key.
- Conversely, secret key cryptography, also known as symmetric cryptography uses a single secret key for both encryption and decryption.
- The two main branches of public key cryptography are:
- Public key encryption—a message encrypted with a recipient's public key cannot be decrypted by anyone except the recipient possessing the corresponding private key. This is used to ensure confidentiality.

- Digital signatures—a message signed with a sender's private key can be verified by anyone who has access to the sender's public key, thereby proving that the sender signed it and that the message has not been tampered with. This is used to ensure authenticity.

The development of public-key cryptography is the greatest and perhaps the only true revolution in the entire history of cryptography. It is asymmetric, involving the use of two separate keys, in contrast to symmetric encryption, which uses only one key. Anyone knowing the public key can encrypt messages or verify signatures, but **cannot** decrypt messages or create signatures, counter-intuitive though this may seem. It works by the clever use of number theory problems that are easy one way but hard the other. Note that public key schemes are neither more nor less secure than private key (security depends on the key size for both), nor do they replace private key schemes (they are too slow to do so), rather they complement them. Both also have issues with key distribution, requiring the use of some suitable protocol.

- probably most significant advance in the 3000 years history of cryptography
- uses **two** keys – a public and a private key.
- **asymmetric** since parties are **not** equal.
- uses clever application of number theoretic concepts to function.
- complements **rather than** replaces private key crypto.
- **public-key/two-key/asymmetric** cryptography involves the use of **two** keys:
  - a **public-key**, which may be known by anybody, and can be used to **encrypt messages**, and **verify signatures**.
  - a **private-key**, known only to the recipient, used to **decrypt messages**, and **sign** (create) **signatures.**
- is **asymmetric** because
  - those who encrypt messages or verify signatures **cannot** decrypt messages or create signatures.

Why Public-Key Cryptography?

The concept of public-key cryptography evolved from an attempt to attack two of the most difficult problems associated with symmetric encryption: key distribution and digital signatures. The idea of public key schemes, and the first practical scheme, which was for key distribution only, was published in 1977 by Diffie and Hellman. The concept had been previously described in a classified report in 1970 by James Ellis (UK CESG)—and subsequently declassified. Its interesting to note that they discovered RSA first, then Diffie—Hellman, opposite to the order of public discovery! There is also a claim that the NSA knew of the concept in the mid-60's.

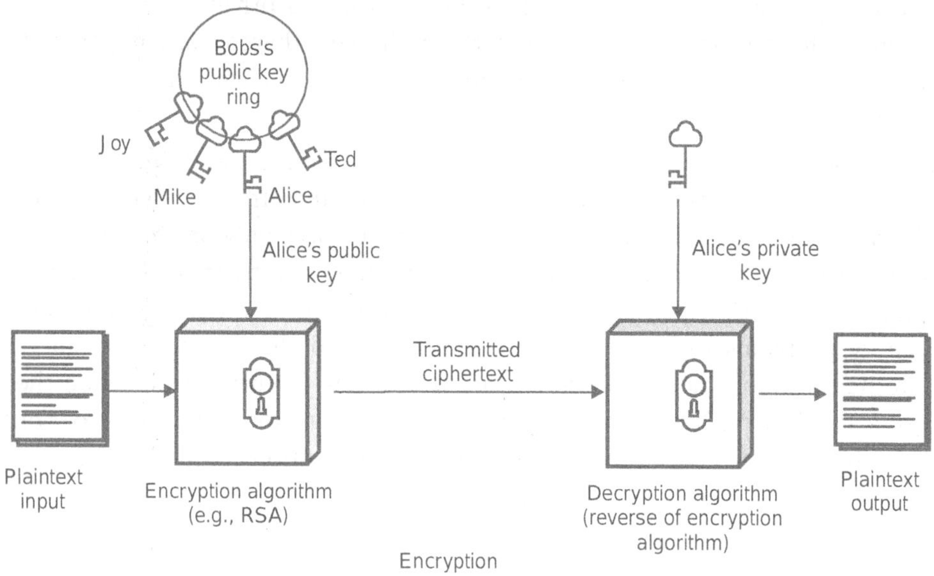

Fig. 6.1. *Public-key encryption.*

The above Fig. 6.1 "Public-Key Cryptography", shows that a public-key encryption scheme has six ingredients: plaintext, encryption algorithm, public and private keys, ciphertext and decryption algorithm.

Consider the following analogy using padlocked boxes: traditional schemes involve the sender putting a message in a box and locking it, sending that to the receiver, and somehow securely also sending them the key to unlock the box. The radical advance in public key schemes was to turn this around, the receiver sends an unlocked box (their public key) to the sender, who puts the message in the box and locks it (easy—and having locked it cannot get at the message), and sends the locked box to the receiver who can unlock it (also easy), having the (private) key. An attacker would have to pick the lock on the box (hard).

6.1.1 Public-Key Characteristics

Asymmetric algorithms rely on one key for encryption and a different but related key for decryption. These algorithms have the following important characteristic: that it is computationally infeasible to determine the decryption key given only knowledge of the cryptographic algorithm and the encryption key. That is public key schemes utilise problems that are easy (P type) one way but hard (NP type) the other way, *e.g.*, exponentiation vs logs, multiplication vs factoring. In addition, some algorithms, such as RSA, are also able to use either key as public and other private.

- Public-Key algorithms rely on two keys where:
  - It is computationally infeasible to find decryption key knowing only algorithm and encryption key.
  - It is computationally easy to en/decrypt messages when the relevant (en/decrypt) key is known.
  - Either of the two related keys can be used for encryption, with the other used for decryption.

6.1.2 Public-Key Cryptosystems

The following Fig. 6.2 "Public-Key Cryptosystems: Secrecy and Authentication" illustrates the essential elements of a public-key encryption scheme.

Note that public-key schemes can be used for either secrecy or authentication, or both (as shown here).

In this case, separate key pairs are used for each of these purposes. The receiver owns and creates secrecy keys, sender owns and creates authentication keys.

In practice typically DO NOT do this, because of the computational cost of public-key schemes. Rather encrypt a session key which is then used with a block cipher to encrypt the actual message, and separately sign a hash of the message as a digital signature – this will be discussed more later.

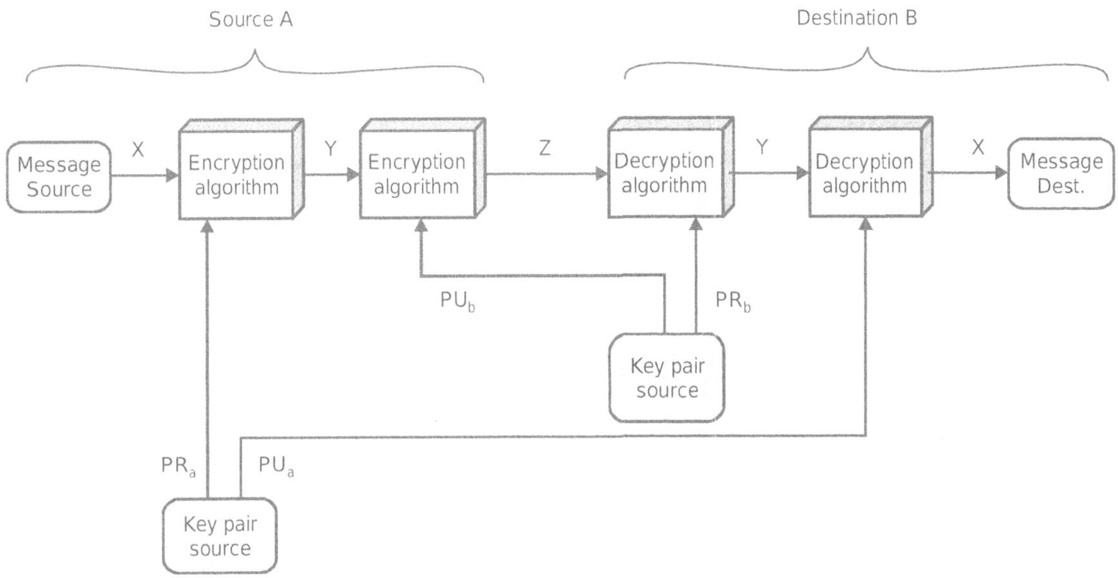

Fig. 6.2. *Public-key cryptosystems.*

6.1.3 Public-Key Applications

Public-key systems are characterized by the use of a cryptographic type of algorithm with two keys. Depending on the application, the sender uses either the sender's private key or the receiver's public key, or both, to perform some type of cryptographic function. In broad terms, we can classify the use of public-key cryptosystems into the three categories:

- **Encryption/decryption:** The sender encrypts a message with the recipient's public key.
- **Digital signature:** The sender "signs" a message with its private key, either to the whole message or to a small block of data that is a function of the message.
- **Key exchange:** Two sides cooperate to exchange a session key. Several different approaches are possible, involving the private key(s) of one or both parties.

Some algorithms are suitable for all three applications, whereas others can be used only for one or two of these applications.

6.1.4 Security of Public-Key Schemes

- Like private key schemes brute force exhaustive search attack is always theoretically possible.
- But keys used are too large (>512 bits).
- Security relies on a large enough difference in difficulty between easy (en/decrypt) and hard (cryptanalyse) problems.
- More generally the hard problem is known, but is made hard enough to be impractical to break.
- Requires the use of very large numbers.
- Hence is slow compared to private key schemes.

6.2 RSA ALGORITHM

In cryptography, RSA is an algorithm for public-key cryptography. It was the first algorithm known to be suitable for signing as well as encryption, and one of the first great advances in public key cryptography. RSA is widely used in electronic commerce protocols, and is believed to be secure given sufficiently long keys and the use of up-to-date implementations.

The RSA algorithm is named after Ron Rivest, Adi Shamir and Len Adleman, who invented it in 1977. The basic technique was first discovered in 1973 by Clifford Cocks of CESG (part of the British GCHQ) but this was a secret until 1997—see The History of ID-PKC.

The RSA algorithm can be used for both public key encryption and digital signatures. Its security is based on the difficulty of factoring large integers.

Operation

RSA involves a public key and a private key. The public key can be known to everyone and is used for encrypting messages. Messages encrypted with the public key can only be decrypted using the private key. The keys for the RSA algorithm are generated the following way.

6.2.1 Key Generation Algorithm

1. Generate two large random primes, p and q, of approximately equal size such that their product $n = pq$ is of the required bit length, *e.g.*, 1024-bits.
2. Compute $n = pq$ and (φ) phi = (p–1)(q–1).
3. Choose an integer e, 1 < e < phi, such that gcd(e, phi) = 1.
4. Compute the secret exponent d, 1 < d < phi, such that

   ed ≡ 1 (mod phi).

5. The public key is (n, e) and the private key is (n, d). The values of p, q and phi should also be kept secret.

- n is known as the *modulus.*
- e is known as the *public exponent or encryption exponent.*
- d is known as the *secret exponent or decryption exponent.*

Encryption

Sender A does the following:

1. Obtains the recipient B's public key (n, e).
2. Represents the plaintext message as a positive integer m [see note 4].
3. Computes the ciphertext c = m^e mod n.
4. Sends the ciphertext c to B.

Decryption

Recipient B does the following:

1. Uses his private key (n, d) to compute m = c^d mod n.
2. Extracts the plaintext from the integer representative m.

A Simple Example

This is an extremely simple example and would not be secure using primes so small, normally the primes p and q would be much larger.

1. Select the prime integers q = 11, q = 3.
2. $n = pq = 33$; $\varphi(n) = (p-1)(q-1) = 20$
3. Choose e = 3
   - Check gcd(3, 20) = 1
4. Compute d=7
   - $(3)d \equiv 1 \pmod{20}$

Therefore the public key is (n, e) = (33, 3) and the private key is (n, d) = (33, 7).

Now say we wanted to encrypt the message M = 7

- $C = M^e \bmod n$
- $C = 7^3 \bmod 33$
- $C = 343 \bmod 33$
- $C = 13$

So now the cyphertext C has been found. The decryption of C is performed as follows:

- $M' = C^d \bmod n$
- $M' = 13^7 \bmod 33$
- $M' = 62{,}748{,}517 \bmod 33$
- $M' = 7$

As you can see after the message has been encrypted and decrypted the final message M′ is the same as the original message M. A more practical way to use the algorithm is to convert the message to hexadecimal and perform the encryption and decryption steps on each octet individually.

6.2.2 Digital Signing

Sender A does the following:

1. Creates a *message digest* of the information to be sent.
2. Represents this digest as an integer m between 0 and n–1. [See note 5].
3. Uses her *private* key (n, d) to compute the signature s = m^d mod n.
4. Sends this signature s to the recipient, B.

Signature Verification

Recipient B does the following:

1. Uses sender A's public key (n, e) to compute integer v = s^e mod n.
2. Extracts the message digest from this integer.
3. Independently computes the message digest of the information that has been signed.
4. If both message digests are identical, the signature is valid.

Notes on Practical Applications

1. To generate the primes p and q, generate a random number of bit length b/2, where b is the required bit length of n; set the low bit (this ensures the number is odd) and set the *two* highest bits (this ensures that the high bit of n is also set); check if prime (use the *Rabin-Miller* test); if not, increment the number by two and check again. This is p. Repeat for q starting with an integer of length b-b/2. If p<q, swop p and q (this only matters if you intend using the CRT form of the private key). In the extremely unlikely event that p = q, check your random number generator. For greater security, instead of incrementing by 2, generate another random number each time.
2. In practice, common choices for e are 3, 17 and 65537 ($2^{16}+1$). These are Fermat primes and are chosen because they make the modular exponentiation operation faster. Also, having chosen e, it is simpler to test whether gcd(e, p–1)=1 and gcd(e, q–1)=1 while generating and testing the primes in step 1. Values of p or q that fail this test can be rejected there and then. (Even better: if e is prime and greater than 2 then you can do the less-expensive test (p mod e)!=1 instead of gcd(p–1, e)==1.)
3. To compute the value for d, use the *Extended Euclidean Algorithm* to calculate d = e^{-1} mod phi (this is known as *modular inversion*).
4. When representing the plaintext octets as the representative integer m, it is usual to add random padding characters to make the size of the integer m large and less susceptible to certain types of attack. If m = 0 or 1 there is no security as the ciphertext has the same value. For more details on how to represent the plaintext

octets as a suitable representative integer m. t is important to make sure that $m < n$ otherwise the algorithm will fail. This is usually done by making sure the first octet of m is equal to 0×00.

5. Decryption and signing are identical as far as the mathematics is concerned as both use the private key. Similarly, encryption and verification both use the same mathematical operation with the public key. That is, mathematically,

   ```
   m = (m^e mod n)^d mod n = (m^d mod n)^e mod n, m < n
   ```

   However, note these important differences in implementation:

   - The signature is derived from a message digest of the original information. The recipient will need to follow exactly the same process to derive the message digest, using an identical set of data.
   - The recommended methods for deriving the representative integers are different for encryption and signing (encryption involves random padding, but signing uses the same padding each time).

Summary of RSA

- $n = pq$, where p and q are distinct primes.
- phi, $\varphi = (p - 1)(q - 1)$
- $e < n$ such that gcd(e, phi) = 1
- d = e^-1 mod phi.
- c = m^e mod n, 1<m<n.
- m = c^d mod n.

6.2.3 Theory and Proof of the RSA Algorithm

Every man and his dog seems to have a proof of the RSA algorithm out there, all requiring varying degrees of understanding of number theory. This is our version of a proof of the RSA algorithm, re-written October 2006 (PDF version) and some hints on understanding it.

A very simple example of RSA encryption

This is an extremely simple example using numbers you can work out on a pocket calculator (those of you over the age of 35 can probably even do it by hand on paper).

1. Select primes p=11, q=3.
2. n = pq = 11.3 = 33

   phi = (p − 1)(q − 1) = 10.2 = 20
3. Choose e=3

   Check gcd(e, p − 1) = gcd(3, 10) = 1 (*i.e.,* 3 and 10 have no common factors except 1),

   and check gcd(e, q − 1) = gcd(3, 2) = 1

   therefore gcd(e, phi) = gcd(e, (p − 1)(q − 1)) = gcd(3, 20) = 1

4. Compute d such that ed ≡1 (mod p hi)

   i.e., compute d = e^-1 mod phi = 3^-1 mod 20

   i.e., find a value for d such that phi divides (ed – 1)

   i.e., find d such that 20 divides 3d–1.

   Simple testing (d = 1, 2, ...) gives d = 7

   Check: ed – 1 = 3.7 – 1 = 20, which is divisible by phi.

5. Public key = (n, e) = (33, 3)

   Private key = (n, d) = (33, 7).

This is actually the smallest possible value for the modulus n for which the RSA algorithm works.

Now say we want to encrypt the message m = 7,

c = m^e mod n = 7^3 mod 33 = 343 mod 33 = 13.

Hence the ciphertext c = 13.

To check decryption we compute

m′ = c^d mod n = 13^7 mod 33 = 7.

Note that we don't have to calculate the full value of 13 to the power 7 here. We can make use of the fact that a = bc mod n = (b mod n).(c mod n) mod n so we can break down a potentially large number into its components and combine the results of easier, smaller calculations to calculate the final value.

One way of calculating m′ is as follows:

m′ = 13^7 mod 33 = 13^(3+3+1) mod 33 = 13^3.13^3.13 mod 33

= (13^3 mod 33).(13^3 mod 33).(13 mod 33) mod 33

= (2197 mod 33).(2197 mod 33).(13 mod 33) mod 33

= 19.19.13 mod 33 = 4693 mod 33

= 7.

Now if we calculate the cipher text c for all the possible values of m (0 to 32), we get

m	0	1	2	3	4	5	6	7	8	9	10	11	12	13	14	15	16
c	0	1	8	27	31	26	18	13	17	3	10	11	12	19	5	9	4
m	17	18	19	20	21	22	23	24	25	26	27	28	29	30	31	32	
c	29	24	28	14	21	22	23	30	16	20	15	7	2	6	25	32	

Note that all 33 values of m (0 to 32) map to a unique code c in the same range in a sort of random manner. In this case we have nine values of m that map to the same value of c—these are known as unconcealed messages. m = 0 and 1 will always do this for any N, no matter how large. But in practice, higher values shouldn't be a problem when we use large values for N.

If we wanted to use this system to keep secrets, we could let A = 2, B = 3, ..., Z = 27. (We specifically avoid 0 and 1 here for the reason given above). Thus the plaintext message "HELLOWORLD" would be represented by the set of integers m_1, m_2, ...

{9,6,13,13,16,24,16,19,13,5}

Using our table above, we obtain cipher text integers c_1, c_2, ...

{3,18,19,19,4,30,4,28,19,26}

Note that this example is no more secure than using a simple Caesar substitution cipher, but it serves to illustrate a simple example of the mechanics of RSA encryption.

Remember that calculating m^e mod n is easy, but calculating the inverse c^-e mod n is very difficult, well, for large n's anyway. However, if we can factor n into its prime factors p and q, the solution becomes easy again, even for large n's. Obviously, if we can get hold of the secret exponent d, the solution is easy, too.

6.3 RSA SECURITY

- Possible approaches to attacking RSA are:
  - Brute force key search (infeasible given size of numbers)
  - Mathematical attacks (based on difficulty of computing ø(n), by factoring modulus n)
  - Timing attacks (on running of decryption)
  - Chosen ciphertext attacks (given properties of RSA)

6.4 RSA FACTORING CHALLENGE

Practical Considerations

1. Key generation

Finding the large primes p and q is usually done by testing random numbers of the right size with probabilistic primality tests which quickly eliminate virtually all non-primes.

p and q should not be 'too close', lest the Fermat factorization for n be successful, if p – q, for instance is less than 2n1/4 (which for even small 1024-bit values of n is 3×1077) solving for p and q is trivial. Furthermore, if either p – 1 or q – 1 has only small prime factors, n can be factored quickly by Pollard's p – 1 algorithm, and these values of p or q should therefore be discarded as well.

It is important that the secret key d be large enough. MichaelJ.Wienershowedin1990 showed in 1990 that if p is between q and 2q (which is quite typical) and d < n1/4/3, then d can be computed efficiently from n and e. There is no known attack against small public exponents such as e=3, provided that proper padding is used. However, when no padding is used or when the padding is improperly implemented then small public exponents have a greater risk of leading to an attack, such as for example the unpadded plaintext vulnerability listed above. 65537 is a commonly used value for e. This value can be regarded as a compromise between avoiding potential small exponent attacks and still allowing efficient encryptions (or signature verification). The NIST Special Publication on Computer Security (SP 800–78 Rev 1 of August 2007) does not allow public exponents e smaller than 65537, but does not state a reason for this restriction.

2. Speed

RSA is much slower than DES and other symmetric cryptosystems. In practice, Bob typically encrypts a secret message with a symmetric algorithm, encrypts the (comparatively short) symmetric key with RSA, and transmits both the RSA-encrypted symmetric key and the symmetrically-encrypted message to Alice.

This procedure raises additional security issues. For instance, it is of utmost importance to use a strong random number generator for the symmetric key, because otherwise Eve (an eavesdropper wanting to see what was sent) could bypass RSA by guessing the symmetric key.

3. Key distribution

As with all ciphers, how RSA public keys are distributed is important to security. Key distribution must be secured against a man-in-the-middle attack. Suppose Eve has some way to give Bob arbitrary keys and make him believe they belong to Alice. Suppose further that Eve can intercept transmissions between Alice and Bob. Eve sends Bob her own public key, which Bob believes to be Alice's. Eve can then intercept any ciphertext sent by Bob, decrypt it with her own secret key, keep a copy of the message, encrypt the message with Alice's public key, and send the new ciphertext to Alice. In principle, neither Alice nor Bob would be able to detect Eve's presence. Defenses against such attacks are often based on digital certificates or other components of a public key infrastructure.

4. Timing attacks

Kocher described a new attack on RSA in 1995: If the attacker Eve knows Alice's hardware in sufficient detail and is able to measure the decryption times for several known ciphertexts, she can deduce the decryption key d quickly. This attack can also be applied against the RSA signature scheme. In 2003, Boneh and Brumley demonstrated a more practical attack capable of recovering RSA factorizations over a network connection (*e.g.,* from a Secure Socket Layer (SSL)-enabled webserver). This attack takes advantage of information leaked by the Chinese remainder theorem optimization used by many RSA implementations.

One way to thwart these attacks is to ensure that the decryption operation takes a constant amount of time for every cipher text. However, this approach can significantly reduce performance. Instead, most RSA implementations use an alternate technique known as cryptographic blinding. RSA blinding makes use of the multiplicative property of RSA. Instead of computing cd mod n, Alice first chooses a secret random value r and computes (rec)d mod n. The result of this computation is r m mod n and so the effect of r can be removed by multiplying by its inverse. A new value of r is chosen for each cipher text. With blinding applied, the decryption time is no longer correlated to the value of the input cipher text and so the timing attack fails.

6.5 KEY TERMS, KEY POINTS AND REVIEW QUESTIONS

Key Terms

Digital Signature	**Public Key**	**RSA**
Key Exchange	**Public Key Cryptography**	**Time Complexity**
One-Way Function	**Public Key Cryptosystems**	**Timing Attack**
Private Key	**Public Key Encryption**	**Trap-Door One-Way Function**

Key Points

➢ The concept of public-key cryptography evolved from an attempt to attack two of the most difficult problems associated with symmetric encryption: key distribution and digital signatures.

➢ Public-key cryptosystems into the three categories:
- Encryption/decryption: The sender encrypts a message with the recipient's public key.
- Digital signature: The sender "signs" a message with its private key, either to the whole message or to a small block of data that is a function of the message.
- Key exchange: Two sides cooperate to exchange a session key. Several different approaches are possible, involving the private key(s) of one or both parties.

➢ RSA involves a public key and a private key.

➢ RSA is block cipher in which the plaintext and ciphertext are integers between 0 and n – 1 for same n.

➢ Sessions keys are transmitted in encrypted form, using a master key that is shared by the key distribution centre and an end system or user.

➢ Asymmetric encryption can be used for confidentiality, authentication or both.

➢ The difficulty of attacking RSA is based on the difficulty of finding the prime factors of a composite number.

Question with Answers *(2 Marks)*

Q. 1. *What is Asymmetric Cryptography?*

Ans. It is a form of cryptography in which a user has a pair of cryptographic keys – a public key and a private key.

Q. 2. *Why Public key Cryptography?*

Ans. The concept of public key cryptography evolved from an attempt to attack two of the most difficult problems associated with symmetric encryption: key distribution and digital signatures.

Q. 3. *What is Public key Encryption?*

Ans. A message encrypted with a recipient's public key cannot be decrypted by anyone except the recipient possessing the corresponding private key. This is used to ensure confidentiality.

Q. 4. *Define Digital signatures.*

Ans. A message signed with a sender's private key can be verified by anyone who has access to the sender's public key, thereby proving that the sender signed it and that the message has not been tampered with. This is used to ensure authenticity.

Q. 5. *List Out the Categories of public key cryptosystems.*

Ans.
- **Encryption/decryption:** The sender encrypts a message with the recipient's public key.
- **Digital signature:** The sender "signs" a message with its private key, either to the whole message or to a small block of data that is a function of the message.
- **Key exchange:** Two sides co-operate to exchange a session key. Several different approaches are possible, involving the private key(s) of one or both parties.

Q. 6. *List out the key used in public key algorithms.*

Ans.
1. It is computationally infeasible to find decryption key knowing only algorithm and encryption key.
2. It is computationally easy to en/decrypt messages when the relevant (en/decrypt) key.

Q. 7. *List out the RSA Security attacks.*

Ans. (*a*) Brute force key search (infeasible given size of numbers)

(*b*) Mathematical attacks (based on difficulty of computing $\phi(n)$, by factoring modulus n)

(*c*) Timing attacks (on running of decryption)

(*d*) Chosen ciphertext attacks (given properties of RSA)

Review Questions

1. Explain briefly Public key Cryptosystem.
2. Why Public key Cryptography? Explain.
3. States the Public key Characteristics.
4. Explain RSA Algorithm.
5. What is Digital Signing?
6. What are the Challenging factors in RSA?

❑❑❑

CHAPTER 7 OTHER PUBLIC KEY CRYPTOSYSTEMS

7.1 DIFFIE-HELLMAN KEY EXCHANGE

Diffie-Hellman (D-H) key exchange is a cryptographic protocol that allows two parties that have no prior knowledge of each other to jointly establish a shared secret key over an insecure communications channel. This key can then be used to encrypt subsequent communications using a symmetric key cipher.

Synonyms of Diffie-Hellman key exchange include:

Diffie-Hellman key agreement

Diffie-Hellman key establishment

Diffie-Hellman key negotiation

Exponential key exchange.

The scheme was first published publicly by Whitfield Diffie and Martin Hellman in 1976, although it later emerged that it had been invented a few years earlier within GCHQ, the British signals intelligence agency, by Malcolm J. Williamson but was kept classified. In 2002, Hellman suggested the algorithm be called Diffie-Hellman-Merkle key exchange in recognition of Ralph Merkle's contribution to the invention of public key cryptography (Hellman, 2002).

Although Diffie-Hellman key agreement itself is an anonymous (non-authenticated) key-agreement protocol, it provides the basis for a variety of authenticated protocols, and is used to provide perfect forward secrecy in Transport Layer Security's ephemeral modes.

7.1.1 History of the Protocol

Diffie-Hellman key agreement was invented in 1976 during a collaboration between Whitfield Diffie and Martin Hellman and was the first practical method for establishing a shared secret over an unprotected communications channel. Ralph Merkle's work on public key distribution was an influence. John Gill suggested application of the discrete logarithm problem. It had been discovered by Malcolm Williamson of GCHQ in the UK some years previously, but GCHQ chose not make it public until 1997, by which time it had no influence on research in academia.

The method was followed shortly afterwards by RSA, another implementation of public key cryptography using asymmetric algorithms.

The system...has since become known as Diffie-Hellman key exchange. While that system was first described in a paper by Diffie and me, it is a public key distribution system, a concept developed by Merkle, and hence should be called 'Diffie-Hellman-Merkle key exchange' if names are to be associated with it. I hope this small pulpit might help in that endeavor to recognize Merkle's equal contribution to the invention of public key cryptography.

7.1.2 Diffie-Hellman Setup

All users agree on global parameters:

Large prime integer or polynomial q

A being a primitive root mod q

Each user (*e.g.*, A) generates their key

Chooses a secret key (number): xA < q

Compute their public key: yA = axA mod q

Each user makes public that key yA

7.1.3 Diffie-Hellman Key Exchange Algorithm

Shared session key for users A and B is KAB:

KAB = axA.xB mod q

= yAxB mod q (which B can compute)

= yBxA mod q (which A can compute)

KAB is used as session key in private-key encryption scheme between Alice and Bob

If Alice and Bob subsequently communicate, they will have the same key as before, unless they choose new public keys

Attacker needs an x, must solve discrete log

7.1.4 Diffie-Hellman Example

Users Alice and Bob who wish to swap keys:

Agree on prime q = 353 and a = 3

Select random secret keys:

A chooses xA = 97, B chooses xB = 233

Compute respective public keys:

yA = 397 mod 353 = 40 (Alice)

yB = 3233 mod 353 = 248 (Bob)

Compute shared session key as:

KAB = yBxA mod 353 = 24897 = 160 (Alice)

KAB = yAxB mod 353 = 40233 = 160 (Bob)

7.1.5 Key Exchange Protocols

- Users could create random private/public D-H keys each time they communicate.
- Users could create a known private/public D-H key and publish in a directory, then consulted and used to securely communicate with them.
- Both of these are vulnerable to a meet-in-the-Middle Attack.
- Authentication of the keys is needed.

Description

The following figure shows a simple protocol that makes use of the Diffe-Hellman Calculation.

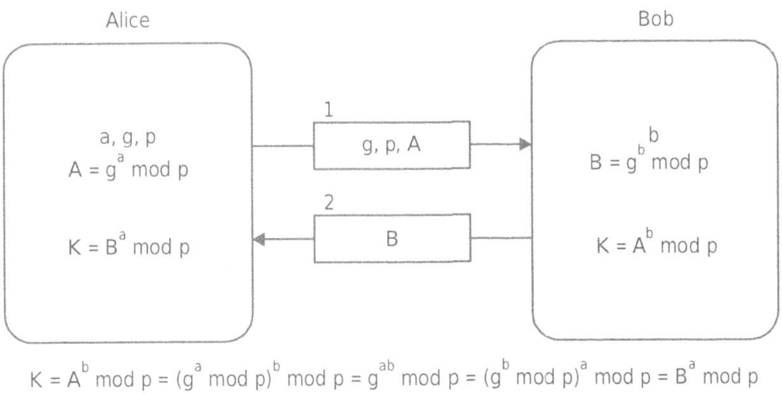

Fig. 7.1. *Diffie-Hellman key exchange.*

The simplest, and original, implementation of the protocol uses the multiplicative group of integers modulo p, where p is prime and g is primitive root mod p. Here is an example of the protocol.

Diffie-Hellman key exchange offers the best of both worlds—It uses public key techniques to allow the exchange of a private encryption key! Let's take a look at how the protocol works, from the perspective of Alice and Bob, two users who wish to establish secure communications. We can assume that Alice and Bob know nothing about each other but are in contact. Here are the nine steps of the process.

Communicating in the clear, Alice and Bob agree on two large positive integers, n and g, with the stipulation that n is a prime number and g is a generator of n.

Alice randomly chooses another large positive integer, XA, which is smaller than n. XA will serve as Alice's private key.

Bob similarly chooses his own private key, XB.

Alice computes her public key, YA, using the formula YA = (g ^XA) mod n.

Bob similarly computes his public key, YB, using the formula YB = (g ^XB) mod n.

Alice and Bob exchange public keys over the insecure circuit.

Alice computes the shared secret key, k, using the formula k = (YB ^XA) mod n.

Bob computes the same shared secret key, k, using the formula k = (YA ^XB) mod n.

Alice and Bob communicate using the symmetric algorithm of their choice and the shared secret key, k, which was never transmitted over the insecure circuit.

The Diffie-Hellman key exchange is vulnerable to a man-in-the-middle attack. In this attack, an opponent Carol intercepts Alice's public value and sends her own public value to Bob. When Bob transmits his public value, Carol substitutes it with her own and sends it to Alice. Carol and Alice thus agree on one shared key and Carol and Bob agree on another shared key. After this exchange, Carol simply decrypts any messages sent out by Alice or Bob, and then reads and possibly modifies them before re-encrypting with the appropriate key and transmitting them to the other party. This vulnerability is present because Diffie-Hellman key exchange does not authenticate the participants. Possible solutions include the use of digital signatures and other protocol variants.

In recent years, the original Diffie-Hellman protocol has been understood to be an example of a much more general cryptographic technique, the common element being the derivation of a shared secret value (that is, key) from one party's public key and another party's private key. The parties' key pairs may be generated a new at each run of the protocol, as in the original Diffie-Hellman protocol. The public keys may be certified, so that the parties can be authenticated and there may be a combination of these attributes.

7.2 CONFIDENTIALITY USING SYMMETRIC ENCRYPTION

7.2.1 Placement of Encryption Function

- Traditionally symmetric encryption is used to provide message confidentiality

If encryption is to be used to counter attacks on confidentiality, need to decide what to encrypt and where the encryption function should be located. Now examine potential locations of security attacks and then look at the two major approaches to encryption placement: link and end to end.

Have many locations where attacks can occur in a typical scenario (Fig. 7.2), such as when have:

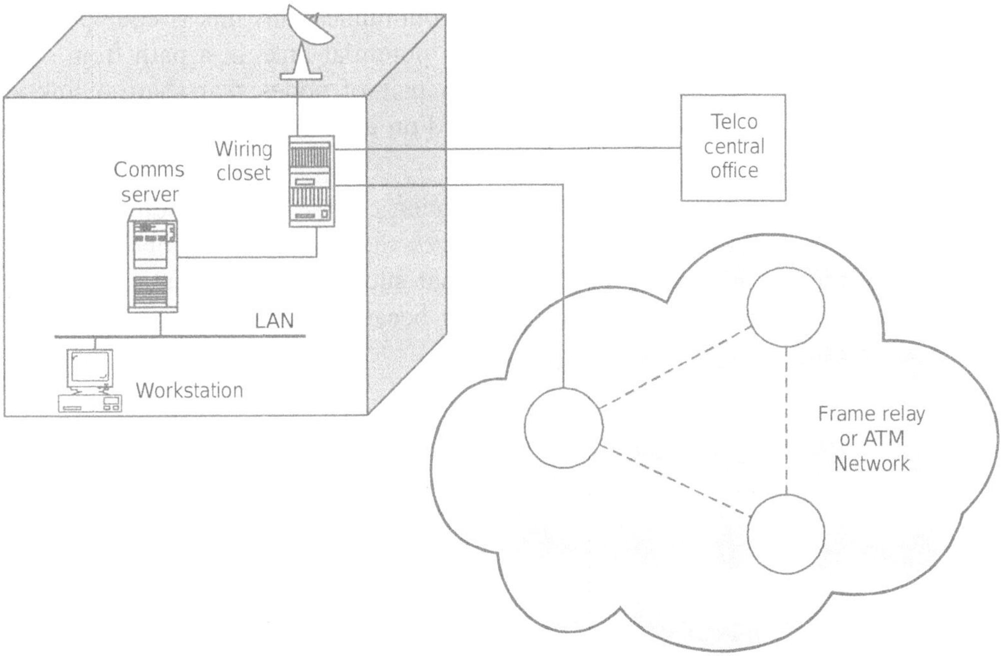

Fig. 7.2. *Workstations on LANs access other workstations and servers on LAN.*

- LANs interconnected using switches/routers
- With external lines or radio/satellite links
- Consider attacks and placement in this scenario
- Snooping from another workstation
- Use dial-in to LAN or server to snoop
- Physically tap line in wiring closet
- Use external router link to enter and snoop
- Monitor and/or modify traffic one external links
- Consider typical scenario
  - workstations on LANs access other workstations and servers on LAN
  - LANs interconnected using switches/routers
  - with external lines or radio/satellite links
- Consider attacks and placement in this scenario
  - snooping from another workstation
  - use dial-in to LAN or server to snoop
  - use external router link to enter and snoop
  - monitor and/or modify traffic one external links

- There are two fundamental encryption placement alternatives: link encryption and end-to-end encryption.
- **With link encryption,** each vulnerable communications link is equipped on both ends with an encryption device. But all the potential links in a path from source to destination must use link encryption. Each pair of nodes that share a link should share a unique key, with a different key used on each link. Thus, many keys must be provided.
- **With end-to-end encryption,** the encryption process is carried out at the two end systems. Thus end-to-end encryption relieves the end user of concerns about the degree of security of networks and links that support the communication. The user data is secure, but the traffic pattern is not because packet headers are transmitted in the clear.

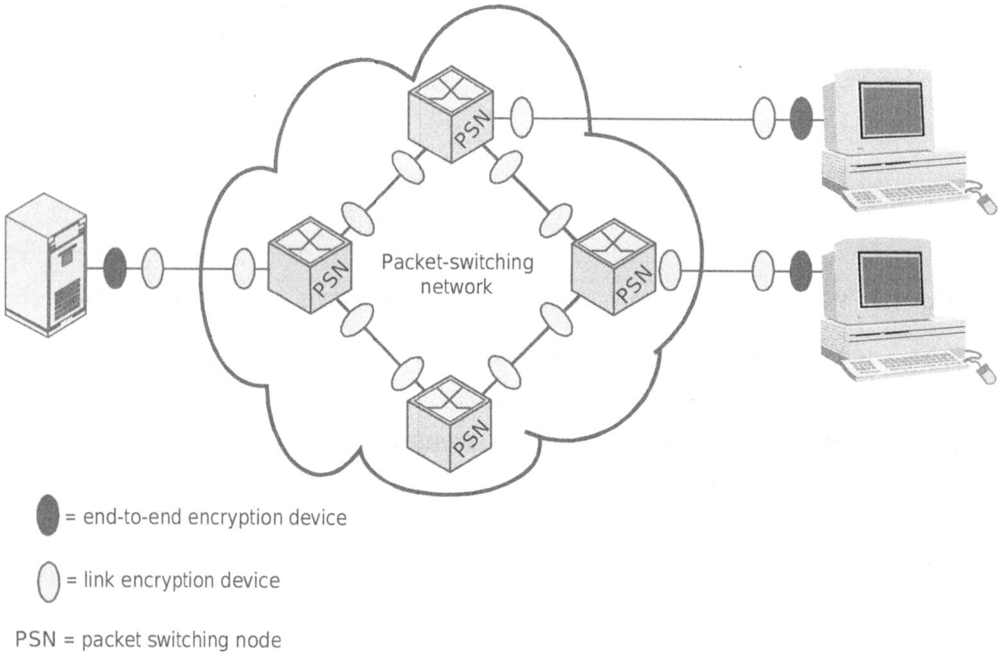

Fig. 7.3. *Contrasts the two encryption placement alternatives, for encryption over a packet net.*

With end-to-end encryption, user data are secure, but the traffic pattern is not because packet headers are transmitted in the clear. However end-to-end encryption does provide a degree of authentication, since a recipient is assured that any message that it receives comes from the alleged sender, because only that sender shares the relevant key. Such authentication is not inherent in a link encryption scheme. To achieve greater security, both link and end-to-end encryption are needed.

7.2.1.1 *Placement of Encryption*

- Can place encryption function at various layers in OSI Reference Model
  - link encryption occurs at layers 1 or 2
  - end-to-end can occur at layers 3, 4, 6, 7
  - as move higher less information is encrypted but it is more secure though more complex with more entities and keys.

7.2.2 Traffic Confidentiality

Some users are concerned with Traffic Analysis, which concerns knowledge about the number and length of messages between nodes which may enable an opponent to determine who is talking to whom, and hence suggest when important information is being exchanged, or to correlate with observed events.

With the use of link encryption, network-layer headers are encrypted, reducing the opportunity for traffic analysis. An effective countermeasure to this attack is traffic padding.

If only end-to-end encryption is employed, then the measures available to the defender are more limited since various protocol headers are visible. Padding of application data and null messages can be used.

Traffic Analysis

- is monitoring of communications flows between parties
  - useful both in military and commercial spheres
  - can also be used to create a covert channel
- link encryption obscures header details
  - but overall traffic volumes in networks and at end-points is still visible
- traffic padding can further obscure flows
  - but at cost of continuous traffic
- when using end-to-end encryption must leave headers in clear
  - so network can correctly route information
- hence although contents protected, traffic pattern flows are not
- ideally want both at once
  - end-to-end protects data contents over entire path and provides authentication
  - link protects traffic flows from monitoring

7.2.3 Key Distribution

For symmetric encryption to work, the two parties to an exchange must share the same key, and that key must be protected from access by others. This is one of the most critical areas in security systems – on many occasions systems have been broken, not because of a poor encryption algorithm, but because of poor key selection or management.

The strength of any cryptographic system thus depends on the key distribution technique. For two parties A and B, key distribution can be achieved in a number of ways:

Physical delivery (1 and 2) is simplest – but only applicable when there is personal contact between recipient and key issuer. This is fine for link encryption where devices and keys occur in pairs, but does not scale as number of parties who wish to communicate grows. 3 is mostly based on 1 or 2 occurring first.

A third party, whom all parties trust, can be used as a trusted intermediary to mediate the establishment of secure communications between them (4). Must trust intermediary not to abuse the knowledge of all session keys. As number of parties grow, some variant of 4 is only practical solution to the huge growth in number of keys potentially needed.

Key Distribution

- Given parties A and B have various key distribution alternatives:
  1. A can select key and physically deliver to B.
  2. Third party can select and deliver key to A and B.
  3. If A and B have communicated previously can use previous key to encrypt a new key.
  4. If A and B have secure communications with a third party C, C can relay key between A and B.

Key Distribution Scenario

The key distribution concept can be deployed in a number of ways. A typical scenario is illustrated below Fig. 7.4, which has a "Key Distribution Center" (KDC) which shares a unique key with each party (user).

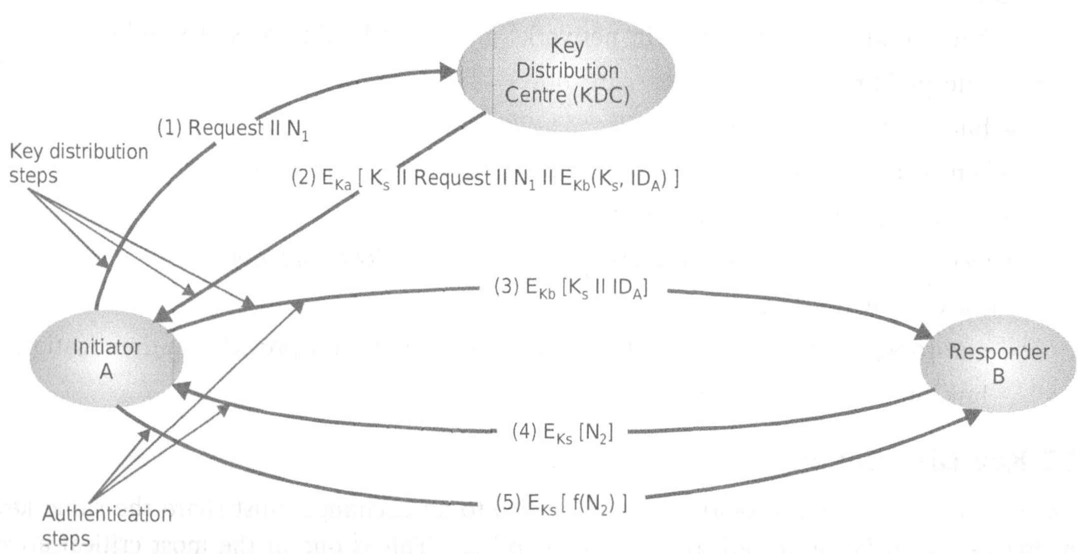

Fig. 7.4. *Key distribution scenario.*

Key Distribution Issues

- Hierarchies of KDC's required for large networks, but must trust each other
- Session key lifetimes should be limited for greater security
- Use of automatic key distribution on behalf of users, but must trust system
- Use of decentralized key distribution
- Controlling purposes keys are used for.

Key Hierarchy

The use of a key distribution center is based on the use of a hierarchy of keys. At a minimum, two levels of keys are used: a session key, used for the duration of a logical connection; and a master key shared by the key distribution center and an end system or user and used to encrypt the session key.

- Typically have a hierarchy of keys
- Session key
  - Temporary key
  - Used for encryption of data between users
  - For one logical session then discarded
- Master key
  - Used to encrypt session keys
  - Shared by user and key distribution center.

7.2.4 Random Numbers

Random numbers play an important role in the use of encryption for various network security applications. Getting good random numbers is important, but difficult. You don't want someone guessing the key you're using to protect your communications because your "random numbers" weren't (as happened in an early release of Netscape SSL). Need such random values to be both statistically random (with uniform distribution and independent) and also to be unpredictable (so that it is not possible to predict future values having observed previous values).

- Many uses of **random numbers** in cryptography
  - Nonces in authentication protocols to prevent replay
  - Session keys
  - Public key generation
  - Keystream for a one-time pad
- In all case its critical that these values be
  - Statistically random, uniform distribution, independent
  - Unpredictability of future values from previous values.

7.2.4.1 Pseudorandom Number Generators (PRNGs)

Cryptographic applications typically make use of deterministic algorithmic techniques for random number generation, producing sequences of numbers that are not statistically random, but if the algorithm is good, the resulting sequences will pass many reasonable tests of randomness. Such numbers are referred to as pseudorandom numbers, created by "Pseudorandom Number Generators (PRNGs)".

- Often use deterministic algorithmic techniques to create "random numbers"
  - Although are not truly random
  - Can pass many tests of "randomness"
- Known as "pseudorandom numbers"
- Created by "Pseudorandom Number Generators (PRNGs)".

7.2.4.2 Linear Congruential Generator

By far the most widely used technique for pseudorandom number generation is the "Linear Congruential Generator", first proposed by Lehmer. It uses successive values from an iterative equation. Given suitable values of parameters can produce a long random-like sequence, but there are only a small number of such good choices. Note that the sequence, whilst looking random, is highly predictable, and an attacker can reconstruct the sequence knowing only a small number of values. There are some approaches to making this harder to do in practice by modifying the numbers in some way.

- Common iterative technique using:

$$Xn+1 = (aXn + c) \bmod m$$

- Given suitable values of parameters can produce a long random-like sequence.
- Suitable criteria to have are:
  - Function generates a full-period
  - Generated sequence should appear random
  - Efficient implementation with 32-bit arithmetic.
- Note that an attacker can reconstruct sequence given a small number of values.
- Have possibilities for making this harder.

Cryptographically Generated Random Numbers

For cryptographically applications it makes some sense to take advantage of the encryption logic available to produce random numbers. A number of means have been used, and in this subsection we look at one representative examples.

7.2.4.3 ANSI X9.17 PRG

One of the strongest (cryptographically speaking) PRNGs is specified in ANSI X9.17. It uses date/time and seed inputs and 3 triple-DES encryptions to generate a new seed and random value. The following Fig. 7.5 illustrates them.

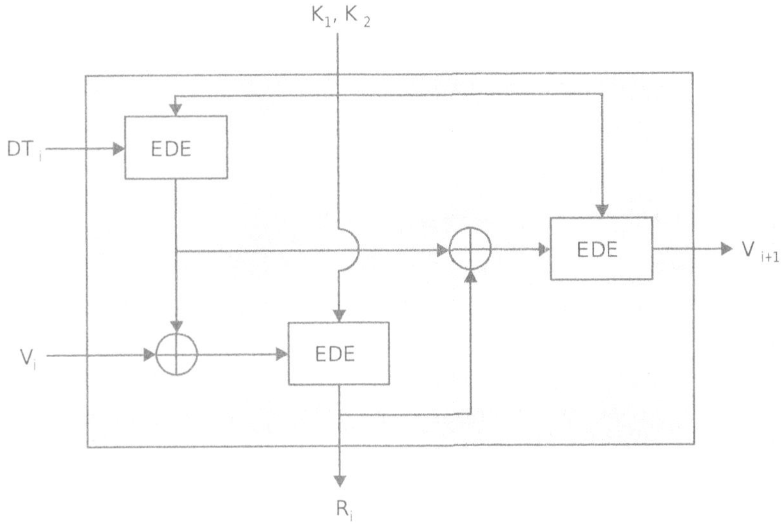

Fig. 7.5. *3-Triple-DES encryption.*

where DT_i = Date/time value at the beginning of *i*th generation stage

V_i = Seed value at the beginning of *i*th generation stage

R_i = Pseudorandom number produced by the *i*th generation stage

K_1, K_2 = DES keys used for each stage

Then compute successive values as:

$$R_i = EDE([K_1, K_2], [V_i \text{ XOR } EDE([K_1, K_2], DT_i)])$$

$$V_{i+1} = EDE([K_1, K_2], [R_i \text{ XOR } EDE([K_1, K_2], DT_i)])$$

Several factors contribute to the cryptographic strength of this method. The technique involves a 112-bit key and three EDE encryptions for a total of nine DES encryptions. The scheme is driven by two pseudorandom inputs, the date and time value, and a seed produced by the generator that is distinct from the pseudorandom number produced by the generator. Thus the amount of material that must be compromised by an opponent is overwhelming.

7.2.4.4. Blum Blum Shub Generator

A popular approach to generating secure pseudorandom number is known as the Blum, Blum, Shub (BBS) generator, after its developers. It has perhaps the strongest public proof of its cryptographic strength of any PRNG. It is based on public key algorithms, and hence is very slow, but has a very high level of security. It is referred to as a cryptographically secure pseudorandom bit generator (CSPRBG), being in practice unpredictable.

- Based on public key algorithms
- Use least significant bit from iterative equation:
  - xi = xi–12 mod n
  - where $n = p, q$ and primes, $p, q = 3 \text{ mod } 4$

- Unpredictable, *passes* **next-bit** *test*
- Security rests on difficulty of factoring N
- Is unpredictable given any run of bits
- Slow, since very large numbers must be used
- Too slow for cipher use, good for key generation.

7.2.4.5. True Random Number Generator (TRNG)

A true random number generator (TRNG) uses a nondeterministic source to produce randomness. Most operate by measuring unpredictable natural processes, such as pulse detectors of ionizing radiation events, gas discharge tubes, and leaky capacitors. Special hardware is usually needed for this. A true random number generator may produce an output that is biased in some way. Various methods of modifying a bit stream to reduce or eliminate the bias have been developed.

- Best source is natural randomness in real world
- Find a regular but random event and monitor
- Do generally need special h/w to do this
  - *e.g.,* radiation counters, radio noise, audio noise, thermal noise in diodes, leaky capacitors, mercury discharge tubes etc.
- Starting to see such h/w in new CPU's.
- Problems of **bias** or uneven distribution in signal
  - have to compensate for this when sample and use
  - best to only use a few noisiest bits from each sample.

7.3 ELLIPTIC CURVE CRYPTOSYSTEMS

Elliptic curve cryptosystems were first proposed independently by Victor Miller and Neal Koblitz in the mid-1980s. At a high level, they are analogs of existing public key cryptosystems in which modular arithmetic is replaced by operations defined over elliptic curves. The elliptic curve cryptosystems that have appeared in the literature can be classified into two categories according to whether they are analogs to the RSA system or to discrete logarithm based systems.

Presently, the methods for computing general elliptic curve discrete logarithms are much less efficient than those for factoring or computing conventional discrete logarithms. As a result, shorter key sizes can be used to achieve the same security of conventional public key cryptosystems, which might lead to better memory requirements and improved performance. One can easily construct elliptic curve encryption, signature, and key agreement schemes by making analogs of ElGamal, DSA, and Diffie-Hellman. These variants appear to offer certain implementation advantages over the original schemes, and they have recently drawn more and more attention from both the academic community and the industry.

7.3.1. Elliptic Curves

The way that the elliptic curve operations are defined is what gives ECC its higher security at smaller key sizes.

An elliptic curve is defined in a standard, two dimensional x, y Cartesian coordinate system by an equation of the form:

$$y^2 = x^3 + ax + b$$

The graphs turns out to be gently looping lines of various forms.

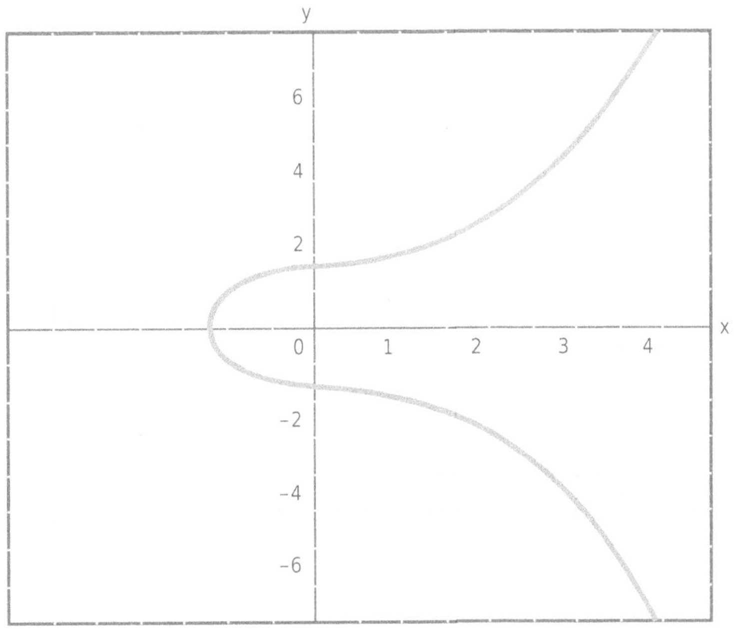

Fig. 7.6. *An elliptic curve.*

In elliptic curve cryptosystems, the elliptic curve is used to define the members of the set over which the group is calculated, as well as the operations between them which define how math works in the group.

It's done as follows: imagine a graph labelled along both axes with the numbers of a large prime field. That is to say: a square graph, $p \times p$ in size, where p is a very large prime number. F_p is the field of integers modulo p, and consists of all the integers from 0 to $p - 1$.

Now the prime numbers actually employed in practical ECC implementations are quite large, so it's difficult to visualize this graph if you use the real kinds of numbers used. But as an exercise, you can imagine a more comprehensible prime — such as 17. So you'd be looking at a graph 17×17 units in size.

Now if you define an elliptic curve—an equation of the form given above—so that there are points (x, y) on the curve that satisfy the condition that both x and y are members of the prime field, you have implicitly created a group from the set of integer points on the curve; it is a subset of all the points in the p by p matrix created when you drew the graph —specifically the ones the curve passes directly through.

Note that unlike the groups used in Diffie-Hellman, the elements of the set aren't integers, but points. But the system that will result is still going to be, in most senses, the same, familiar arithmetic system as those discussed above. It contains a set of elements (points, in this case), and when you add one point to another, or subtract one from another, there are rules that say what point in the set you wind up at when you do so—just as for the integers in the groups used in Diffie-Hellman. And these rules still follow many of the familiar rules for the arithmetic you already know.

7.3.2 Elliptic Curve Over Real Numbers

An elliptic curve over real numbers may be defined as the set of points (x, y) which satisfy an elliptic curve equation of the form:

$y^2 = x^3 + ax + b$, where x, y, a and b are real numbers.

Each choice of the numbers a and b yields a different elliptic curve. For example, $a = -4$ and $b = 0.67$ gives the elliptic curve with equation $y^2 = x^3 - 4x + 0.67$; the graph of this curve is shown follows:

If $x^3 + ax + b$ contains no repeated factors, or equivalently if $4a^3 + 27b^2$ is not 0, then the elliptic curve $y^2 = x^3 + ax + b$

Can be used to form a group. An elliptic curve group over real numbers consists of the points on the corresponding elliptic curve, together with a special point O called the point at infinity.

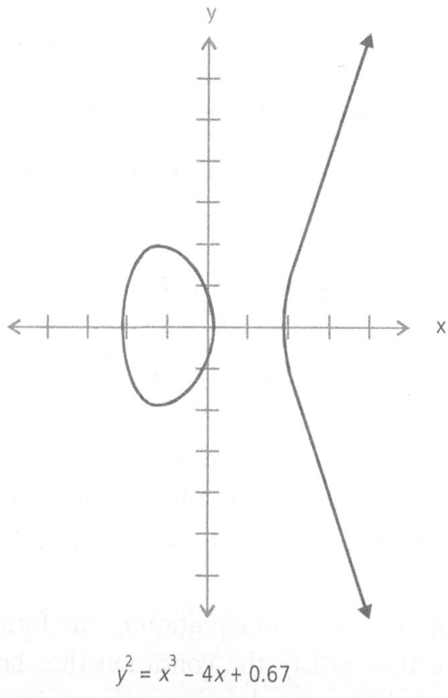

$y^2 = x^3 - 4x + 0.67$

Fig. 7.7

7.3.3 Elliptic Curve Groups over F_p

Calculations over the real numbers are slow and inaccurate due to round-off error. Cryptographic applications require fast and precise arithmetic; thus elliptic curve groups over the finite fields of F_p and F_2m are used in practice.

Recall that the field F_p uses the numbers from 0 to $p - 1$, and computations end by taking the remainder on division by p. For example, in F_{23} the field is composed of integers from 0 to 22, and any operation within this field will result in an integer also between 0 and 22.

An elliptic curve with the underlying field of F_p can formed by choosing the variables a and b within the field of F_p. The elliptic curve includes all points (x, y) which satisfy the elliptic curve equation modulo p (where x and y are numbers in F_p).

For example, $y^2 \bmod p = x^3 + ax + b \bmod p$ has an underlying field of F_p if a and b are in F_p.

If $x^3 + ax + b$ contains no repeating factors (or, equivalently, if $4a^3 + 27b^2 \bmod p$ is not 0), then the elliptic curve can be used to form a group. An elliptic curve group over F_p consists of the points on the corresponding elliptic curve, together with a special point O called the point at infinity. There are finitely many points on such an elliptic curve.

7.3.4 Elliptic Curve Groups over F_2m

Elements of the field F_2m are m-bit strings. The rules for arithmetic in F_2m can be defined by either polynomial representation or by optimal normal basis representation. Since F_2m operates on bit strings, computers can perform arithmetic in this field very efficiently.

An elliptic curve with the underlying field F_2m is formed by choosing the elements a and b within F_2m (the only condition is that b is not 0). As a result of the field F_2m having a characteristic 2, the elliptic curve equation is slightly adjusted for binary representation:

$$y^2 + xy = x^3 + ax^2 + b$$

The elliptic curve includes all points (x, y) which satisfy the elliptic curve equation over F_2m (where x and y are elements of F_2m). An elliptic curve group over F_2m consists of the points on the corresponding elliptic curve, together with a point at infinity, O. There are finitely many points on such an elliptic curve.

7.3.5 Example of an Elliptic Curve Group over F_2m

As a very small example, consider the field F_24, defined by using polynomial representation with the irreducible polynomial $f(x) = x^4 + x + 1$.

The element $g = (0010)$ is a generator for the field. The powers of g are:

$$g^0 = (0001)\ g^1 = (0010)\ g^2 = (0100)\ g^3 = (1000)\ g^4 = (0011)\ g^5 = (0110)$$
$$g^6 = (1100)\ g^7 = (1011)\ g^8 = (0101)\ g^9 = (1010)\ g^{10} = (0111)\ g^{11} = (1110)$$
$$g^{12} = (1111)\ g^{13} = (1101)\ g^{14} = (1001)\ g^{15} = (0001)$$

In a true cryptographic application, the parameter m must be large enough to preclude the efficient generation of such a table otherwise the cryptosystem can be broken. In today's practice, m = 160 is a suitable choice. The table allows the use of generator notation (g^e) rather than bit string notation, as used in the following example. Also, using generator notation allows multiplication without reference to the irreducible polynomial

$$f(x) = x^4 + x + 1.$$

Consider the elliptic curve $y^2 + xy = x^3 + g^4x^2 + 1$. Here $a = g^4$ and $b = g^0 = 1$. The point (g^5, g^3) satisfies this equation over F_2m:

$$y^2 + xy = x^3 + g^4x^2 + 1$$
$$(g^3)^2 + g^5g^3 = (g^5)^3 + g^4g^{10} + 1$$
$$g^6 + g^8 = g^{15} + g^{14} + 1$$

$$(1100) + (0101) = (0001) + (1001) + (0001)$$
$$(1001) = (1001)$$

The fifteen points which satisfy this equation are:

$(1, g^{13})$ (g^3, g^{13}) (g^5, g^{11}) (g^6, g^{14}) (g^9, g^{13}) (g^{10}, g^8) (g^{12}, g^{12})
$(1, g^6)$ (g^3, g^8) (g^5, g^3) (g^6, g^8) (g^9, g^{10}) (g^{10}, g) $(g^{12}, 0)$ $(0, 1)$

These points are graphed below:

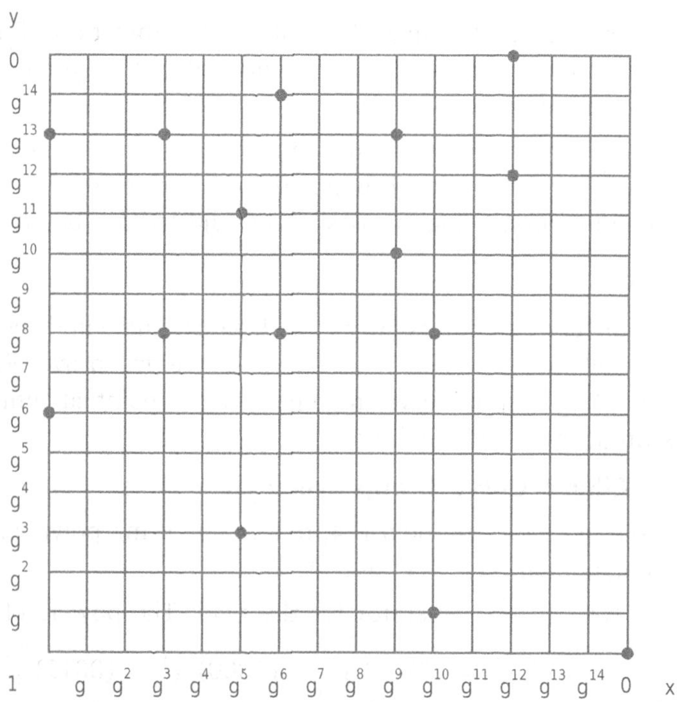

$y^2 + xy = x^3 + g^4x^2 + 1$ over F_{2^4}

Fig. 7.8

ECC Encryption/Decryption

Several approaches to encryption/ decryption using elliptic curves have been analyzed. This paper describes one of them. The first task in this system is to encode the plaintext message m to be sent as an $x - y$ point Pm. It is the point Pm that will be encrypted as a cipher text and subsequently decrypted. Note that we cannot simply encode the message as the x or y coordinate of a point, because not all such coordinates are in Ep(a, b). There are approaches to encoding. We developed a scheme that will be reported elsewhere. As with the key exchange system, an encryption/decryption system requires a point G and an elliptic group Ep(a, b) as parameters. Each user A selects a private key nA and generates a public key

$$PA = nA\ xG. \quad (6)$$

To encrypt and send a message Pm to B, A chooses a random positive integer x and produces the cipher text Cm consisting to the pair of points

$$Cm = \{xG,\ Pm + xPB\}$$

Note that A has used B's public key PB. To decrypt the cipher text, B multiplies the first point in the pair by B's secret key and subtracts the result from the second point:

$$Pm + xPB - nB(xG) = Pm + x(nBG) - nB(xG) = Pm \quad (8)$$

A has masked the message Pm by adding xPB to it. Nobody but A knows the value of x, so even though PB is a public key, nobody can remove the mask xPB. However, A also includes a "clue," which is enough to remove the mask if one knows the private key nB. For an attacker to recover the message, the attacker would have to compute x given G and xG, which is hard.

7.4 KEY TERMS, KEY POINTS AND REVIEW QUESTIONS

Key Terms

Abelian Group	**Eliptic Curve Cryptography**	**Primitive Root**
Cubic Equation	**Eliptic Curve Arithmetic**	**Public key Certificate**
Diffie-Hellman Key Exchange	**Finite Field**	**Public key Directory**
Discrete Logarithm	**Key Distribution**	**Zero Point**
Eliptic Curve	**Key Management**	

Key Points

- Diffie-Hellman key agreement was invented in 1976 during a collaboration between Whitfield Diffie and Martin Hellman
- Diffie-Hellman (D-H) key exchange is a cryptographic protocol that allows two parties that have no prior knowledge of each other to jointly establish a shared secret key over an insecure communications channel.

➢ The Diffie-Hellman key exchange is vulnerable to a man-in-the-middle attack.

➢ Traditionally symmetric encryption is used to provide message confidentiality

➢ Traffic Analysis is monitoring of communications flows between parties

➢ The strength of any cryptographic system thus depends on the key distribution technique.

➢ Random numbers play an important role in the use of encryption for various network security applications.

➢ Many uses of random numbers in cryptography
  - nonces in authentication protocols to prevent replay
  - session keys
  - public key generation

➢ A popular approach to generating secure pseudorandom number is known as the Blum, Blum, Shub (BBS) generator, after its developers

➢ True random number generator (TRNG) uses a nondeterministic source to produce randomness.

➢ Presently, the methods for computing general elliptic curve discrete logarithms are much less efficient than those for factoring or computing conventional discrete logarithms.

➢ Elliptic curve arithmetic can be used develop a variety of elliptic curve cryptography schemes, including key exchange, encryption and digital signature.

Question with Answers *(2 Marks)*

Q. 1. *Define Diffie-Hellman key exchange.*

Ans. **Diffie-Hellman (D-H)** key exchange is a cryptographic protocol that allows two parties that have no prior knowledge of each other to jointly establish a shared secret key over an insecure communications channel. This key can then be used to encrypt subsequent communications using a symmetric key cipher.

Q. 2. *Write down the steps of Diffie-Hellman key exchange.*

Ans. Diffie-Hellman key agreement.

Diffie-Hellman key establishment.

Diffie-Hellman key negotiation.

Exponential key exchange.

Q. 3. *List out the steps of key exchange protocols.*

Ans.
1. Users could create random private/public D-H keys each time they communicate.
2. Users could create a known private/public D-H key and publish in a directory, then consulted and used to securely communicate with them.
3. Both of these are vulnerable to a meet-in-the-Middle Attack.
4. Authentication of the keys is needed.

Q. 4. *Write down the placement encryption fundamentals.*

Ans. There are two fundamental encryption placement alternatives: link encryption and end-to-end encryption.

Q. 5. *What is traffic analysis?*

Ans. **Traffic Analysis** is monitoring of communications flows between parties and useful both in military and commercial spheres. It can also be used to create a covert channel.

Q. 6. *List out the key distribution issues.*

Ans.
- Hierarchies of KDC's required for large networks, but must trust each other.
- Session key lifetimes should be limited for greater security.
- Use of automatic key distribution on behalf of users, but must trust system.
- Use of decentralized key distribution.
- Controlling purposes keys are used for.

Q. 7. *List out uses of random numbers in cryptography.*

Ans.
1. Nonces in authentication protocols to prevent replay.
2. Session keys.
3. Public key generation.
4. Keystream for a one-time pad.

Q. 8. *What is TRNG?*

Ans. A true random number generator (TRNG) uses a nondeterministic source to produce randomness.

Review Questions

1. Explain Diffie-Hellman Key Exchange.
2. Explain Diffie-Hellman Key Exchange Algorithm.
3. States the Example for Diffie-Hellman Key Exchange.
4. Explain Key Exchange Protocol.
5. Explain the Key Management.
6. Explain Eliptic Curve Cryptosystems briefly.
7. Explain the placement of encryption function.
8. Explain the Random Numbers briefly.

❑❑❑

PART 3
CRYPTOGRAPHIC DATA INTEGRITY ALGORITHMS

Chapter

CHAPTER 8

CRYPTOGRAPHIC HASH FUNCTIONS

8.1 AUTHENTICATION REQUIREMENTS

Principles of Message Authentication

- Message Authentication is concerned with:
  - Protecting the integrity of a message
  - Validating identity of originator
  - Non-repudiation of origin (dispute resolution)

In the context of communications across a networks, the following Attacks Against message security can be identified.

- **Disclosure.** Release of message contents to any person or process not possessing the appropriate cryptographic key.

- **Traffic Analysis.** Discovery of the pattern of traffic between parties.
- **Masquerade.** Insertion of message into the network from a fraudulent source.
- **Content Modification.** Changes to the contents of a message, including insertion, deletion, transposition and modification.
- **Sequence Modification.** Any modification to a sequence of messages between parties including insertion, deletion and reordering.
- **Timing Modification.** Delay or replay of messages.
- **Source Repudiation.** Denial of transmission of message by source.
- **Destination Repudiation.** Denial of receipt of message

In summary message authentication is a procedure to verify that received message come from the alleged source and have not been altered. Message authentication may also verify sequencing and timeliness.

8.2 AUTHENTICATION FUNCTIONS

Authentication functions are cryptographic primitives which are used by message authentication protocols between two parties, sender and receiver. Sender attaches to the message an authenticator. Receiver uses the authenticator to verify authenticity of the message.

- **Authentication Functions:**

  Message encryption: The ciphertext of the entire message serves as its authenticator.

  Message authentication code (MAC): A public function of the message and a secret key that produces a fixed-length value that serves as the authenticator.

  Hash functions: A public function that maps a message of any length into a fixed-length hash value, which serves as the authenticator.

8.2.1 Message Encryption

Message encryption by itself can provide a measure of authentication. The analysis differs for symmetric and public key encryption schemes. The following points to focused for message encryption.

- Conventional encryption can provide confidentiality as well as authentication.
- Message encryption by itself also provides a measure of authentication
- If symmetric encryption is used then:
  - receiver know sender must have created it
  - since only sender and receiver now key used
  - know content cannot of been altered
  - if message has suitable structure, redundancy or a checksum to detect any changes
- If public key encryption is used:
  - Encryption provides no confidence of sender
  - Since anyone potentially knows public key

- However if
  - sender signs message using their private key
  - then encrypts with recipients public key
  - have both secrecy and authentication
- Again need to recognize corrupted messages
- But at cost of two public key uses on message

8.2.2 Symmetric Encryption

- Symmetric encryption provides *authentication* as well as *confidentiality*
- Requires recognizable plaintext or other *structure* to distinguish between well-formed legitimate plaintext and meaningless random bits, *e.g.,* ASCII text, an appended checksum, or use of layered protocols

The following Fig. 8.1 shows the basic issues of message encryption.

A message M Transmitted from source A to destination B is encrypted using a secret key K shared by A and B. If no other party knows the key, then confidentiality is provided: No other party can recover the plaintext of the message.

Let's start with symmetric encryption. As shown in Fig. 8.1 (*a*), A sends B a message M encrypted by their shared secret key K. Because a third party is unable to recover the plaintext of the message without the knowledge of K, confidentiality is provided. Now let's examine how encryption mechanism can provide message authentication. Generally, B is assured that the message is from A, because A is the only person (other than B) who is able to generate the ciphertext that can be decrypted using K. Further, if M is fully recovered, B knows none of the bits of M have been altered. However, to achieve this goal B needs to be able to identify the "correct plaintext" from the ones that is decrypted from an altered ciphertext, or the ciphertext generated with a different key. A d there are several scenarios:

- If M is in ordinary English, then B can recognize the message by reading off it. But this "plaintext" is difficult to be recognized automatically.
- If M is in binary code, and can be any arbitrary bit pattern, then there is no way to determine automatically, whether the recovered message is legitimate or not.

Lacking of an automatic way to verify the recovered message limits the usage of symmetric encryption as a mechanism for message authentication. Moreover, if a block cipher (such as DES, AES) is used then modes of operations need to be applied for messages whose length is larger than a block. As we have discussed in the previous lectures, no data integrity protection is provided by any mode of operation. This means that an attacker is able to alter the message (such as re-arranging the blocks) without being detected by the receiver. Then modes of operations need to be applied for messages whose length is larger than a block. As we have discussed in the previous lectures, no data integrity protection is provided by any mode of operation. This means that an attacker is able to alter the message (such as re-arranging the blocks) without being detected by the receiver.

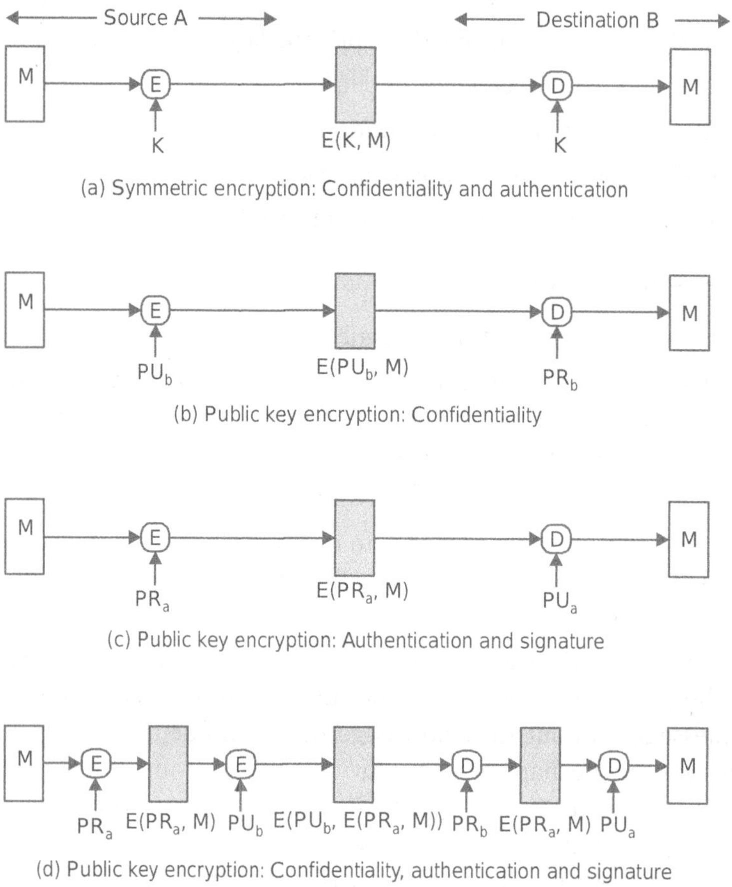

Fig. 8.1. *Basic uses of message encryption.*

Now let's proceed with public key encryption. As shown in Fig. 8.1 (*b*), if A sends a message M to B, which is encrypted with B's public key KU_b , then message confidentiality can be preserved. This is because the ciphertext of M can only be decrypted by B's private key. However no authentication is provided, as any one may have access to B's public key and generate such a ciphertext of M. If M is encrypted by A's private key as shown in Fig. 8.1 (*c*), the encryption provides both authentication and source non-repudiation in limited scenarios. This is because only A could have prepared the ciphertext of M. Since any other person with the knowledge of A's public key is able to decrypt the message, confidentiality is not provided. Due to the same reasoning as symmetric encryption, the authentication is only provided in limited scenarios such as (1) receiver is able to distinguish the well-formed plaintext and random bits, and (2) modes of operation are not used in encryption procedure. A double use of the public key and private key encryption is needed to achieve confidentiality, authentication, and non-repudiation simultaneously.

The symmetric encryption provides authentication as well as confidentiality . However, this flat statement needs to be qualified. Consider exactly what is happening at B. Given a decryption function D and a secret key K, the destination will accept any input X and produce output Y = D(K, X).

For example suppose that we are transmitting English language messages using a Caesar cipher with a shift of one (K = 1). A sends the following legitimate ciphertext:

neuqweardxscvpotvbxcm

B decrypts to produce the following plaintext:

mqastfwecxzkiytrpnsdwqb

8.2.3 Public Key Encryption

Use of public key encryption provides confidentiality but not authentication. The source(A) uses the public key Pub of the destination (B) to encrypt M. Because only B has the corresponding private key PRb only B can decrypt the message. This scheme provides no authentication because any opponent could also use B's public key to encrypt a message, claiming to be A.

The following table summarizes the confidentiality and authentication implication of these various approaches to message encryption.

Table 8.1 Confidentially and Authentication Implication of Message Encryption

(*a*) Symmetric encryption

$A \rightarrow B$: $E(K, M)$

- Provides confidentiality
  - Only A and B share K
- Provides a degree of authentication
  - Could come only from A
  - Has not been altered in transit
  - Requires some formatting/redundancy
- Does not provide signature
  - Receiver could forge message
  - Sender could deny message

(*b*) Public key (asymmetric) encryption: Confidentiality

$A \rightarrow B$: $E(PU_b, M)$

- Provides confidentiality
  - Only B has PR_b to decrypt
- Provides no authentication
  - Any party could use PU_b to encrypt message and claim to be A

(*c*) Public key encryption: Authentication and signature

$A \rightarrow B$: $E(PR_a, M)$
- Provides authentication and signature
  - Only A has PR_a to encrypt
  - Has not been altered in transit
  - Requires some formatting/redundancy
  - Any party can use PU_a to verify signature

(*d*) Public key encryption: Confidentiality, authentication and signature

$A \rightarrow B$: $E(PU_b, E(PR_a, M))$
- Provides confidentiality because of PU_b
- Provides authentication and signature because of PR_a

To provide both confidentiality and authentication, A can encrypt M first using its private key, which provides the digital signature, and then using B's public key, which provides confidentiality. The disadvantage of this approach is that the public key algorithm, which is complex, must be exercised four times rather than two in each communication.

8.3 MESSAGE AUTHENTICATION CODE

A cryptographic **message authentication code (MAC)** is a short piece of information used to authenticate a message. A MAC algorithm accepts as input a secret key and an arbitrary-length message to be authenticated, and outputs a MAC (sometimes known as a *tag*). The MAC value protects both a message's integrity as well as its authenticity, by allowing verifiers (who also possess the secret key) to detect any changes to the message content.

We understand that the authentication support from the encryption mechanism (including symmetric and asymmetric encryption) is (1) limited; (2) inefficient. So additional message authentication mechanism needs to be developed. In what follows, we will study message authentication code, which is one of such mechanisms.

Why use a MAC?

- Sometimes only authentication is needed
- Sometimes need authentication to persist longer than the encryption (*e.g.*, archival use)
  - Note that a MAC is not a digital signature

8.3.1 Concept and Model

Essentially, the message authentication code (MAC) is a small fixed-size block of data that is generated based on a message M of variable length using secret key K as follows. It is also called cryptographic checksum.

$$MAC = C(K, M)$$

where M = Input message

C = MAC function

K = Shared secret key

If A wishes to send B a message M, and protects it via a MAC, they first need to share a secret key K. Then A calculates code MAC as a function of M and K. Then the message M plus the code MAC are transmitted to B. B performs the same calculation on M, using K to generate a new code MAC_2. The received code MAC is compared to the calculated code MAC_2 to verify the data integrity. As only A is able to generate MAC, source authentication is also achieved. This procedure is shown in Fig. 8.2.

Fig. 8.2 (*b*) and (*c*) illustrate how to provide confidentiality and authentication simultaneously using MAC. Note that two different keys need to be used.

MAC provides an efficient way to message authentication. It also separates the authentication function from confidentiality. This is an attractive feature for many applications (such as software package distribution) where confidentiality is not necessary. Note that MAC can not be used as a digital signature to provide non-repudiation.

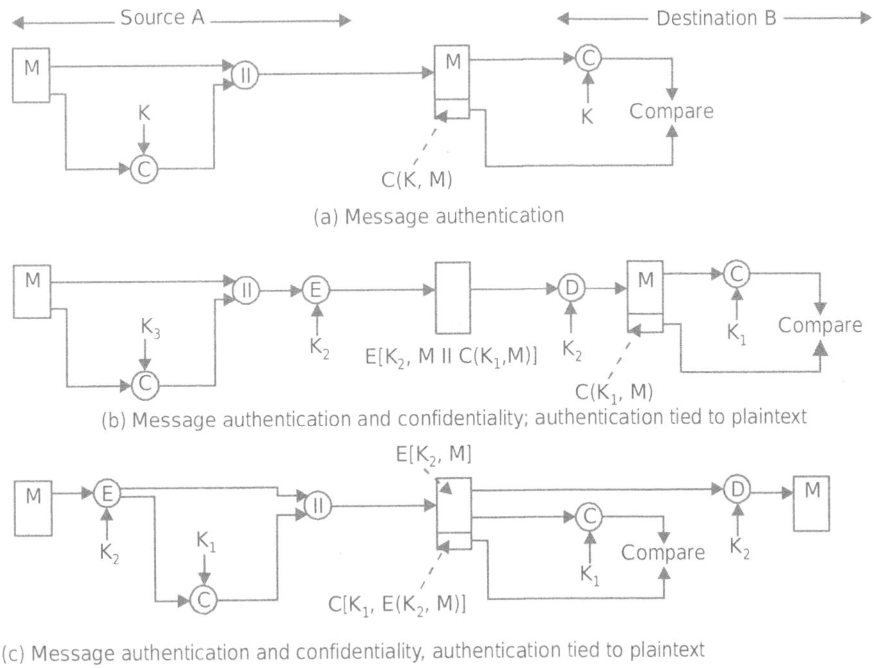

Fig. 8.2. *Usages of message encryption*

8.3.2 MAC Properties

MAC, also known as a cryptographic checksum, is generated by a function C. The MAC is appended to the message at the source at a time when the message is assumed or known to be correct. The receiver authenticates that message by re-computing the MAC.

The MAC function is a many-to-one function, since potentially many arbitrarily long messages can be condensed to the same summary value, but don't want finding them to be easy!

- a MAC is a cryptographic checksum

  MAC = CK(M)

  - condenses a variable-length message M
  - using a secret key K
  - to a fixed-sized authenticator
- is a many-to-one function
  - potentially many messages have same MAC
  - but finding these needs to be very difficult

8.3.3 Requirements for MACs

In asessing the security of a MAC function, we need to consider the types of attacks that may be mounted against it. Hence it needs to satisfy the listed requirements.

The first requirement deals with message replacement attacks, in which an opponent is able to construct a new message to match a given MAC, even though the opponent does not know and does not learn the key.

The second requirement deals with the need to thwart a brute-force attack based on chosen plaintext.

The final requirement dictates that the authentication algorithm should not be weaker with respect to certain parts or bits of the message than others.

- Taking into account the types of attacks
- Need the MAC to satisfy the following:
  1. Knowing a message and MAC, is infeasible to find another message with same MAC
  2. MACs should be uniformly distributed
  3. MAC should depend equally on all bits of the message

8.4 HASH FUNCTION

In cryptography, a **cryptographic hash function** is a transformation that takes an input and returns a fixed-size string, which is called the hash value. Hash functions with this property are used for a variety of computational purposes, including cryptography. The hash value is a concise representation of the longer message or document from which it was computed. The message digest is a sort of "digital fingerprint" of the larger document. Cryptographic hash functions are used to do message integrity checks and digital signatures in various information security applications, such as authentication and message integrity.

A hash function takes a long string (or 'message') of any length as input and produces a fixed length string as output, sometimes termed a **message digest** or a **digital**

fingerprint. A hash value (also called a "digest" or a "checksum") is a kind of "signature" for a stream of data that represents the contents. One analogy that explains the role of the hash function would be the "tamper-evident" seals used on a software package.

A hash function H is a transformation that takes a variable-size input m and returns a fixed-size string, which is called the hash value h

$$h = H(M)$$

where M = Variable length of message

H(M) = Fixed-length hash value

Hash functions with just this property have a variety of general computational uses, but when employed in cryptography the hash functions are usually chosen to have some additional properties.

8.4.1 Requirements for a Hash Function are

The input can be of any length,

The output has a fixed length,

H(x) is relatively easy to compute for any given x,

H(x) is one-way,

H(x) is collision-free.

A hash function H is said to be one-way if it is hard to invert, where "hard to invert" means that given a hash value h, it is computationally infeasible to find some input x such that H(x) = h.

If, given a message x, it is computationally infeasible to find a message y not equal to x such that H(x) = H(y) then H is said to be a weakly collision-free hash function.

A strongly collision-free hash function H is one for which it is computationally infeasible to find any two messages x and y such that H(x) = H(y).

The hash value represents concisely the longer message or document from which it was computed; one can think of a message digest as a "digital fingerprint" of the larger document. Examples of well-known hash functions are MD2 and MD5 and SHA.

Perhaps the main role of a cryptographic hash function is in the provision of digital signatures. Since hash functions are generally faster than digital signature algorithms, it is typical to compute the digital signature to some document by computing the signature on the document's hash value, which is small compared to the document itself. Additionally, a digest can be made public without revealing the contents of the document from which it is derived. This is important in digital timestamping where, using hash functions, one can get a document timestamped without revealing its contents to the timestamping service.

Simple Hash Functions

All hash functions operate using the following general principles. The input (message, file, etc.) is viewed as a sequence of n-bit blocks, processed one block at a time in an iterative fashion to produce an n-bit hash function. Can construct a range of possible simple hash functions by just XOR'ing blocks with rotates etc. None of these are secure, since can predict how changes to message affect the resulting hash.

8.4.2 Hash Functions

- There are several proposals for simple functions, based on XOR of message blocks:
  e.g., longitudinal redundancy check:
    - xor of columns of n-bit block arranged in rows

  e.g., above + circular left shift of hash after each row
    - effect of rotated XOR (RXOR) is to randomize the input
- But these lack weak collision resistance
  - simply "add a block" to obtain desired hash
- Need a stronger cryptographic function.

8.4.3 Birthday Attacks

The Birthday Attack exploits the birthday paradox – the chance that in a group of people two will share the same birthday – only 23 people are needed for a Pr>0.5 of this. Can generalize the problem to one wanting a matching pair from any two sets, and show need 2 m/2 in each to get a matching m-bit hash.

The idea behind this attack is that for a group of 23 people the probability that at least two people have a common birthday exceeds 1/2 [106]. Because this number of people is significantly smaller than what one would expect, this has also been called the "birthday paradox". For some applications a related problem is relevant: if two groups of people have 17 persons each, the probability that two people in the two different groups have a common birthday will also exceed 1/2. Note that these results assume that birthdays are randomly distributed over the year; as this is not the case the probability will be even higher. This can be generalized as follows. If two samples of size r_1 and r_2 are drawn from a set of n elements, and if r_1r_2 = n with r_1, r_2 = O(pn), then the probability of a match equals 1 – 1/e or 63%. Note that if the attacker is unlucky, it is sufficient to increase the size of r_1 and r_2 slightly, which will increase the success probability significantly. If $r_1 + r_2$ has to be minimized, one can show that this corresponds to $r_1 = r_2$ = pn. This explains why attacks based on this property have also been called "square root" attacks.

The first attack based on this property was proposed by G. Yuval. He showed how to attack a digital signature scheme of Rabin, more in particular he shows that it is easier to construct collisions for a one-way function than to find a preimage of a given element in the range. A collision can be produced in the following way.

- The adversary generates r_1 variations on a bogus message and r_2 variations on a genuine message. This is very easy, even if r_1 and r_2 are large: it is sufficient to have $\log_2(r_1)$ respectively $\log_2(r_2)$ positions where one has two alternatives or synonyms. If $r_1 = r_2 = r$ = pn the probability of the existence of a match will be 63%. Note that in case of a MAC the opponent is unable to generate the MAC of a message. He could however obtain these MAC's with a chosen plaintext attack. A second possibility is that he collects a large number of messages and corresponding MAC's and divides them in two categories, which corresponds to a known plaintext attack.
- The search for a match does not require r_2 operations: after sorting the data, which requires O(r log r) operations, comparison is easy.

The following points to remember the importance issues in Brithday Attack:

- Might think a 64-bit hash is secure
- But by Birthday Paradox is not
- Birthday attack works thus:
  - Opponent generates 2 m/2 variations of a valid message all with essentially the same meaning
  - Opponent also generates 2 m/2 variations of a desired fraudulent message
  - Two sets of messages are compared to find pair with same hash (probability > 0.5 by birthday paradox)
  - Have user sign the valid message, then substitute the forgery which will have a valid signature
- Conclusion is that need to use larger MAC/hash

8.4.4 Block Chaining Technique Hash Function

- A number of proposals for hash functions based on using a cipher block chaining technique, but without the secret key.
- Ravin's proposal:
  - Divide a message M into fixed-size blocks M_1, M_2, ..., M_N and use a conventional encryption system such as DES to compute the hash code G as follows
    - ⋆ H0 = initial value
    - ⋆ Hi = EMi[Hi-1]
    - ⋆ G = HN
  - Similar to CBC technique, but no secret key
  - As with any hash code, subject to the birthday attack
    - ⋆ If DES is used, and only a 64-bit hash code is produced, then the system is vulnerable
  - Another version of birthday attack is possible

8.4.5 Birthday Attack to Block Chaining Techniques

- Assume the opponent intercepts a message with a signature in the form of an encrypted hash code and the unencrypted hash code is m bits long
  1. Use the algorithm (Ravin's) to calculate the unencrypted hash code G
  2. Construct any desired message in the form Q_1, Q_2, ..., Q_{N-2}
  3. Compute Hi = EQi[Hi–1] for 1 £ i £ (N–2)
  4. Generate 2 m/2 random blocks; for each block X, compute EX[HN–2]. Generate an additional 2 m/2 random blocks; for each block Y, compute DY[G].
  5. Based on birthday paradox, with high probability there will be an X and Y s.t. EX[HN–2] = DY[G]
  6. Form the message Q_1, Q_2, ..., Q_{N-2}, X, Y. This message has the hash code G and therefore can be used with the intercepted encrypted signature.

8.5 SHA HASH FUNCTIONS

The SHA hash functions are five cryptographic hash functions designed by the National Security Agency (NSA) and published by the NIST as a U.S. Federal Information Processing Standard. SHA stands for Secure Hash Algorithm. Hash algorithms compute a fixed-length digital representation (known as a message digest) of an input data sequence (the message) of any length. They are called "secure" when (in the words of the standard), "it is computationally infeasible to: ind a message that corresponds to a given message digest, or find two different messages that produce the same message digest. Any change to a message will, with a very high probability, result in a different message digest."

The five algorithms are denoted SHA-1, SHA-224, SHA-256, SHA-384, and SHA-512. The latter four variants are sometimes collectively referred to as SHA-2. SHA-1 produces a message digest that is 160-bits long; the number in the other four algorithms' names denote the bit length of the digest they produce.

SHA-1 is employed in several widely used security applications and protocols, including TLS and SSL, PGP, SSH, S/MIME, and IPsec. It was considered to be the successor to MD5, an earlier, widely-used hash function.

The security of SHA-1 has been somewhat compromised by cryptography researchers. Although no attacks have yet been reported on the SHA-2 variants, they are algorithmically similar to SHA-1 and so efforts are underway to develop improved alternative hashing algorithms. An open competition for a new SHA-3 function was formally announced in the Federal Register on November 2, 2007. "NIST is initiating an effort to develop one or more additional hash algorithms through a public competition, similar to the development process for the Advanced Encryption Standard (AES)." Submissions are due October 31, 2008 and the proclamation of a winner and publication of the new standard are scheduled to take place in 2012.

8.5.1 SHA-0 and SHA-1

The original specification of the algorithm was published in 1993 as the Secure Hash Standard, FIPS PUB 180, by US government standards agency NIST (National Institute of Standards and Technology). This version is now often referred to as SHA-0. It was withdrawn by the NSA shortly after publication and was superseded by the revised version, published in 1995 in FIPS PUB 180-1 and commonly referred to as SHA-1. SHA-1 differs from SHA-0 only by a single bitwise rotation in the message schedule of its compression function; this was done, according to the NSA, to correct a flaw in the original algorithm which reduced its cryptographic security. However, the NSA did not provide any further explanation or identify what flaw was corrected. Weaknesses have subsequently been reported in both SHA-0 and SHA-1. SHA-1 appears to provide greater resistance to attacks, supporting the NSA's assertion that the change increased the security.

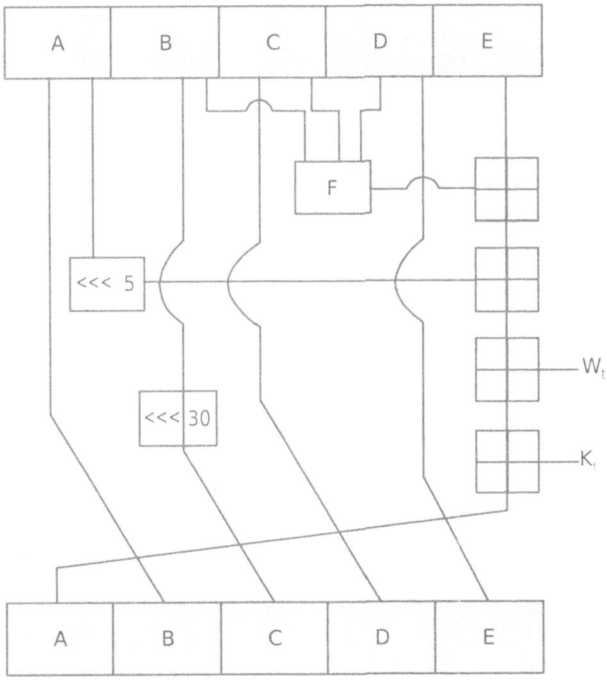

Fig. 8.3. *SHA-0 and SHA-1.*

One iteration within the SHA-1 compression function. A, B, C, D and E are 32-bit words of the state; F is a nonlinear function that varies; <<<n denotes a left bit rotation by n places; n varies for each operation. ∃ denotes addition modulo 232. K_t is a constant.

SHA-1 (as well as SHA-0) produces a 160-bit digest from a message with a maximum length of (264 – 1) bits and is based on principles similar to those used by Ronald L. Rivest of MIT in the design of the MD4 and MD5 message digest algorithms.

8.5.2 Cryptanalysis

For an ideal hash function, violating the first criterion listed above, finding a message that corresponds to a given message digest, can always be done using a brute force search in 2L evaluations, where L is the number of bits in the message digest. This is called a preimage attack. The second criterion, finding two different messages that produce the same message digest, known as a collision, requires only 2L/2 evaluations using a birthday attack. For the later reason the strength of a hash function is usually compared to a symmetric cipher of half the message digest length. Thus SHA-1 was originally considered to have 80-bit strength.

Cryptographers have produced collision pairs for SHA-0 and have found algorithms that should produce SHA-1 collisions in far fewer than the intended 280 evaluations.

8.6 MD5 (MESSAGE-DIGEST ALGORITHM 5)

In cryptography, MD5 (Message-Digest Algorithm 5) is a widely used cryptographic hash function with a 128-bit hash value. As an Internet standard (RFC 1321), MD5 has been employed in a wide variety of security applications, and is also commonly used to check the integrity of files. An MD5 hash is typically expressed as a 32-character hexadecimal number.

MD5 was designed by Ronald Rivest in 1991 to replace an earlier hash function, MD4. In 1996, a flaw was found with the design of MD5; while it was not a clearly fatal weakness, cryptographers began recommending the use of other algorithms, such as SHA-1 (which has since been found vulnerable itself). In 2004, more serious flaws were discovered making further use of the algorithm for security purposes questionable.

8.6.1 History and Cryptanalysis

Message Digest is a series of message digest algorithms designed by Professor Ronald Rivest of MIT (Rivest, 1994). When analytic work indicated that MD5's predecessor—MD4—was likely to be insecure, MD5 was designed in 1991 to be a secure replacement. (Weaknesses were indeed later found in MD4 by Hans Dobbertin.)

In 1993, Den Boer and Bosselaers gave an early, although limited, result of finding a "pseudo-collision" of the MD5 compression function; that is, two different initialization vectors which produce an identical digest.

In 1996, Dobbertin announced a collision of the compression function of MD5 (Dobbertin, 1996). While this was not an attack on the full MD5 hash function, it was close enough for cryptographers to recommend switching to a replacement, such as WHIRLPOOL, SHA-1 or RIPEMD-160.

The size of the hash—128 bits—is small enough to contemplate a birthday attack. MD5CRK was a distributed project started in March 2004 with the aim of demonstrating that MD5 is practically insecure by finding a collision using a birthday attack.

MD5CRK ended shortly after 17 August 2004, when collisions for the full MD5 were announced by Xiaoyun Wang, Dengguo Feng, Xuejia Lai, and Hongbo Yu. Their analytical attack was reported to take only one hour on an IBM p690 cluster.

On 1 March 2005, Arjen Lenstra, Xiaoyun Wang, and Benne de Weger demonstrated construction of two X.509 certificates with different public keys and the same MD5 hash, a demonstrably practical collision. The construction included private keys for both public keys. A few days later, Vlastimil Klima described an improved algorithm, able to construct MD5 collisions in a few hours on a single notebook computer. On 18 March 2006, Klima published an algorithm that can find a collision within one minute on a single notebook computer, using a method he calls tunneling.

Because MD5 makes only one pass over the data, if two prefixes with the same hash can be constructed, a common suffix can be added to both to make the collision more reasonable.

Because the current collision-finding techniques allow the preceding hash state to be specified arbitrarily, a collision can be found for any desired prefix; that is, for any given string of characters X, two colliding files can be determined which both begin with X.

All that is required to generate two colliding files is a template file, with a 128-byte block of data aligned on a 64-byte boundary, that can be changed freely by the collision-finding algorithm.

Recently, a number of projects have created MD5 "rainbow tables" which are easily accessible online, and can be used to reverse many MD5 hashes into strings that collide with the original input, usually for the purposes of password cracking. However, if passwords are combined with a salt before the MD5 digest is generated, rainbow tables become much less useful.

The use of MD5 in some websites' URLs means that Google can also sometimes function as a limited tool for reverse lookup of MD5 hashes. This technique is rendered ineffective by the use of a salt.

8.6.2 Applications

MD5 digests have been widely used in the software world to provide some assurance that a transferred file has arrived intact. For example, file servers often provide a pre-computed MD5 checksum for the files, so that a user can compare the checksum of the downloaded file to it. Unix-based operating systems include MD5 sum utilities in their distribution packages, whereas Windows users use third-party applications.

However, now that it is easy to generate MD5 collisions, it is possible for the person who created the file to create a second file with the same checksum, so this technique cannot protect against some forms of malicious tampering. Also, in some cases the checksum cannot be trusted (for example, if it was obtained over the same channel as the downloaded file), in which case MD5 can only provide error-checking functionality: it will recognize a corrupt or incomplete download, which becomes more likely when downloading larger files.

MD5 is widely used to store passwords. To mitigate against the vulnerabilities mentioned above, one can add a salt to the passwords before hashing them. Some implementations may apply the hashing function more than once—see key strengthening.

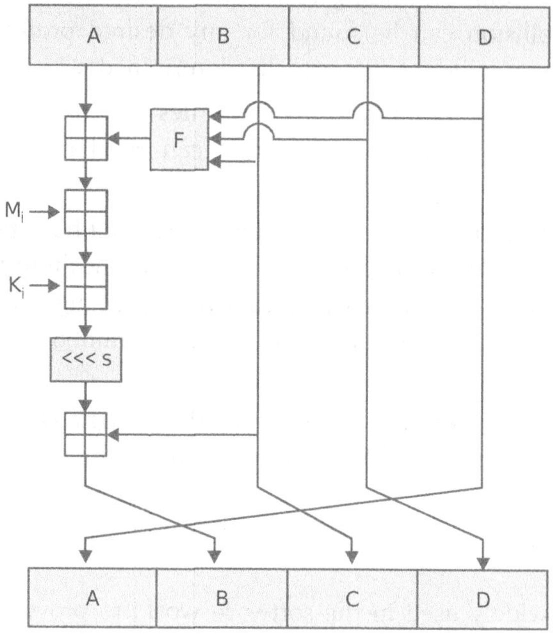

Fig. 8.4. *MD5.*

Fig. 8.4 One MD5 operation-MD5 consists of 64 of these operations, grouped in four rounds of 16 operations. F is a nonlinear function; one function is used in each round. M_i denotes a 32-bit block of the message input, and K_i denotes a 32-bit constant, different for each operation.

MD5 processes a variable-length message into a fixed-length output of 128-bits. The input message is broken up into chunks of 512-bit blocks (sixteen 32-bit little endian integers); the message is padded so that its length is divisible by 512. The padding works as follows: first a single bit, 1, is appended to the end of the message. This is followed by as many zeros as are required to bring the length of the message up to 64-bits fewer than a multiple of 512. The remaining bits are filled up with a 64-bit integer representing the length of the original message, in bits.

The main MD5 algorithm operates on a 128-bit state, divided into four 32-bit words, denoted A, B, C and D. These are initialized to certain fixed constants. The main algorithm then operates on each 512-bit message block in turn, each block modifying the state. The processing of a message block consists of four similar stages, termed rounds; each round is composed of 16 similar operations based on a non-linear function F, modular addition, and left rotation. Fig. 8.4 illustrates one operation within a round. There are four possible functions F; a different one is used in each round:

$$F(X, Y, Z) = (X \wedge Y) \vee (\neg X \wedge Z)$$
$$G(X, Y, Z) = (X \wedge Z) \vee (Y \wedge \neg Z)$$
$$H(X, Y, Z) = X \oplus Y \oplus Z$$
$$I(X, Y, Z) = Y \oplus (X \vee \neg Z)$$

$\oplus$, $\wedge$, $\vee$, $\neg$ denote the XOR, AND, OR and NOT operations respectively.

8.6.3 MD5 Algorithm Description

We begin by supposing that we have a b-bit message as input, and that, we wish to find its message digest. Here b is an arbitrary nonnegative integer; b may be zero, it need not be a multiple of eight, and it may be arbitrarily large. We imagine the bits of the message written down as follows:

m_0 m_1 ... m_{b-1}

The following five steps are performed to compute the message digest of the message.

Step 1. Append Padding Bits

The message is "padded" (extended) so that its length (in bits) is congruent to 448, modulo 512. That is, the message is extended so that it is just 64-bits shy of being a multiple of 512-bits long. Padding is always performed, even if the length of the message is already congruent to 448, modulo 512.

Padding is performed as follows: a single "1" bit is appended to the message, and then "0" bits are appended so that the length in bits of the padded message becomes congruent to 448, modulo 512. In all, at least one bit and at most 512-bits are appended.

Step 2. Append Length

A 64-bit representation of b (the length of the message before the padding bits were added) is appended to the result of the previous step. In the unlikely event that b is greater than 2^64, then only the low-order 64-bits of b are used. (These bits are appended as two 32-bit words and appended low-order word first in accordance with the previous conventions.)

At this point the resulting message (after padding with bits and with b) has a length that is an exact multiple of 512-bits. Equivalently, this message has a length that is an exact multiple of 16 (32-bit) words. Let M[0 ... N-1] denote the words of the resulting message, where N is a multiple of 16.

Step 3. Initialize MD Buffer

A four-word buffer (A, B, C, D) is used to compute the message digest. Here each of A, B, C, D is a 32-bit register. These registers are initialized to the following values in hexadecimal, low-order bytes first):

word A: 01 23 45 67

word B: 89 ab cd ef

word C: fe dc ba 98

word D: 76 54 32 10

Step 4. Process Message in 16-Word Blocks

We first define four auxiliary functions that each take as input three 32-bit words and produce as output one 32-bit word.

F(X, Y, Z) = XY v not(X) Z

G(X, Y, Z) = XZ v Y not(Z)

H(X, Y, Z) = X xor Y xor Z

I(X, Y, Z) = Y xor (X v not(Z))

In each bit position F acts as a conditional: if X then Y else Z. The function F could have been defined using + instead of v since XY and not(X)Z will never have 1's in the same bit position. It is interesting to note that if the bits of X, Y and Z are independent and unbiased, the each bit of F(X, Y, Z) will be independent and unbiased.

The functions G, H and I are similar to the function F, in that they act in "bitwise parallel" to produce their output from the bits of X, Y and Z, in such a manner that if the corresponding bits of X, Y and Z are independent and unbiased, then each bit of G(X, Y, Z), H(X, Y, Z), and I(X, Y, Z) will be independent and unbiased. Note that the function H is the bit-wise "xor" or "parity" function of its inputs.

This step uses a 64-element table T[1 ... 64] constructed from the sine function. Let T[i] denote the *i*th element of the table, which is equal to the integer part of 4294967296 times abs(sin(i)), where i is in radians.

Do the following:

```
    /* Process each 16-word block. */
            For i = 0 to N/16-1 do

    /* Copy block i into X. */
            For j = 0 to 15 do
            Set X[j] to M[i*16+j].
            end /* of loop on j */

    /* Save A as AA, B as BB, C as CC, and D as DD. */
            AA = A
            BB = B
            CC = C
            DD = D

  /* Round 1. */
  /* Let [abcd k s i] denote the operation
  a = b + ((a + F(b,c,d) + X[k] + T[i]) <<< s). */
  /* Do the following 16 operations. */
  [ABCD 0 7 1] [DABC 1 12 2] [CDAB 2 17 3] [BCDA 3 22 4]
  [ABCD 4 7 5] [DABC 5 12 6] [CDAB 6 17 7] [BCDA 7 22 8]
  [ABCD 8 7 9] [DABC 9 12 10] [CDAB 10 17 11] [BCDA 11 22 12]
  [ABCD 12 7 13] [DABC 13 12 14] [CDAB 14 17 15] [BCDA 15 22 16]

  /* Round 2. */
  /* Let [abcd k s i] denote the operation
```

```
a = b + ((a + G(b, c, d) + X[k] + T[i]) <<< s). */
/* Do the following 16 operations. */
[ABCD 1 5 17] [DABC 6 9 18] [CDAB 11 14 19] [BCDA 0 20 20]
[ABCD 5 5 21] [DABC 10 9 22] [CDAB 15 14 23] [BCDA 4 20 24]
[ABCD 9 5 25] [DABC 14 9 26] [CDAB 3 14 27] [BCDA 8 20 28]
[ABCD 13 5 29] [DABC 2 9 30] [CDAB 7 14 31] [BCDA 12 20 32]

/* Round 3. */
/* Let [abcd k s t] denote the operation
a = b + ((a + H(b, c, d) + X[k] + T[i]) <<< s). */
/* Do the following 16 operations. */
[ABCD 5 4 33] [DABC 8 11 34] [CDAB 11 16 35] [BCDA 14 23 36]
[ABCD 1 4 37] [DABC 4 11 38] [CDAB 7 16 39] [BCDA 10 23 40]
[ABCD 13 4 41] [DABC 0 11 42] [CDAB 3 16 43] [BCDA 6 23 44]
[ABCD 9 4 45] [DABC 12 11 46] [CDAB 15 16 47] [BCDA 2 23 48]

/* Round 4. */
/* Let [abcd k s t] denote the operation
a = b + ((a + I(b, c, d) + X[k] + T[i]) <<< s). */
/* Do the following 16 operations. */
[ABCD 0 6 49] [DABC 7 10 50] [CDAB 14 15 51] [BCDA 5 21 52]
[ABCD 12 6 53] [DABC 3 10 54] [CDAB 10 15 55] [BCDA 1 21 56]
[ABCD 8 6 57] [DABC 15 10 58] [CDAB 6 15 59] [BCDA 13 21 60]
[ABCD 4 6 61] [DABC 11 10 62] [CDAB 2 15 63] [BCDA 9 21 64]

/* Then perform the following additions. (That is increment each
of the four registers by the value it had before this block
was started.) */
A = A + AA
B = B + BB
C = C + CC
D = D + DD

end /* of loop on i *
```

The message digest produced as output is A, B, C, D. That is, we begin with the low-order byte of A, and end with the high-order byte of D.

Step 5. Summary

The MD5 message-digest algorithm is simple to implement, and provides a "fingerprint" or message digest of a message of arbitrary length. It is conjectured that the difficulty of coming up with two messages having the same message digest is on the order of 2^64 operations, and that the difficulty of coming up with any message having a given message digest is on the order of 2^128 operations. The MD5 algorithm has been carefully scrutinized for weaknesses. It is, however, a relatively new algorithm and further security analysis is of course justified, as is the case with any new proposal of this sort.

8.6.4. Differences between MD4 and MD5

The following are the differences between MD4 and MD5:

1. A fourth round has been added.
2. Each step now has a unique additive constant.
3. The function g in round 2 was changed from (XY v XZ v YZ) to (XZ v Y not(Z)) to make g less symmetric.
4. Each step now adds in the result of the previous step. This promotes a faster "avalanche effect".
5. The order in which input words are accessed in rounds 2 and 3 is changed, to make these patterns less like each other.
6. The shift amounts in each round have been approximately optimized, to yield a faster "avalanche effect." The shifts in different rounds are distinct.

8.7 RIPEMD (RACE INTEGRITY PRIMITIVES EVALUATION MESSAGE DIGEST)

The main contribution of MD4 is that it is the first cryptographic hash function which made optimal use of the structure of current 32-bit processors. The use of serial operations and the favorable treatment of little-endian architectures show that MD4 is tuned towards software implementations.

Early '95 H. Dobbertin found collisions for the last two out of three (and later for the first two) rounds of RIPEMD. While this is not an immediate threat to RIPEMD with three rounds, the attack was quite surprising. Moreover, it introduced a new technique to cryptanalyze this type of functions. In the Fall of '95, H. Dobbertin was able to extend these techniques to produce collisions for MD4, and for the compression function of the extended version of MD4. The attack on MD4 requires only a few seconds on a PC, and still leaves some freedom to the message; it clearly rules out the use of MD4 as a collision resistant function.

It is anticipated that these techniques can be used to produce collisions for MD5 and perhaps also for RIPEMD. This will probably require an additional effort, but it no longer seems as far away as it was a year ago.

An independent reason to upgrade RIPEMD is the limited resistance against a brute force collision search attack. P. van Oorschot and M. Wiener present in a design for a $10 million collision search machine for MD5 that could find a collision in 24 days. If only a $1 million budget is available, and the memory of an existing computer network is used, the computation would require about 6 months. Taking into account the fact that the cost of computation and memory is divided by four every three years (this observation is known as Moore's law), one can conclude that a 128-bit hash-result does not offer sufficient protection for the next ten years. Note that collisions obtained in this way need less than 10 random looking bytes; the rest of the inputs can be chosen arbitrarily. RIPEMD is in use in several banking applications, and is (together with SHA-1) currently under consideration as a candidate for standardization within ISO/IEC JTC1/SC27. However, the current situation brings us to the conclusion that it would be prudent to upgrade current implementations, and to consider a more secure scheme for standardization. Therefore the authors designed a strengthened version of RIPEMD-160 which should be secure for ten years or more. Also, an improved 128-bit version is proposed, which should only be used to replace RIPEMD in current applications.

8.7.1 RIPEMD-160

RIPEMD-160 is a 160-bit cryptographic hash function, designed by Hans Dobbertin, Antoon Bosselaers, and Bart Preneel. It is intended to be used as a secure replacement for the 128-bit hash functions MD4, MD5, and RIPEMD. MD4 and MD5 were developed by Ron Rivest for RSA Data Security, while RIPEMD was developed in the framework of the EU project RIPE (RACE Integrity Primitives Evaluation, 1988–1992). There are three good reasons to consider such a replacement:

- A 128-bit hash result does not offer sufficient protection anymore. A brute force collision search attack on a 128-bit hash result requires 2^{64} or about 2.10^{19} evaluations of the function. In 1994 Paul van Oorschot and Mike Wiener showed that this brute-force job can be done in less than a month with a $10 million investment. This cost is expected to halve every 18 months.
- In the first half of 1995 Hans Dobbertin found collisions for a version of RIPEMD restricted to two rounds out of three. Using similar techniques Hans produced in the Fall of 1995 collisions for (all 3 rounds of class) MD4. The attack on MD4 requires only a few seconds on a PC, and still leaves some freedom as to the choice of the message, clearly ruling out MD4 as a collision resistant hash function. Shortly afterwards, in the Spring of 1996, Hans also found collisions for the compression function of MD5. Although not yet extended to collisions for MD5 itself, this attack casts serious doubts on the strength of MD5 as a collision resistant hash function. RSA Data Security, for which Ron Rivest developed MD4 and MD5, recommend that MD4 should not longer be used, and that MD5 should not be used for future applications that require the hash function to be collision-resistant.
- At the rump session of Crypto 2004 it was announced that Xiaoyun Wang, Dengguo Feng, Xuejia Lai and Hongbo Yu found collisions for MD4, MD5, RIPEMD, and the 128-bit version of HAVAL. No details of this attack are public yet.

RIPEMD-160 is a strengthened version of RIPEMD with a 160-bit hash result, and is expected to be secure for the next ten years or more. The design philosophy is to build as much as possible on experience gained by evaluating MD4, MD5, and RIPEMD. Like its predecessors, RIPEMD-160 is tuned for 32-bit processors, which we feel will remain important in the coming decade.

RIPEMD-128 is a plug-in substitute for RIPEMD (or MD4 and MD5, for that matter) with a 128-bit result. In view of the result of Paul van Oorschot and Mike Wiener mentioned earlier, 128-bit hash results do not offer sufficient protection for the next ten years, and applications using 128-bit hash functions should consider upgrading to a 160-bit hash function.

RIPEMD-256 and RIPEMD-320 are optional extensions of, respectively, RIPEMD-128 and RIPEMD-160, and are intended for applications of hash functions that require a longer hash result without needing a larger security level.

How fast is RIPEMD-160?

The following table gives an idea of the performance of the different MD4-like hash functions. The implementations are written in 80 × 86 assembly language and are optimized for the Pentium processor. It is assumed that both code and data resides in the on-chip caches. Under these conditions the cycle figures are independent of the clock speed, and the throughput figures scale with the clock speed.

Table 8.2. Performance of optimized assembly language implementations of MD4-like hash functions on a 90 MHz Pentium using a 32-bit flat memory model (*i.e.*, running in native protected mode).

Algorithm	*Cycles*	*Mbit/sec*	*Mbyte/sec*	*Relative performance*
MD4	241	191.2	23.90	1.00
MD5	337	136.7	17.09	0.72
RIPEMD	480	96.0	12.00	0.50
RIPEMD-128	592	77.8	9.73	0.41
SHA-1	837	55.1	6.88	0.29
RIPEMD-160	1013	45.5	5.68	0.24

8.8 HMAC

In cryptography, a **Keyed-Hash Message Authentication Code**, or HMAC, is a type of message authentication code (MAC) calculated using a cryptographic hash function in combination with a secret key. As with any MAC, it may be used to simultaneously verify both the data integrity and the authenticity of a message. Any iterative cryptographic hash function, such as MD5 or SHA-1, may be used in the calculation of an HMAC; the resulting MAC algorithm is termed HMAC-MD5 or HMAC-SHA-1 accordingly. The cryptographic strength of the HMAC depends upon the cryptographic strength of the underlying hash function, on the size and quality of the key and the size of the hash output length in bits.

An iterative hash function breaks up a message into blocks of a fixed size and iterates over them with a compression function. For example, MD5 and SHA-1 operate on 512-bit blocks. The size of the output of HMAC is the same as that of the underlying hash function (128 or 160-bits in the case of MD5 and SHA-1), although it can be truncated if desired. Truncating the hash image reduces the security of the MAC which is upper bound by the birthday attack.

The construction and analysis of HMACs was first published in 1996 by Mihir Bellare, Ran Canetti, and Hugo Krawczyk, who also wrote RFC 2104. FIPS PUB 198 generalizes and standardizes the use of HMACs. HMAC-SHA-1 and HMAC-MD5 are used within the IPsec and TLS protocols.

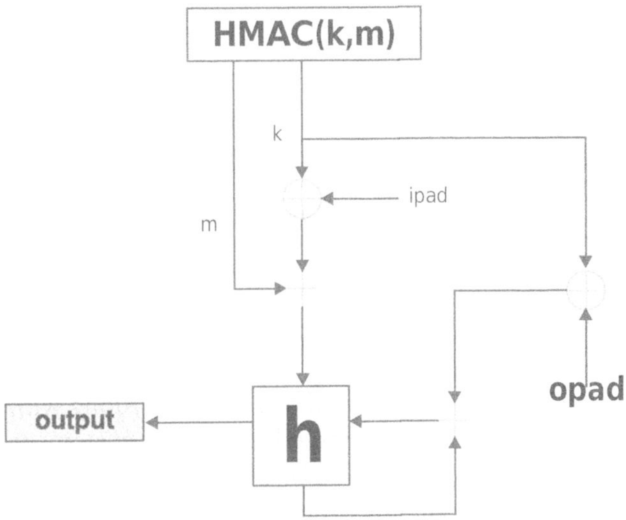

Fig. 8.5. *HMAC.*

8.8.1 Definition

HMAC is merely a specific type of MAC function. It works by using an underlying hash function over a message and a key. It is currently one of the predominant means to ensure that secure data is not corrupted in transit over unsecure channels (like the internet).

$$HMAC_K(m) = h\left((K \oplus \text{opad}) \,||\, h((K \oplus \text{ipad}) \,||\, m)\right)$$

where h is a cryptographic hash function, K is a secret key padded with extra zeros to the block size of the hash function, m is the message to be authenticated, || denotes concatenation, + denotes exclusive or (XOR), and the outer padding opad = 0 × 5c5c5c...5c5c and inner padding ipad = 0 × 363636...3636 are two one-block long hexadecimal constants.

8.8.2 Implementation

The following pseudocode demonstrates how HMAC may be implemented.

```
function hmac (key, message)
  opad = [0 × 5c * blocksize] // where blocksize is that of the underlying hash function
  ipad = [0 × 36 * blocksize]
  if (length(key) > blocksize), then
    key = hash(key) // where 'hash' is the underlying hash function
  end if
  if (length(key) < blocksize), then
    key = key || [0 × 00 * (blocksize - length(key))] // Pad the key if shorter than blocksize
  end if
  for i from 0 to length(key) – 1 step 1
    ipad[i] = ipad[i] XOR key[i]
    opad[i] = opad[i] XOR key[i]
  end for
  return hash(opad || hash(ipad || message)) // where || is concatenation
end function
```

8.8.3 Example Usage

A pizza restaurant that suffers from attackers that place fraudulent Internet orders may insist that all its customers deposit a secret key with the restaurant. Along with an order, a customer must supply the order's HMAC digest, computed using the customer's symmetric key. The restaurant, knowing the customer's symmetric key, can then verify that the order originated from the stated customer and has not been tampered with.

8.8.4 Security

The cryptographic strength of the HMAC depends upon the cryptographic strength of the underlying hash function, on the size and quality of the key and the size of the hash output length in bits. As outlined in "Keying Hash Functions for Message Authentication", MACs can be vulnerable to birthday, collision, extension, and other attacks.

In the recently (2006) published paper "On the Security of HMAC and NMAC Based on HAVAL, MD4, MD5, SHA-0 and SHA-1", by Jongsung Kim, Alex Biryukov, Bart Preneel, Seokhie Hong, claim to have devised: "two new distinguishers of the structure of HMAC, called differential and rectangle distinguishers, and use them to discuss the security of HMAC based on HAVAL, MD4, MD5, SHA-0 and SHA-1. We show how to distinguish HMAC with reduced or full versions of these cryptographic hash functions from a random function or from HMAC with a random function. We also show how to use our differential distinguisher to devise a forgery attack on HMAC. Our distinguishing and forgery attacks can also be mounted on NMAC based on HAVAL, MD4, MD5, SHA-0 and SHA-1. Furthermore, we show that our differential and rectangle distinguishers can lead to second-preimage attacks on

HMAC and NMAC.". They go on to claim: "With these distinguishing and forgery attacks we have shown that HMAC with the full versions of 3-pass HAVAL and SHA-0 can be distinguished from HMAC with a random function, and HMAC with the full version of MD4 can be forged. These distinguishing and forgery attacks have also been applied to HMAC based on reduced versions of MD5 and SHA-1. All these attacks do not contradict the security proof of HMAC, but they improve our understanding of the security of HMAC based on existing cryptographic hash functions."

8.9 DIGITAL SIGNATURES

The most important development from the work on public key cryptography is the digital signature. Message authentication protects two parties who exchange messages from any third party. However, it does not protect the two parties against each other. A digital signature is analogous to the handwritten signature, and provides a set of security capabilities that would be difficult to implement in any other way. It must have the following properties:

- It must verify the author and the date and time of the signature
- It must to authenticate the contents at the time of the signature
- It must be verifiable by third parties, to resolve disputes

Thus, the digital signature function includes the authentication function.

A digital signature scheme typically consists of three algorithms:

A key generation algorithm G that randomly produces a "key pair" (PK, SK) for the signer. PK is the verifying key, which is to be public, and SK is the signing key, to be kept private.

A signing algorithm S, that on input of a message m and a signing key SK, produces a signature σ.

A signature verifying algorithm V, that on input a message m, a verifying key PK, and a signature σ, either accepts or rejects.

Two main properties are required. First, signatures computed honestly should always verify. That is, V should accept (m, PK, S (m, SK)) where SK is the secret key related to PK, for any message m. Secondly, it should be hard for any adversary, knowing only PK, to create valid signature(s)

8.9.1 Digital Signature Properties

On the basis of the properties, we can formulate the requirements for a digital signature as shown. A variety of approaches has been proposed for the digital signature function. These approaches fall into two categories: direct and arbitrated.

- Must depend on the message signed
- Must use information unique to sender
  - to prevent both forgery and denial
- Must be relatively easy to produce

- Must be relatively easy to recognize and verify
- Be computationally infeasible to forge
  - With new message for existing digital signature
  - With fraudulent digital signature for given message
- Be practical save digital signature in storage.

8.9.2 Digital Signature Algorithm

The Digital Signature Algorithm (DSA) is a United States Federal Government standard or FIPS for digita signatures. It was proposed by the National Institute of Standards and Technology (NIST) in August 1991 for use in their Digital Signature Standard (DSS), specified in FIPS 186, adopted in 1993. A minor revision was issued in 1996 as FIPS 186-1, and the standard was expanded further in 2000 as FIPS 186-2. Key generation.

DSA differs from RSA in how the message signature is generated and validated. RSA signatures encrypt the message hash with the private key to create a signature, which is then verified by being decrypted with the public key to compare to a recreated hash value.

DSA signatures use the message hash, global public values, private key and random k to create a 2 part signature (s, r). This is verified by computing a function of the message hash, public key, r and s, and comparing the result with r. The proof that this works is complex, but it achieves its aims!

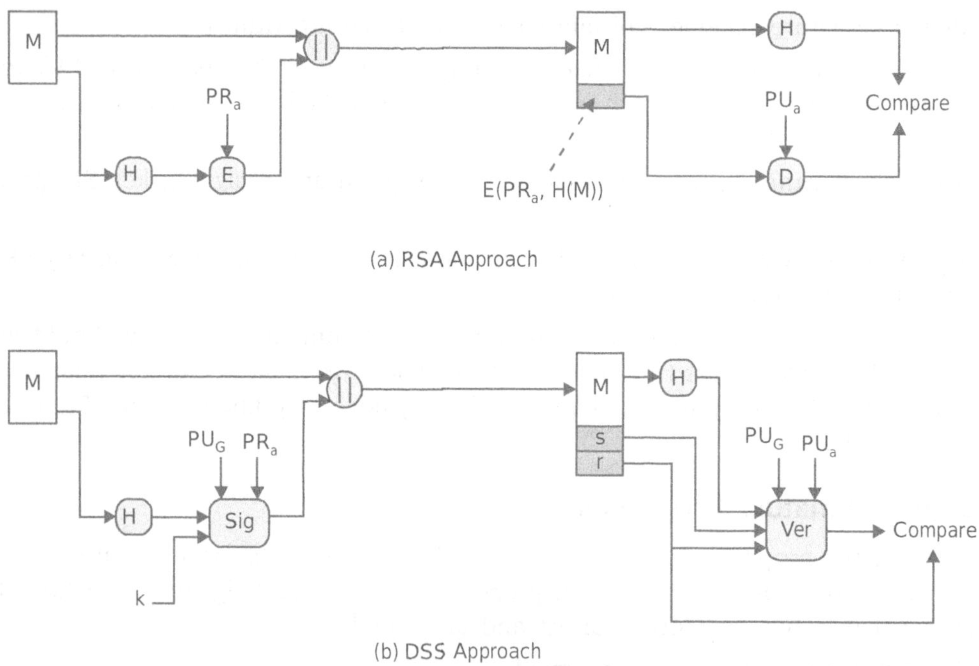

Fig. 8.6. *Digital signature.*

The following steps for digital signature algorithm

- Key generation
- Signing
- Verifying
- Correctness of the algorithm.

Key Generation

Key generation has two phases. The first phase is a choice of algorithm parameters which may be shared between different users of the system:

- Choose a cryptographic hash function H. In the original DSS, H was always SHA-1, but stronger hash functions from the SHA family are also in use. Sometimes the output of a newer hash function is truncated to the size of an older one for compatibility with existing key pairs.
- Decide on a key length L. This is the primary measure of the cryptographic strength of the key. The original DSS constrained L to be a multiple of 64 between 512 and 1024 (inclusive). Later, FIPS-186-2, change notice 1 specifies that L should always be 1024. Later yet, NIST 800-57 recommends lengths of 2048 (or 3072) for keys with security lifetimes extending beyond 2010 (or 2030).
- Choose a prime q with the same number of bits as the output of H.
- Choose a L-bit prime p such that p–1 is a multiple of q.
- Choose g, a number whose multiplicative order modulo p is q. This may be done by setting g = h(p–1)/q mod p for some arbitrary h (1 < h < p–1), and trying again if the result comes out as 1. Most choices of h will lead to a usable g; commonly h=2 is used.

  The algorithm parameters (p, q, g) may be shared between different users of the system. The second phase computes private and public keys for a single user:
- Choose x by some random method, where 0 < x < q.
- Calculate y = gx mod p.
- Public key is (p, q, g, y). Private key is x.

The forthcoming FIPS 186-3 (available as a draft) uses SHA-224/256/384/512 as the hash function, q of size 224 and 256 bits, and L equal to 2048 and 3072, respectively.

There exist efficient algorithms for computing the modular exponentiations ha mod p and gx mod p.

Signing

- Generate a random per-message value k, where 0 < k < q
- Calculate r = (gk mod p) mod q
- Calculate s = (k–1(H(m) + x*r)) mod q
- Recalculate the signature in the unlikely case that r=0 or s=0
- The signature is (r, s)
- The extended Euclidean algorithm can be used to compute the modular inverse k–1 mod q.

Verifying

- Reject the signature if either 0< r <q or 0< s <q is not satisfied.
- Calculate w = (s)–1 mod q
- Calculate u1 = (H(m)*w) mod q
- Calculate u2 = (r*w) mod q
- Calculate v = ((gu1*yu2) mod p) mod q
- The signature is valid if v = r

DSA is similar to the ElGamal signature scheme.

Correctness of the Algorithm

The signature scheme is correct in the sense that the verifier will always accept genuine signatures. This can be shown as follows:

First, if g = h(p–1)/q mod p it follows that gq ≡ hp–1 ≡ 1 (mod p) by Fermat's little theorem. Since g>1 and q is prime, g must have order q.

8.9.3 DSA Signature Verification

At the receiving end, verification is performed using the formulas shown. The receiver generates a quantity v that is a function of the public key components, the sender's public key, and the hash of the incoming message. If this quantity matches the r component of the signature, then the signature is validated. Note that the difficulty of computing discrete logs is why it is infeasible for an opponent to recover k from r, or x from s. Note also that nearly all the calculations are mod q, and hence are much faster save for the last step.

The structure of this function is such that the receiver can recover r using the incoming message and signature, the public key of the user, and the global public key. It is certainly not obvious that such a scheme would work.

Having received M and signature (r, s) to verify a signature, recipient computes:

w = s–1(mod q)

u1 = (H(M).w)(mod q)

u2 = (r.w)(mod q)

v = (gu1.yu2(mod p)) (mod q)

if v = r then signature is verified

8.10 AUTHENTICATION PROTOCOLS

Authentication Protocols are used to convince parties of each others identity and to exchange session keys. They may be one-way or mutual. Central to the problem of authenticated key exchange are two issues: confidentiality and timeliness. To prevent masquerade and to prevent compromise of session keys, essential identification and session key information must be communicated in encrypted form. This requires the prior existence of secret or public keys that can be used for this purpose. The second issue, timeliness, is important because of the threat of message replays. A number of protocols that appeared secure but were revised after additional analysis. These examples highlight the difficulty of getting things right in the area of authentication.

8.10.1 Replay Attacks

Replay Attacks are where a valid signed message is copied and later resent. Such replays, at worst, could allow an opponent to compromise a session key or successfully impersonate another party. At minimum, a successful replay can disrupt operations by presenting parties with messages that appear genuine but are not.

Lists the examples above of replay attacks.

Possible countermeasures include the use of:

- Sequence numbers (generally impractical since must remember last number used with every communicating party)
- Timestamps (needs synchronized clocks amongst all parties involved, which can be problematic)
- Challenge/response (using unique, random, unpredictable nonce, but not suitable for connectionless applications because of handshake overhead)

8.10.2 Using Symmetric Encryption

A two-level hierarchy of symmetric encryption keys can be used to provide confidentiality for communication in a distributed environment.

Usually involves the use of a trusted key distribution center (KDC). Each party in the network shares a secret master key with the KDC. The KDC is responsible for generating session keys, and for distributing those keys to the parties involved, using the master keys to protect these session keys.

8.10.3 Needham-Schroeder Protocol

The Needham-Schroeder Protocol is the original, basic key exchange protocol. Used by 2 parties who both trusted a common key server, it gives one party the info needed to establish a session key with the other. Note that since the key server chooses the session key, it is capable of reading/forging any messages between A and B, which is why they need to trust it absolutely!

Note that all communications is between A and KDC and A and B, B and KDC don't talk directly (though indirectly a message passes from KDC via A to B, encrypted in B's key so that A is unable to read or alter it). Other variations of key distribution protocols can involve direct communications between B and KDC.

- Protocol overview is:

  1. A->KDC: IDA || IDB || N1
  2. KDC -> A: EK_a[Ks || IDB || N1 || EK_b[Ks||IDA]]
  3. A -> B: EKb[Ks||IDA]
  4. B -> A: EKs[N2]
  5. A -> B: EKs[f(N2)]

There is a critical flaw in the protocol, as shown. It can be corrected by either using timestamps, or an additional nonce, with respective advantages and limitations.

This example emphasises the need to be extremely careful in codifying assumptions, and tracking the timeliness of the flow of info in protocols. Designing secure protocols is not easy, and should not be done lightly. Great care and analysis is needed.

8.10.4 Using Public key Encryption

Have a range of approaches based on the use of public key encryption, which generally assume that each of the two parties is in possession of the current public key of the other. The central system is known as an Authentication Server (AS). Have various protocols using timestamps or nonces, and again flaws were found in a number of the original proposals.

8.10.5 Denning AS Protocol

- Denning 81 presented the following:
  1. A -> AS: IDA || IDB
  2. AS -> A: EPR_{as}[IDA||PU_a||T] || EPR_{as}[IDB||PU_b||T]
  3. A -> B: EPR_{as}[IDA||PU_a||T] || EPR_{as}[IDB||PU_b||T] || EPU_b[EPR_{as}[Ks||T]]
- note session key is chosen by A, hence AS need not be trusted to protect it
- timestamps prevent replay but require synchronized clocks

A protocol using timestamps is provided in [DENN81] is shown above. The central authentication server (AS) only provides public key certificates. The session key is chosen and encrypted by A; hence, there is no risk of exposure by the AS. The timestamps protect against replays of compromised keys. This protocol is compact but, as before, requires synchronization of clocks.

8.10.6 One-Way Authentication

One application for which encryption is growing in popularity is electronic mail (e-mail). The very nature of electronic mail, and its chief benefit, is that it is not necessary for the sender and receiver to be online at the same time. Instead, the e-mail message is forwarded to the receiver's electronic mailbox,where it is buffered until the receiver is available to read it. The "envelope" or header of the e-mail message must be in the clear so that the message can be handled by the store-and-forward e-mail protocol. However it is often desirable that e-mail message be encrypted such that the mail-handling system is not in possession of the decryption key. A second requirement is that of authentication, where the recipient wants some assurance that the message is from the alleged sender. One-Way Authentication addresses these requirements.

8.10.7 Using Symmetric Encryption

- Can refine use of KDC but can't have final exchange of nonces, vis:
  1. A->KDC: IDA || IDB || N1
  2. KDC -> A: EKa[Ks || IDB || N1 || EKb[Ks||IDA]]
  3. A -> B: EKb[Ks||IDA] || EKs[M]

- does not protect against replays
  - could rely on timestamp in message, though email delays make this problematic

Using symmetric encryption, with some refinement, the KDC strategy is a candidate for encrypted electronic mail. Because we wish to avoid requiring that the recipient be on line at the same time as the sender, steps 4 and 5 must be eliminated, leaving the protocol as shown.

This approach guarantees that only the intended recipient of a message will be able to read I, and also provides a level of authentication that the sender is A. As specified, the protocol does not protect against replays. You could rely on timestamp in the message, though email delays make this problematic.

8.10.8 Public key Approaches

- Have seen some public key approaches
- if confidentiality is major concern, can use:

  A->B: EPU_b[Ks] || EKs[M]

  - has encrypted session key, encrypted message
- if authentication needed use a digital signature with a digital certificate:

  A->B: M || EPR_a[H(M)] || EPR_{as}[T||IDA||PU_a]

  - with message, signature, certificate

Have already presented public key encryption approaches that are suited to electronic mail, including the straight forward encryption of the entire message for confidentiality, authentication, or both. These approaches require that either the sender know the recipient's public key (confidentiality) or the recipient know the sender's public key (authentication) or both (confidentiality plus authentication). In addition, the public key algorithm must be applied once or twice to what may be a long message.

If confidentiality is the primary concern, then the message can be encrypted with a one-time secret key, which in turn is encrypted with B's public key.

To achieve authentication, and to validate the senders public key, the signature can be encrypted with the recipient's public key, and for assurance A's public key is sent in a digital certificate, as shown. To obtain confidentiality as well, the message can be encrypted with a session key, combining both options above.

8.11 DIGITAL SIGNATURE STANDARD

Digital Signature Standard (DSS) is the digital signature algorithm (DSA) developed by the U.S. National Security Agency (NSA) to generate a digital signature for the authentication of electronic documents. DSS was put forth by the National Institute of Standards and Technology (NIST) in 1994, and has become the United States government standard for authentication of electronic documents. DSS is specified in Federal Information Processing Standard (FIPS) 186.

DSA is a pair of large numbers that are computed according to the specified algorithm within parameters that enable the authentication of the signatory, and as a consequence, the integrity of the data attached. Digital signatures are generated through DSA, as well as verified. Signatures are generated in conjunction with the use of a private key; verification takes place in reference to a corresponding public key. Each signatory has their own paired public (assumed to be known to the general public) and private (known only to the user) keys. Because a signature can only be generated by an authorized person using their private key, the corresponding public key can be used by anyone to verify the signature.

A data summary of the information (called a *message digest*) is created through the use of a hash function (called the *Secure Hash Standard*, or *SHS*, and specified in FIPS 180). The data summary is used in conjuntion with the DSA algorithm to create the digital signature that is sent with the message. Signature verification involves the use of the same hash function.

8.11.1 Direct Digital Signatures

Direct Digital Signatures involve the direct application of public key algorithms involving only the communicating parties. A digital signature may be formed by encrypting the entire message with the sender's private key, or by encrypting a hash code of the message with the sender's private key. Confidentiality can be provided by further encrypting the entire message plus signature using either public or private key schemes. It is important to perform the signature function first and then an outer confidentiality function, since in case of dispute, some third party must view the message and its signature. But these approaches are dependent on the security of the sender's private key. Will have problems if it is lost/stolen and signatures forged. Need time-stamps and timely key revocation.

8.11.2 Arbitrated Digital Signatures

The problems associated with direct digital signatures can be addressed by using an arbiter, in a variety of possible arrangements.

The arbiter plays a sensitive and crucial role in this sort of scheme, and all parties must have a great deal of trust that the arbitration mechanism is working properly.

These schemes can be implemented with either private or public key algorithms, and the arbiter may or may not see the actual message contents. It has the following issues:

- involves use of arbiter A
  - validates any signed message
  - then dated and sent to recipient
- requires suitable level of trust in arbiter
- can be implemented with either private or public key algorithms
- arbiter may or may not see message

8.12 KEY TERMS, KEY POINTS AND REVIEW QUESTIONS

Key Terms

Big Endian	**MD4**	**SHA-256**
Compression Function	**MD5**	**SHA-384**
HMAC	**RIPEMD-160**	**SHA-512**
Little Endian	**SHA-1**	

Key Points

- ➢ Message Authentication is concerned with:
  - Protecting the integrity of a message
  - Validating identity of originator
  - Non-repudiation of origin (dispute resolution)
- ➢ Message encryption by itself can provide a measure of authentication. The analysis differs for symmetric and public key encryption schemes.
- ➢ Authentication functions are cryptographic primitives which are used by message authentication protocols between two parties, sender and receiver.
- ➢ A **digital** signature scheme typically consists of three algorithms:
  - A *key generation* algorithm *G* that randomly produces a "key pair" (*PK*, *SK*) for the signer. *PK* is the verifying key, which is to be public, and *SK* is the signing key, to be kept private.
  - A *signing* algorithm *S*, that on input of a message *m* and a signing key *SK*, produces a signature σ.
  - A *signature verifying* algorithm *V*, that on input a message *m*, a verifying key *PK*, and a signature σ, either accepts or rejects.
- ➢ **HMAC**, is a type of message authentication code (MAC) calculated using a cryptographic hash function in combination with a secret key.
- ➢ RIPEMD-160 is a 160-bit cryptographic hash function, designed by Hans Dobbertin, Antoon Bosselaers, and Bart Preneel.
- ➢ MD5 (Message-Digest algorithm 5) is a widely used cryptographic hash function with a 128-bit hash value.
- ➢ A hash function H is a transformation that takes a variable-size input m and returns a fixed-size string, which is called the hash value h

$$h = H(M)$$

where M = Variable length of message

H(M) = Fixed-length hash value

- Types of digital signature
  - Directed Digital Signature
  - Arbitrated Digital Signatures
- Authentication functions:
  - Message encryption:
  - Message authentication code (MAC)
  - Hash functions

Question with Answers *(2 Marks)*

Q. 1. *What is a hash function?*

Ans. A hash function H is a transformation that takes a variable-size input m and returns a fixed-size string, which is called the hash value (h = H(m)). Hash functions with just this property have a variety of general computational uses.

Q. 2. *What primitive operations are used in Blowfish?*

Ans. Blowfish uses two primitive operations:

- Addition: Addition of words, denoted by +, is performed modulo 2^{32}
- Bitwise Exclusive-OR: This operation is denoted by $\oplus$

Q. 3. *What are symmetric and asymmetric ciphers?*

Ans. Symmetric systems are also known as shared secret systems or private key systems. Asymmetric cipher the key is negotiated betweet the parties during communication. In asymmetric system each person has two keys. One key the public key-shared key other key is private key – nerver shared.

Q. 4. *What types of attack are addressed by message authentication?*

Ans.
- Content modification: Changes to the contents of the message.
- Sequence modification: Any modification to a sequence of messages between parties, including insertion, deletion, and recording.
- Timing modification: Delay or replay of message

Q. 5. *What primitive operation is used in RC4?*

Ans. The primitive operation used in RC4 is bitwise Exclusive-OR (XOR) operation.

Q. 6. *What is the use of digital signature?*

Ans. Data appended to or a data unit that allows a recipent of the data unit to prove the source and integrity of the data unit and protect against forgery.

Q. 7. *What types of information might be derived from a traffic analysis attack?*

Ans.
- Identities of partners
- How frequently the partners are communicating
- Message pattern, message length
- Events that correlate with special conversations between particular partners.

Q. 8. *What is traffic padding and what is its purpose?*

Ans. Traffic padding produces ciphertext output continuously, even in the absence of plaintext. A continuous random data stream is generated. When plaintext is available, it is encrypted and transmitted. When input plaintext is not present random data are encrypted and transmitted.

Q. 9. *What is Message Authentication Code?*

Ans. An alternative authentication technique involves the use of a small fixed size block of data known as cryptographic checksum or MAC that is appended to the message.

Q. 10. *What is the difference between MAC and One-Way hash function?*

Ans. The difference between a MAC and a one-way hash function is that unlike a MAC, a hash code does not use a key but is a function only of the input message.

Q. 11. *What is the purpose of the State array?*

Ans. A single 128-bit is depcited as a square matrix of bytes. This block is copies into the State array, which is modified at each stage of encryption or decryption. After the final stage, State is copied to an output matrix.

Q. 12. *List ways in which secret keys can be distributed to two communicating parties.*

Ans.
- A can selected a key and physically deliver it to B
- A thrid party can select the key and physically deliver it A and B

Q. 13. *What is a birthday attack?*

Ans. A birthday attack is a name used to refer to class of brute-force attacks. It gets its name from the surprising result that the probability that two or more people in a group of 23 share the same birthday is greater than ½ such a result is called a birthday paradox.

Q. 14. *What is utility of detached signature?*

Ans. A detached signautre may be stored and transmitted separately from the message it signs. This is useful in serveral contexts. A user may wish to maintain a separate signature log of all message sent or received.

Q. 15. *What is Nonce?*

Ans. Consider A issues a request to the KDC for a session key to protect a logical connection to B. The message includes the identity of A and B and q unique identifer, N1, for this transaction, which we refer to as nonce. The nonce may be timestamp, a counter, or a random number.

Q. 16. *What is key distribution centre?*

Ans. A key distribution centre is responsible for distributing keys to pairs of users such as hosts, processes, application. Each user must share a unique key with the key distribution centre for purposes of key distribution.

Review Questions

1. Explain is MAC.
2. Differentiate Message Authentication and One-Way Hash function.
3. What is the difference between weak and strong collision resistance?
4. List out types of attacks are addressed by message authentication.
5. What are some approaches to producing message authentication?
6. List out characteristics are needed in a secure hash function.
7. Write a short note on secure hash algorithm.
8. Explain the design objective of HMAC.
9. Explain Briefly MD5.
10. What is RIPEMD? Explain.
11. What are the requirements for a digital signature?
12. List the properties of digital signature.
13. What is a direct digital signature?
14. What is a reply attack?
15. Define Authentication.

❑❑❑

PART 4
MUTUAL TRUST

Chapter

CHAPTER 9

KEY MANAGEMENT AND DISTRIBUTION

9.1 KERBEROS

What is Kerberos?

Kerberos is a network authentication protocol. It is designed to provide strong authentication for client/server applications by using secret-key cryptography. A free implementation of this protocol is available from the Massachusetts Institute of Technology. Kerberos is available in many commercial products as well.

The Internet is an insecure place. Many of the protocols used in the Internet do not provide any security. Tools to "sniff" passwords off of the network are in common use by malicious hackers. Thus, applications which send an unencrypted password over the network are extremely vulnerable. Worse yet, other client/server applications rely on the client program to be "honest" about the identity of the user who is using it. Other applications rely on the client to restrict its activities to those which it is allowed to do, with no other enforcement by the server.

Some sites attempt to use firewalls to solve their network security problems. Unfortunately, firewalls assume that "the bad guys" are on the outside, which is often a very bad assumption.

Most of the really damaging incidents of computer crime are carried out by insiders. Firewalls also have a significant disadvantage in that they restrict how your users can use the Internet. (After all, firewalls are simply a less extreme example of the dictum that there is nothing more secure then a computer which is not connected to the network — and powered off!) In many places, these restrictions are simply unrealistic and unacceptable.

Kerberos was created by MIT as a solution to these network security problems. The Kerberos protocol uses strong cryptography so that a client can prove its identity to a server across an insecure network connection. After a client and server has used Kerberos to prove their identity, they can also encrypt all of their communications to assure privacy and data integrity as they go about their business.

Kerberos is freely available from MIT, under copyright permissions very similar those used for the BSD operating system and the X Window System. MIT provides Kerberos in source form so that anyone who wishes to use it may look over the code for themselves and assure themselves that the code is trustworthy. In addition, for those who prefer to rely on a professionally supported product, Kerberos is available as a product from many different vendors.

In summary, Kerberos is a solution to your network security problems. It provides the tools of authentication and strong cryptography over the network to help you secure your information systems across your entire enterprise. We hope you find Kerberos as useful as it has been to us. At MIT, Kerberos has been invaluable to our Information/Technology architecture.

Kerberos provides a centralized authentication server whose function is to authenticate users to servers and servers to users. Unlike most other authentication schemes, Kerberos relies exclusively on symmetric encryption, making no use of public key encryption. Two versions of Kerberos are in common use: v4 and v5.

9.1.1 The Kerberos Protocol

Kerberos provides a means of verifying the identities of principals, (*e.g.*, a workstation user or a network server) on an open (unprotected) network. This is accomplished without relying on assertions by the host operating system, without basing trust on host addresses, without requiring physical security of all the hosts on the network, and under the assumption that packets travelling along the network can be read, modified, and inserted at will. Kerberos performs authentication under these conditions as a trusted third-party authentication service by using conventional (shared secret key) cryptography. Extensions to Kerberos (outside the scope of this document) can provide for the use of public key cryptography during certain phases of the authentication protocol. Such extensions support Kerberos authentication for users registered with public key certification authorities and provide certain benefits of public key cryptography in situations where they are needed.

The basic Kerberos authentication process proceeds as follows: A client sends a request to the authentication server (AS) for "credentials" for a given server. The AS responds with these credentials, encrypted in the client's key. The credentials consist of a "ticket" for the server and a temporary encryption key (often called a "session key"). The client transmits the ticket (which contains the client's identity and a copy of the session key, all encrypted in the server's key) to the server. The session key (now shared by the client and server) is used to authenticate the client and may optionally be used to authenticate the server. It may also be used to encrypt further communication between the two parties or to exchange a separate sub-session key to be used to encrypt further communication. Note that many applications use Kerberos' functions only upon the initiation of a stream-based network connection. Unless an application performs encryption or integrity protection for the data stream, the identity verification applies only to the initiation of the connection, and it does not guarantee that subsequent messages on the connection originate from the same principal.

Implementation of the basic protocol consists of one or more authentication servers running on physically secure hosts. The authentication servers maintain a database of principals (*i.e.*, users and servers) and their secret keys. Code libraries provide encryption and implement the Kerberos protocol. In order to add authentication to its transactions, a typical network application adds calls to the Kerberos library directly or through the Generic Security Services Application Programming Interface (GSS-API) described in a separate document. These calls result in the transmission of the messages necessary to achieve authentication.

9.1.2 Kerberos Requirements

- Its first report identified requirements as:
  - Secure
  - Reliable
  - Transparent
  - Scalable
- Implemented using an authentication protocol based on Needham-Schroeder

The first published report on Kerberos listed the requirements shown above. To support these requirements, Kerberos is a trusted third-party authentication service that uses a protocol.

9.1.3 Kerberos v4 Overview

- A basic third-party authentication scheme
- Have an Authentication Server (AS)
  - Users initially negotiate with AS to identify self
  - AS provides a non-corruptible authentication credential [ticket granting ticket (TGT)]
- Have a Ticket Granting Server (TGS)
  - Users subsequently request access to other services from TGS on basis of users TGT

The core of Kerberos is the Authentication and Ticket Granting Servers – these are trusted by all users and servers and must be securely administered. The protocol includes a sequence of interactions between the client, AS, TGT and desired server.

9.1.4 Kerberos Realms

- A Kerberos environment consists of:
  - A Kerberos server

  - A number of clients, all registered with server
  - Application servers, sharing keys with server
- This is termed a realm
  - Typically a single administrative domain
- If have multiple realms, their Kerberos servers must share keys and trust

A full-service Kerberos environment consisting of a Kerberos server, a number of clients, and a number of application servers is referred to as a Kerberos realm. A Kerberos realm is a set of managed nodes that share the same Kerberos database, and are part of the same administrative domain. If have multiple realms, their Kerberos servers must share keys and trust each other.

9.2 X.509 AUTHENTICATION SERVICE

History and Usage

X.509 was initially issued in July 3, 1988 and was begun in association with the X.500 standard. It assumes a strict hierarchical system of certificate authorities (CAs) for issuing the certificates. This contrasts with web of trust models, like PGP, where anyone (not just special CAs) may sign, and thus attest to the validity of others' key certificates. Version 3 of X.509 includes the flexibility to support other topologies like bridges and meshes. It can be used in a peer-to-peer, OpenPGP-like web of trust, but is rarely used that way as of 2004. The X.500 system has never been fully implemented, and the IETF's Public Key Infrastructure (X.509), or PKIX, working group has adapted the standard to the more flexible organization of the Internet. In fact, the term X.509 certificate usually refers to the IETF's PKIX Certificate and CRL Profile of the X.509 v3 certificate standard, as specified in RFC 3280, commonly referred to as PKIX for Public Key Infrastructure (X.509).

9.2.1 X.509 Certificates

The X.509 certificate is the heart of the standard. There are 3 versions, with successively more info in the certificate—must be v2 if either unique identifier field exists, must be v3 if any extensions are used. These user certificates are assumed to be created by some trusted certification authority (CA) and placed in the directory by the CA or by the user. The directory server itself is not responsible for the creation of public keys or for the certification function; it merely provides an easily accessible location for users to obtain certificates. The certificate includes the elements shown.

The standard uses the notation for a certificate of: CA<<A>> where the CA signs the certificate for user A with its private key.

9.2.2 Structure of a Certificate

The structure of a X.509 v3 digital certificate is as follows:

- Certificate
  - Version

  - Serial Number
  - Algorithm ID
  - Issuer
  - Validity
    - Not Before
    - Not After
  - Subject
  - Subject Public Key Info
    - Public Key Algorithm
    - Subject Public Key
  - Issuer Unique Identifier (Optional)
  - Subject Unique Identifier (Optional)
  - Extensions (Optional)
    - ...
- Certificate Signature Algorithm
- Certificate Signature

What's Inside an X.509 Certificate?

The X.509 standard defines what information can go into a certificate, and describes how to write it down (the data format). All X.509 certificates have the following data, in addition to the signature:

Version

This identifies which version of the X.509 standard applies to this certificate, which affects what information can be specified in it. Thus far, three versions are defined.

Serial Number

The entity that created the certificate is responsible for assigning it a serial number to distinguish it from other certificates it issues. This information is used in numerous ways, for example when a certificate is revoked its serial number is placed in a Certificate Revocation List (CRL).

Signature Algorithm Identifier

This identifies the algorithm used by the CA to sign the certificate.

Issuer Name

The X.500 name of the entity that signed the certificate. This is normally a CA. Using this certificate implies trusting the entity that signed this certificate. (Note that in some cases, such as *root or top-level* CA certificates, the issuer signs its own certificate.)

Validity Period

Each certificate is valid only for a limited amount of time. This period is described by a start date and time and an end date and time, and can be as short as a few seconds or almost as long as a century. The validity period chosen depends on a number of factors, such as the strength of the private key used to sign the certificate or the amount one is willing to pay for a certificate. This is the expected period that entities can rely on the public value, if the associated private key has not been compromised.

Subject Name

The name of the entity whose public key the certificate identifies. This name uses the X.500 standard, so it is intended to be unique across the Internet. This is the Distinguished Name (DN) of the entity, for example,

CN=Java Duke, OU=Java Software Division, O=Sun Microsystems Inc, C=US

(These refer to the subject's Common Name, Organizational Unit, Organization, and Country.)

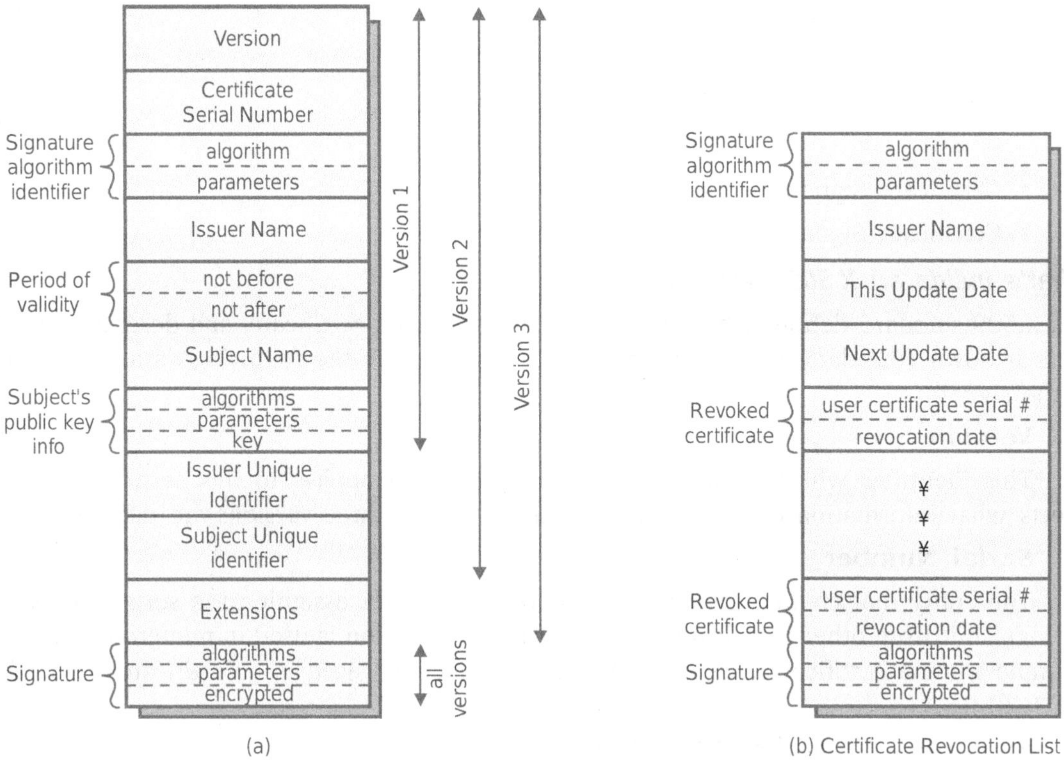

Fig. 9.1. *Shows the format of an X.509 certificate and CRL.*

Certificate File Extensions

Common filename extensions for X.509-certificates are:

- .CER - CER encoded certificate, sometimes sequence of certificates
- .DER - DER encoded certificate
- .PEM - (Privacy Enhanced Mail) Base64 encoded DER certificate, enclosed between "........BEGIN CERTIFICATE........" and "........END CERTIFICATE........"

- .P7B - See .p7c
- .P7C - PKCS#7 SignedData structure without data, just certificate(s) or CRL(s)
- .PFX - See .p12
- .P12 - PKCS#12, may contain certificate(s) (public) and private keys (password protected)
- PKCS #7 is a standard for signing or encrypting (officially called "enveloping") data. Since the certificate is needed to verify signed data, it is possible to include them in the SignedData structure. A .P7C-file is just a degenerated SignedData structure, without any data to sign.
- PKCS #12 evolved from the PFX (Personal inFormation eXchange) standard and is used to exchange public and private objects in a single file.

A .PEM-file may contain certificate(s) or private key(s), enclosed between the appropriate BEGIN/END-lines (CERTIFICATE or RSA PRIVATE KEY).

X.509 Version 3 is the most recent (1996) and supports the notion of extensions, whereby anyone can define an extension and include it in the certificate. Some common extensions in use today are: *KeyUsage* (limits the use of the keys to particular purposes such as "signing-only") and *AlternativeNames* (allows other identities to also be associated with this public key, *e.g.,* DNS names, Email addresses, IP addresses). Extensions can be marked *critical* to indicate that the extension should be checked and enforced/used. For example, if a certificate has the KeyUsage extension marked critical and set to "keyCertSign" then if this certificate is presented during SSL communication, it should be rejected, as the certificate extension indicates that the associated private key should only be used for signing certificates and not for SSL use.

Obtaining a Certificate

- Any user with access to CA can get any certificate from it.
- Only the CA can modify a certificate.
- Because cannot be forged, certificates can be placed in a public directory.

User certificates generated by a CA have the characteristics that any user with access to the public key of the CA can verify the user public key that was certified, and no party other than the certification authority can modify the certificate without this being detected. Because certificates are unforgeable, they can be placed in a directory without the need for the directory to make special efforts to protect them.

CA Hierarchy

If both parties use the same CA, they know its public key and can verify others certificates. If not, then there has to be some means to form a chain of certifications between the CA's used by the two parties, by the use of client and parent certificates. It is assumed that each client trusts its parents certificates.

CA Hierarchy Use

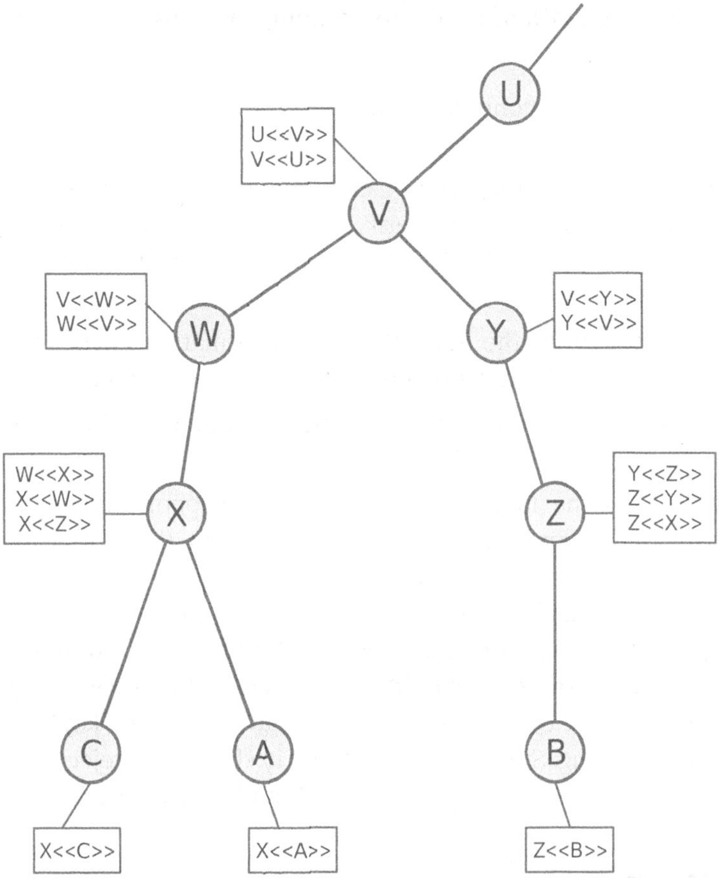

Fig. 9.2. *Illustrates the use of an X.509 hierarchy to mutually verify clients' certificates.*

Track chains of certificates:

A acquires B certificate using chain: X<<W>>W<<V>>V<<Y>>Y<<Z>>Z<<B>>

B acquires A certificate using chain: Z<<Y>>Y<<V>>V<<W>>W<<X>>X<<A>>

Certificate Revocation

A certificate includes a period of validity. Typically a new certificate is issued just before the expiration of the old one.

In addition, it may be desirable on occasion to revoke a certificate before it expires, for one of a range of reasons, such as those shown above.

To support this, each CA must maintain a list consisting of all revoked but not expired certificates issued by that CA, known as the certificate revocation list (CRL).

When a user receives a certificate in a message, the user must determine whether the certificate has been revoked, by checking the directory CRL each time a certificate is received, this often does not happen in practice.

Authentication Procedures

X.509 also includes three alternative authentication procedures that are intended for use across a variety of applications, used when obtaining and using certificates. 1-way for unidirectional messages (like email), 2-way for interactive sessions when timestamps are used, 3-way for interactive sessions with no need for timestamps (and hence synchronised clocks).

9.3 IPSEC (IP SECURITY)

IPsec (IP security) is a suite of protocols for securing Internet Protocol (IP) communications by authenticating and/or encrypting each IP packet in a data stream. IPsec also includes protocols for cryptographic key establishment.

IPsec protocols operate at the network layer, layer 3 of the OSI model. Other Internet security protocols in widespread use, such as SSL, TLS and SSH, operate from the transport layer up (OSI layers 4–7). This makes IPsec more flexible, as it can be used for protecting layer 4 protocols, including both TCP and UDP, the most commonly used transport layer protocols. IPsec has an advantage over SSL and other methods that operate at higher layers: For an application to use IPsec no code change in the applications is required whereas to use SSL and other higher level protocols, applications must undergo code changes.

Network architecture is usually explained as a stack of different layers. Fig. 9.3 explains the OSI (Open System Interconnect) model stack and IP (Internet Protocol) model stack. TCP is Transmission Control Protocol, IP is Internet Protocol, UDP is User Datagram Protocol, data link including Ethernet, PPP, FDDI etc.

<table>
<tr><th>OSI model</th><th>IP model</th></tr>
<tr><td>Application</td><td rowspan="2">Application</td></tr>
<tr><td>Presentation</td></tr>
<tr><td>Session</td><td rowspan="2">TCP/UDP</td></tr>
<tr><td>Transport</td></tr>
<tr><td>Network</td><td>IP</td></tr>
<tr><td>Data link</td><td>Data link</td></tr>
<tr><td>Physical</td><td>Physical</td></tr>
</table>

Fig. 9.3. *Network layer stack.*

9.3.1 Security Architecture

IPsec is implemented by a set of cryptographic protocols for (1) securing packet flows, (2) mutual authentication and (3) establishing cryptographic parameters.

The IP security architecture uses the concept of a security association as the basis for building security functions into IP. A security association is simply the bundle of algorithms and parameters (such as keys) that is being used to encrypt and authenticate a particular flow in one direction. Therefore, in normal bi-directional traffic, the flows are secured by a pair of security associations. The actual choice of encryption and authentication algorithms (from a defined list) is left to the IPsec administrator.

In order to decide what protection is to be provided for an outgoing packet, IPsec uses the security parameter index (SPI), an index to the security association database (SADB), along with the destination address in a packet header, which together uniquely identify a security association for that packet. A similar procedure is performed for an incoming packet, where IPsec gathers decryption and verification keys from the security association database.

For multicast, a security association is provided for the group, and is duplicated across all authorized receivers of the group. There may be more than one security association for a group, using different SPIs, thereby allowing multiple levels and sets of security within a group. Indeed, each sender can have multiple security associations, allowing authentication, since a receiver can only know that someone knowing the keys sent the data. Note that the relevant standard does not describe how the association is chosen and duplicated across the group; it is assumed that a responsible party will have made the choice.

9.3.2 Protocol Structure—IPsec: Security Architecture for IP Network

IPsec Architecture included many protocols and algorithms. The relationships of these protocols are displayed as follows in Fig. 9.4.

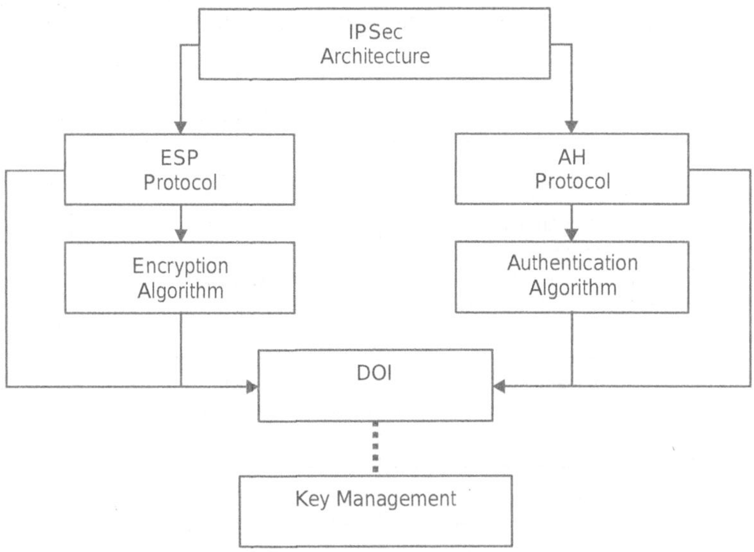

Fig. 9.4. *IPsec Architecture – Relationship between the protocols.*

9.3.3 Current Status as a Standard

IPsec is a mandatory part of IPv6 (mandatory to implement, not mandatory to use), and is optional for use with IPv4. While the standard is designed to be indifferent to IP versions, current widespread deployment and experience concerns IPv4 implementations.

IPsec protocols were originally defined by RFCs 1825–1829, published in 1995. In 1998, these documents were obsoleted by RFCs 2401–2412, which are not compatible with 1825–1829, although they are conceptually identical. In December 2005, third-generation documents, RFCs 4301–4309, were produced. They are largely a superset of 2401–2412, but provide a second Internet Key Exchange standard. These third-generation documents standardized the abbreviation of IPsec to uppercase "IP" and lowercase "sec".

9.3.4 Design Intent

IPsec was intended to provide either transport mode (end-to-end) security of packet traffic in which the end-point computers do the security processing, or tunnel mode (portal-to-portal) communications security in which security of packet traffic is provided to several machines (even to whole LANs) by a single node.

IPsec can be used to create Virtual Private Networks (VPN) in either mode, and this is the dominant use. Note, however, that the security implications are quite different between the two operational modes.

Since the Internet Protocol does not inherently provide any security capabilities, IPsec was introduced to provide security services such as the following:

- Encrypting traffic (so it cannot be read by parties other than those for whom it is intended)
- Integrity validation (ensuring traffic has not been modified along its path)
- Authenticating the peers (ensuring that traffic is from a trusted party)
- Anti-replay (protecting against replay of the secure session).

9.3.5 Modes

There are two modes of IPsec operation: transport mode and tunnel mode.

1. Transport mode

In transport mode, only the payload (the data you transfer) of the IP packet is encrypted and/or authenticated. The routing is intact, since the IP header is neither modified nor encrypted; however, when the authentication header is used, the IP addresses cannot be translated, as this will invalidate the hash value. The transport and application layers are always secured by hash, so they cannot be modified in any way (for example by translating the port numbers). Transport mode is used for host-to-host communications.

A means to encapsulate IPsec messages for NAT traversal has been defined by RFC documents describing the NAT-T mechanism.

2. Tunnel mode

In tunnel mode, the entire IP packet (data plus the message headers) is encrypted and/or authenticated. It must then be encapsulated into a new IP packet for routing to work. Tunnel mode is used for network-to-network communications (secure tunnels between routers, *e.g.*, for VPNs) or host-to-network and host-to-host communications over the Internet.

9.3.6 Technical Details

Two protocols have been developed to provide packet-level security for both IPv4 and IPv6:

The IP Authentication Header provides integrity and authentication and non-repudiation, if the appropriate choice of cryptographic algorithms is made.

The IP Encapsulating Security Payload provides confidentiality, along with optional (but strongly recommended) authentication and integrity protection.

9.3.7 Authentication Header (AH)

The AH is intended to guarantee connectionless integrity and data origin authentication of IP datagrams. Further, it can optionally protect against replay attacks by using the sliding window technique and discarding old packets. AH protects the IP payload and all header fields of an IP datagram except for mutable fields, *i.e.,* those that might be altered in transit. In IPv4, mutable (and therefore unauthenticated) IP header fields include TOS, Flags, Fragment Offset, TTL and Header Checksum. AH operates directly on top of IP, using IP protocol number 51.

0–7 bit	8–15 bit	16–23 bit	24–31 bit
Next header	Payload length	RESERVED	
Security parameters index (SPI)			
Sequence number			
Authentication data (variable)			

Fig. 9.5. *An AH packet diagram.*

Field meanings:

Next header

Identifies the protocol of the transferred data.

Payload length

Size of AH packet.

RESERVED

Reserved for future use (all zero until then).

Sequence number

A monotonically increasing number, used to prevent replay attacks.

Authentication data

Contains the integrity check value (ICV) necessary to authenticate the packet; it may contain padding.

Encapsulating Security Payload (ESP)

The ESP protocol provides origin authenticity, integrity, and confidentiality protection of a packet. ESP also supports encryption-only and authentication-only configurations, but using encryption without authentication is strongly discouraged because it is insecure. Unlike AH, the IP packet header is not protected by ESP. (Although in tunnel mode ESP, protection is afforded to the whole inner IP packet, including the inner header; the outer header remains unprotected.) ESP operates directly on top of IP, using IP protocol number 50.

0–7 bit	8–15 bit	16–23 bit	24–31 bit
Security parameters index (SPI)			
Sequence number			
Payload data (variable)			
	Padding (0–255 bytes)		
		Pad Length	Next Header
Authentication Data (variable)			

Fig. 9.6. *An ESP packet.*

Field meanings:

Security parameters index (SPI)

  Identifies the security parameters in combination with IP address.

Sequence number

  A monotonically increasing number, used to prevent replay attacks.

Payload data

  The data to be transferred.

Padding

  Used with some block ciphers to pad the data to the full length of a block.

Pad length

  Size of padding in bytes.

Next header

  Identifies the protocol of the transferred data.

Authentication data

  Contains the data used to authenticate the packet.

9.3.8 Implementations

IPsec support is usually implemented in the kernel with key management and ISAKMP/IKE negotiation carried out from user-space. Existing IPsec implementations tend to include both of these functionalities. However, as there is a standard interface for key management, it is possible to control one kernel IPsec stack using key management tools from a different implementation.

Because of this, there is confusion as to the origins of the IPsec implementation that is in the Linux kernel. The FreeS/WAN project made the first complete and open source implementation of IPsec for Linux. It consists of a kernel IPsec stack (KLIPS), as well as a key management daemon (pluto) and many shell scripts. The FreeS/WAN project was disbanded in March 2004. Openswan and strongSwan are continuations of FreeS/WAN. The KAME project also implemented complete IPsec support for NetBSD, FreeBSD. Its key management daemon is called racoon. OpenBSD made its own ISAKMP/IKE daemon, simply named isakmpd (which was also ported to other systems, including Linux).

However, none of these kernel IPsec stacks were integrated into the Linux kernel. Alexey Kuznetsov and David S. Miller wrote a kernel IPsec implementation from scratch for the Linux kernel around the end of 2002. This stack was subsequently released as part of Linux 2.6, and is referred to variously as "native" or "NETKEY".

Therefore, contrary to popular belief, the Linux IPsec stack did not originate from the KAME project. As it supports the standard PF_KEY protocol (RFC 2367) and the native XFRM interface for key management, the Linux IPsec stack can be used in conjunction with either pluto from Openswan/strongSwan, isakmpd from OpenBSD project, racoon from the KAME project or without any ISAKMP/IKE daemon (using manual keying).

The new architectures of network processors, including multi-core processors with integrated encryption engines, change the way the IPsec stacks are designed. A dedicated Fast Path is used in order to offload the processing of the IPsec processing (SA, SP lookups, encryption, etc.). These Fast Path stacks must be co-integrated on dedicated cores with Linux or RTOS running on other cores. These OS are the control plane that runs ISAKMP/IKE of the Fast Path IPsec stack.

9.4 KEY MANAGEMENT

In AH and ESP, secret keys are required for communications. An important part of IPSec is key management.

IPSec supports two types of key management for both AH and ESP

1. **Manual:** A system administrator manually configures each system with its own keys and with the keys of other communicating systems.
2. **Automated:** An automated system enables the on-demand creation of keys for SA and facilities the use of keys in a large system. IPSec's default automated key management protocol is ISAKMP/Oakley. The Oakley key exchange protocol was discussed before, which is based on Deffie-Hellman key exchange scheme. Now we introduce ISAKMP key management.

ISAKMP provides a framework for internet key management. It does not dictate a specific key exchange algorithm. Other key exchange algorithm scan also be used with SAKMP.ISAKMP (Internet Security Association and Key Management Protocol) defines procedures and packet formats to establish, negotiate, modify and delete security associations.

The ISAKMP header format is shown in Fig. 9.7.

0	8		16	24 31
Initiator Cookie				
Responder Cookie				
Next payload	MjVer	MnVer	Exchange Type	Flags
Message ID				
Length				

Fig. 9.7. *ISAKMP header.*

Initiator Cookie (64-bits) initiated SA establishment, SA notification, or SA deletion. Responder Cookie(64-bits) is used for responding; null in the first message from initiator. Next Payload (8-bits) indicates the type of the first payload in the message, which is followed the ISAKMP header. Major Version (4-bits) indicates major version of ISAKMP in use and Minor Version (4-bits) indicates minor version in use. Exchange Type (8-bits) indicates the type of exchange. Flags (8-bits) indicates specific options set for this ISAKMP exchange. Message ID (32-bits) is the unique ID for this message. Length (32-bits) is the length of total message (header plus all payloads) in octets.

ISAKMP Payload is followed the ISAKMP header. All ISAKMP payloads begin with the same generic payload header which is shown in Fig. 9.8.

0	8	16 31
Net Payload	Reserved	Payload Length

Fig. 9.8. *ISAKMP payload header.*

Next Payload field uses 8-bits which has value 0 if this is the last payload in the message, otherwise its value is the type of the next payload. The Payload length field indicates the length in octets of this payload, including the generic payload header.

The payload types defined for ISAKMP are as follows:

- **SA payload (SA):** Used to begin the establishment of an SA. Parameters include Domain of Interpretation (*e.g.,* IPSec DOI), and a situation parameter which defines the security policy for this negotiation.
- **Proposal payload (P):** Contains information used during SA negotiation. The payload indicates the protocol for this SA (ESP or AH),entity's SPI and the number of transforms.
- **Transform payload (T):** Includes a transform number which identifies this particular payload. The payload also contains the transform ID and Attributes to specify the transform (*e.g.,* 3DES for ESP, HMACSHA-1-96 for AH) with its associated attribution (*e.g.,* hash length).
- **Key Exchange payload (KE):** Used for key exchange (Oakley, PGPetc.). The payload contains the data required to generate a session key.

- **Identification payload (ID):** Used to identify the communicating peers.
- The Data field will contain an IPv4 of IPv6 address.
- **Certificate payload (CERT):** Transfers public-key certificate. The payload indicates the type of certificate of certificate-related information.
- **Certificate Request payload (CR):** Requests the certificate of the other communicating entity. Lists certificate types and certificate authorities that are acceptable.
- **Hash payload (HASH):** Contains data generated by a hash function
- Over some message.
- **Signature payload (SIG):** Contains data generated by a digital signature scheme.
- **Nonce payload (NONCE):** Contains random data to protect against
- Replay attacks.
- **Notification payload (N):** Contains either error or status information associated with this SA.
- **Delete payload (D):** Indicates one or more SAs that sender has deleted from its database.

9.5 WEB SECURITY

Web security includes three parts: security of server, security of client, and network traffic security between a browser and a server. Security of server and security of client are problems of computer security. In this chapter we consider the traffic security.

Network security can considered at different levels, for example:

Network level: Use IPSec.

Transport level: Use SSL (Secure Socket Layer) or TLS (Transport Layer Security).

Application level: Use PGP, S/MIME, SET(Secure Electronic Transaction).

In this chapter we discuss some schemes related to the web security.

9.5.1 SSL

Secure Socket Layer (SSL) is developed by Netscape. The main parts of SSL contains several protocols: SSL Handshake Protocol, SSL Change Cipher Spec Protocol, SSL Alert Protocol, SSL Record Protocol. We give the outline of these protocols in the follows.

(a) SSL Record Protocol

This protocol defines how to transmit an application message in SSL. The sender of a message does the following:

Fragmentation: The message is fragmented into blocks of 214 bytes or less.

Compression: (optional).

Add MAC: Compute a MAC using a shared secret key *K* and add the resulting MAC to the fragment. The MAC function used in SSL is similar to HMAC. A hash function *h* and a shared secret key *K* is used. The MAC value is computed as follows.

h(Kjjpad2jjh(Kjjpad1jjseqnumjjtypejjlengthjjM))

where *seqnum* is the sequence number of the message, *type* is the highlevel protocol used to process this fragment, *length* is the length of the fragment and *M* is the content of the fragment. *pad*1 and *pad*2 are fixed paddings which are repeating of fixed bytes.

Encrypt: Encrypt the compresses message plus the MAC using symmetric encryption (block cipher or stream cipher). The block cipher used in SSL are IDEA, DES, 3-DES, RC4, Fortezza. The stream cipher used are RC4s.

Append SSL record header: The header consists: Content Type (8 bits), Major Version (8 bits), minor version (8 bits) and Compressed Length (16 bits). The compressed length is the length of the plaintext (or compressed plaintext) fragment in bytes. The maximum value is 214 +2048: The content types are change cipher spec, alert, handshake and application data.

The SSL record format is illustrated in Fig. 9.9.

The following Change Cipher Spec Protocol and Alert Protocol are capsulated by Record Protocol.

(b) Change Cipher Spec Protocol

This protocol consists of a single byte with the value 1. This message causes the pending state to be copied into the current state, which updates the cipher suite. Usually, it is sent during the handshake sequence (we will discuss Handshake protocol later) after key exchange and certificate certificate verification (optional).

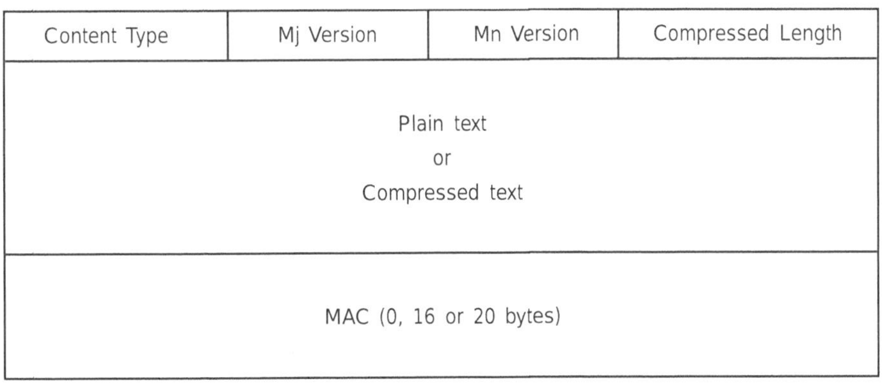

Fig. 9.9. *SSL record format.*

(c) Alert Protocol

Each message of this protocol consists of two bytes. The first byte takes the value waning (1) or fatal (2). The second byte contains a code which indicates the specific alert such as unexpected message, bad record mac, bad certificate, etc.

(d) Handshake Protocol

This protocol is more complicated than other SSL protocols. The protocol consists of a series of messages exchanged by client and server. Each message has three fields:

Type (1 byte): Indicates the message type such as hello request, client hello, server key exchange, certificate verify, etc.

Length (3 bytes): The length of the message in bytes.

Content (1 byte): The parameters associated with this message.

The protocol can be viewed as having four phases of exchanges. Now we give description of these exchanges.

Phase 1. Establish Security Capabilities

The client initiates the exchange by sending a client hello message (in SSL record format) which contains: version, random number (nonce), session ID, CipherSuite which is a list of cryptographic algorithms supported by the client, compression method which is a list of compression methods the client supports.

After sending the client hello message, the client waits for the server hello message which contains the same parameters as the client hello message but only one CipherSuite and one compression method are chosen. The elements of Cipher Suite are key exchange method and CipherSpec which includes cipher algorithm, MAC algorithm, cipher type (stream or block), hash size, key material, IV size etc.

Phase 2. Server Authentication and Key Exchange

Server first sends its certificate message. Then a server key exchange message may be sent if it is required. The certificate request message may be followed to request the client's certificate. Finally, server sends the server done message which indicates the end of server hello.

Phase 3. Client Authentication and Key Exchange

Upon receipt of the server done message, the client should verify the certificate and server hello parameters. If everything is fine, then the client sends back messages to the server. First the client sends certificate message or no certificate alert according whether the server requested a certificate. Next the client sends the client key exchange message which contains a 48-byte pre-master secret if RSA is used or public parameters of Diffie-Hellman scheme. We will explain pre-master secret later. Finally, the client may sends a certificate verify message which provides verification of a client certificate.

Phase 4. Finish

This phase completes the setting up of a secure connection. The client sends a change cipher spec message and copies the pending CiperSpec into the current CipherSpec. Then the client sends the finished message under the new algorithms, keys, and secrets. The finished message is hash value of master secret, handshake message (which consists of all of the data from handshake messages up to but not including this message) and some other codes. The master secret is computed from the pre-master secret. The master secret is then used to generate the session keys which are used for encryption and authentication.

9.6 SECURE ELECTRONIC TRANSACTION (SET)

SET is an open encryption and security specification designed to protect credit card transactions on the Internet. SSL secures communications between a client and a server. However, if we use SSL for credit card transaction, some problems might occur. For example, the information of a credit card might be used by the server for some purpose not desired for the client. On the other hand, a client might supply an invalid credit card number. SET is designed as a secure credit card payment system over internet, which protect both customers and merchants. SET is more complicated than SSL. A full description of SET needs a hundred pages. In this section, we just give a brief description of SET.

SET participants include the following:

- **Cardholder:** Who hold a payment card (credit card)issued by an issuer.

  A cardholder will use the card to purchase over the internet.
- **Merchant:** A person or organization that has goods or service to sell to the cardholder. A merchant that accepts payment cards must have a relationship with an acquirer.
- **Issuer:** A financial institution that provides the cardholder with the payment card.
- **Acquirer:** A financial institute that establishes an account with a merchant and processes payment card authorizations and payments. Merchants will usually accept more than one credit card brand but do not want to deal with multiple bankcard associations or with multiple issuers. The acquirer provides authorization to the merchant that a given card is fine. The acquirer also pays the merchant's account and then reimbursed by the issuer.
- **Payment gateway:** A function operated by the acquirer or a third party that processes merchant payment messages. The payment gateway interfaces between SET and the existing bankcard payment network.

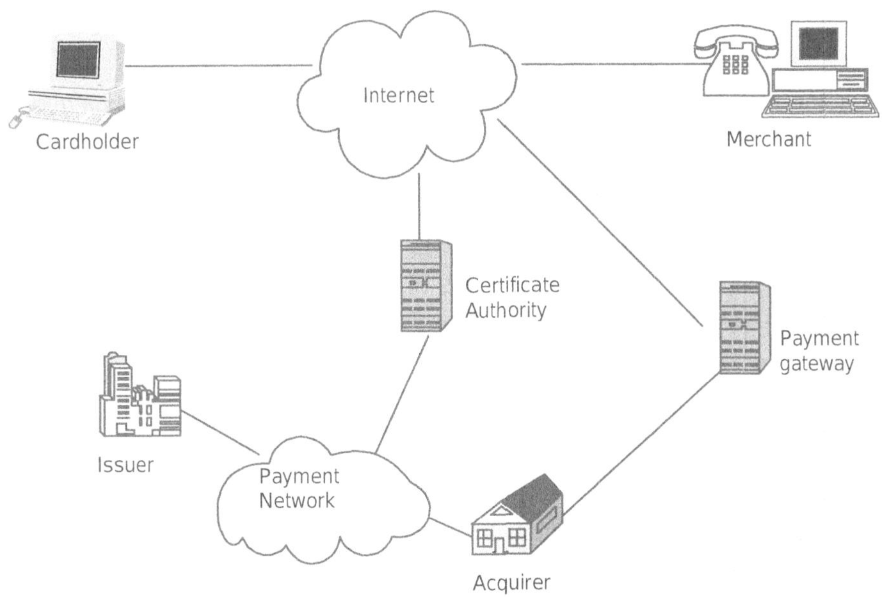

Fig. 9.10. *SET components.*

- **Certification authority (CA):** An entity that is trust to issue public key certificates (X. 509) for card holders, merchants, and payment gateways.

The components of SET can be described as in Fig. 9.10. Next we give an outline of the sequence of the events for a transaction using SET.

1. The customer opens an account. The customer obtains a credit card that supports electronic payment and SET.
2. The customer receives a certificate. The customer receives an digital certificate (X. 509) signed by the bank. The certificate verifies the customer's RSA public key and its expiration date. It also establishes a relationship between the customer's key pair and his/her credit card.
3. Merchants have their own certificates. A merchant must have two certificates for two public keys: one for signing messages and one for key exchange. The merchant also needs a copy of the payment gateway's public key certificate.
4. The customer places an order. The customer sends a list of the items to be purchased to the merchant through web site, who returns an order form containing the list of items, their price, and an order number.
5. The merchant is verified. The merchant sends a copy of its certificate, so that the customer can verify that he is dealing with a valid store.
6. The order and payment are sent. The customer sends both order and payment information to the merchant, along with the customer's certificate. The payment is encrypted in such a way that it cannot be read by the merchant. The customer's certificate enables the merchant to verify the customer.
7. The merchant requests payment authentication. The merchant sends the payment information to the payment gateway, requesting the authorization for this purchase.
8. The merchant confirms the order. The merchant sends confirmation of the order to the customer.
9. The merchant provides the goods or service.
10. The merchant requests payment. This request is sent to the payment gateway, which handles all of the payment processing.

Now we discuss some interesting innovation introduced in SET: the dual signature. The purpose of dual signature is to link two messages that are intended for two different recipients. In this case, the customer has two messages: the order information (OI) and the payment information (PI). OI is sent to merchant while PI is sent to the bank. However, there must be a link between OI and PI. For example, a customer does not want the merchant to know the PI but the merchant need to know that the customer provided the PI for the specific OI. SET uses a dual signature to solve that problem. Let h be a hash function (SHA-1). The dual signature (DS) is as follows.

$$\mathrm{DS} = SigKc(h(h(\mathrm{PI})jjh(\mathrm{OI}))$$

where Kc is the customer's private signature key.

Then customer can give OI, h(PI) and DS to the merchant and give PI, h(OI) and DS to the bank. Both merchant and bank can verify the signature since they know the customer's public key of the signature scheme. However, the merchant cannot substitute another OI in this transaction for its advantage, since it is difficult to find another OI which has the same hash digest.

To encrypt the PI, the customer will choose a session key and uses that key for encryption. The session key is then encrypted using the payment gateway's public key. In this way, the merchant cannot decrypt the PI. However, the payment gateway can get the information after the merchant forwards these information to it. SET provided 14 transaction types. We omit the details here. Unlike SSL and SSH, the cryptographic algorithms used in SET are fixed. It uses DES, RSA signature using SHA-1, HMAC based on SHA-1 and X. 509v3 digital certificate.

SET is a very comprehensive and complicated security protocol. It addresses all the parties involved in typical credit card transactions. To realize SET, every party needs to have some part of the software, even very expensive hardware. That is why SET is not widely spread although people believe that it is safe. How to simplify the SET while keep the main security features is still an open problem?

9.7 E-MAIL SECURITY

Electronic mail is one of the most heavily used network-based applications. With the explosively growing reliance on e-mail, there grows a demand for security e-mail systems. In an e-mail system, there are a sender and a receiver. However, usually the receiver is not on-line. So in an e-mail system, usually there is no massage interchange when the sender sends an e-mail. On the other hand, some e-mail system (*e.g.*, SMTP) only can deliver ASCII codes. We need to consider how to provide authentication and confidentiality services in this situation. We will examine two most widely used systems.

9.7.1 Pretty Good Privacy

Pretty good privacy or PGP was developed by Phil Zimmermann. PGP uses public key encryption, signature scheme, hash function, secret key encryption, compression function and e-mail compatibility. We can outline the algorithm as follows.

When Alice (A) wants to send a message M to Bob (B), she does the following:

1. Computes $H(M)$, where H is a hash function.
2. Signs the digest. So A computes $sig_A(H(M))$.
3. Compression the message. A computes $CM = zip(sig_A(H(M))jjM)$.
4. Chooses a session key K (random number) and encrypts CM using the session key. A computes $eK(CM)$.
5. Uses B's public key to encrypt K. She computes $eK_B(K)$.
6. Concatenates $eK(CM)jjeK_B(K)$.
7. Uses Radix-64 conversion (explained later) to convert $eK(CM)jjeK_B(K)$ to printable characters.
8. Sends out the above message. The message is split into segment before sending, if necessary.

Bob does the following, when he received the message:

1. Uses Radix-64 to convert the message into binary version.
2. Decrypts $eK_B(K)$ to obtain session key K.
3. Decrypts $eK(CM)$ to obtain CM.
4. Unzips CM to obtain $sig_A(H(M))jjM$.
5. Computes $H(M)$ from M
6. Verifies $sig_A(H(M))$.

The PGP has many nice features. We give some further discussions about the operations of PGP.

Confidentiality: PGP uses secret session key to encrypt (CAST, IDEA, AES, Blowfish, 3-key DES etc.) and the session key actually is a onetime key. The session key is sent by public key encryption (RSA or ElGamal). So key exchange is not needed and we don't need handshaking to assure that both sides have the same session key.

Authentication: PGP uses a hash function (SHA-1 or MD5) to obtain digest of the message. Then a public key signature scheme (RSA or DSS) is used to sign the digest.

Compression: PGP uses zip (or zlib) to compression the message and the signature. A message encryption is applied after compression to strengthen the security. This is because the compressed message has less redundancy than the original text. The basic idea of zip compression is to replace a repeated string by a short code. For example, consider the following text the more he read the letter the more he confused by the letter they wrote the zip program will search the text to find repeated sequences. The second appearance of "the more he " will be replaced as a code (18; 10), where 18 is a pointer pointed to 18 characters before and 10 is the length of the sequence. Similarly, the second appearance of "the letter the" will be replaced as a code (38; 16). In this way, the compressed message will be shorter and have less redundancy than the original message.

E-mail compatibility. Since many email system only permits the use of block consisting of ASCII text, PGP uses Radix-64 (also called base 64) to convert the raw 8-bit binary stream to a stream of ASCII characters as follows.

Suppose there is a 24-bit:

001000 110101 110010 010001

which is divided into four 6-bit. Each of the 6-bit can be converted into a number between 0 and 63. In the above example, the 24-bit is converted to numbers 8; 53; 50; 17. Then the following correspondence is used. The numbers from 0 to 25 are corresponding to the characters from A to Z. The numbers from 26 to 51 are corresponding to the characters from a to z. The numbers from 52 to 61 are corresponding to the characters from 0 to 9. The number 62 is corresponding to the character + and the number 63 is corresponding to the character =. Thus the numbers 8; 53; 50; 17 are corresponding to $I1yR$. If the binary stream is not divided by 6, then four or two "0" need to padded. In these cases, two or one "=" are padded as a indicator. Finally, radix- 64 outputs the characters as 8-bit ASCII codes. So radix-64 expands 24-bit to 32-bit. However, since PGP uses zip compression which is of an average compression rate of about 2.0, the overall compression is about one-third.

Alice in PGP involves three types of keys: a session key, her keys of a public key system and Bob's public key. So we need to consider key management and public key certificates.

For a session key, PGP defined a random number generation algorithm. CAST-128 uses a key of size 128-bits.

Since a public key system has two keys, one public key and one private key, how to securely store a private key is a problem. In PGP, when the system generates a new public/private key pair, it asks the user for a passphrase. The SHA-1 is then used to the passphrase to get a 160-bit digest. This digest is used as a key to encrypt the private key of the public system. The ciphertext is then stored in a file (called secret-key ring or private key ring). Subsequently, when the user wants to retrieve the private key, he or she must supply the passphrase. PGP will retrieve the encrypted private key, generate the digest of the passphrase, and decrypt the ciphertext to obtain the private key.

The structure of private key ring is as follows, where the records are indexed by Key ID or User ID.

Timestamp	*Key ID*	*Public key*	*Encrypted private key*	*User ID*
. .	. .	. .	. .	. .

For the public key, there are more things we need to consider. First a public key ID is used in PGP to indicate which public key is used. This is necessary if Bob has more than one public keys. PGP uses the last 64 bits of the public key as key ID. Most difficult and complicated thing for the public key is how to certificate it. PGP uses a referral method for certification. PGP uses a public-key ring to record public keys of other users that are known to this user. In each entry of the record, several fields are listed which include timestamp (the date/time of the generating of this entry), key ID, public key, user ID (the owner of this key), owner trust (a trust flag indicating the user's assessment of the trust to the owner of the public key), key legitimacy, signature(s), signature trust, etc. A certificate of PGP can be signed by several users. These signatures are collected in signature fields. For each signature there is a trust flag of the signature recorded in signature trust field. Based on these information, PGP computes a value of the trust level to the public key and records the value at the legitimacy field. The higher the level of trust, the stronger is the binding of this user ID to this key. The structure of a public-key ring is as follows.

Time-Stamp	*Key ID*	*Public key*	*Owner trust*	*User ID*	*Key legitimacy*	*Signature*	*Signature Trusts*
. .	. .	. .	. .	. .	. .	. .	. .

The PGP also considers how to revoke public keys. Usually a user will revoke a key after some time or by some reasons. On the other hand, the system will not let a user revoke other users' public keys.

The format of PGP message is described in Fig. 9.11.

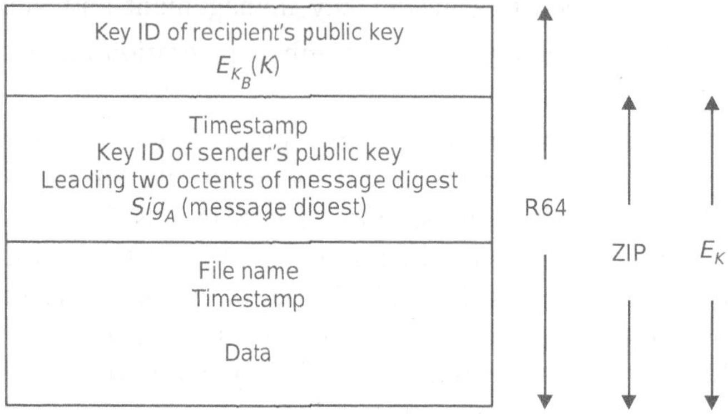

Notation:

K_B: Receiver's public key

K: Session key

Sig_A: Sender's signature

R64: Radix-64

Fig. 9.11. *General format of PGP message.*

This format includes three components: session key, signature, and message. The timestamp indicates the time at which the signature (or the message) was made. The leading two octects of message digest is used for the receiver to check the signature.

The message component and optional signature component may be compressed using ZIP and may be encrypted using a session key. The entire block is usually encoded with the redix-64. In the implementation of PGP, several requirements are considered such as the flexibility which allows the user using or not using encryption or authentication, the revoking public keys etc. We omitted the details here.

RFC 2440 described a standard of PGP called OpenPGP. RFC 3156 describes how the OpenPGP Message Format can be used to provide privacy and authentication using the Multipurpose Internet Mail Extensions (MIME) security content types described in RFC 1847.

9.7.2 S/MIME

Secure/Multipurpose Internet Mail Extension (S/MIME) is another security enhanced email system. S/MIME is similar to PGP which uses signature scheme, session key and secret key encryption. S/MIME version 3 message specification is given in RFC 2633. It appears likely that S/MIME will emerge as the industry standard for commercial and organizational use, while PGP will remain the choice for personal use.

MIME is specified in RFCs 2045 through 2049. MIME is an extension of Simple Mail Transfer Protocol (SMTP) that is specified in RFC 822. MIME is more flexible and powerful than SMTP. MIME uses different transfer encodings such as 7-bit, 8-bit, binary, base64, etc. So MIME can be used to send texts, mixed messages, images, video and audio files, executable files, etc, while SMTP only can transfer ASCII codes.

S/MIME is very similar to PGP. It also offers the ability to encrypt and authenticate messages. The hash functions used in S/MIME are SHA-1 and MD5. The signature schemes used in S/MIME are DSS and RSA signature scheme. The public key encryption system used is ElGamal cryptosystem or RSA encryption with key sizes 512 bits to 1024 bits. The data encryption method used is triple DES or RC2.

S/MIME provides the following functions.

- **Enveloped data:** This consists of encrypted content of any type and encrypted content encryption keys for one or more recipients. To prepare an enveloped data, the sender generates a pseudo random session key and then for each recipient, encrypted the session key with the recipient's public RSA key. For each recipient, the sender prepares an RecipientInfo that contains the sender's public key certificate, an identifier of public key system used to encrypt the session key, and the encrypted session key. The message content is encrypted using the session key. The RecipientInfo blocks followed by the encrypted message content constitute the enveloped data. It is then encoded into base64.
- **Signed data:** A digital signature is formed for the message. The sender selects a hash function and computes the digest of the message content. Then the sender sign the message digest using a signature scheme. A block known as SignerInfo is formed, which contains the signer's public key certificate, an identifier of the hash function, an identifier of the signature scheme and the signature. The content and the SignerInfo are then encoded into base64.
- **Clear-signed data:** Use the same method of signed data to form a signature. However, in this case, only the digital signature is encoded into base64. The message content is not encoded so that the recipients without S/MIME can view the message, although they cannot verify the signature. The data consist two part, one part is the message content and the other part is an attached digital signature.
- **Signed and enveloped data:** Signed-only and encrypted-only entities may be nested, so that encrypted data may be signed and signed data or clear-signed data may be encrypted.

Since there is no interaction between a sender and a recipient when a sender sends an e-mail, there are some decisions about the algorithm used for the content to be made by the sender. First, the sending agent must determine if the receiving agent is able to decrypt the message using a given encryption algorithm. Second, if the receiving agent is only capable of accepting weakly encrypted content, the sending agent must decide if it is acceptable to send using weak encryption. To support this decision process, a sending agent may announce its decrypting capabilities in order of preference. A receiving agent may store that information for future use. Usually, the sending agent should use the first method in the intended receiver's list or the method used on the last message received from that intended recipient. If the sending agent has no knowledge about the decryption capabilities of the intended recipient, then the sending agent uses triple DES when the sender is willing to risk that the recipient may not be able to decrypt the message, or uses RC2 otherwise. The certificates used in S/MIME is X.509.

RFC 2634 defined Enhanced Security Services for S/MIME, which is a set of extensions to S/MIME to allow signed receipts, security labels, and secure mailing lists.

9.8 KEY TERMS, KEY POINTS AND REVIEW QUESTIONS

Key Terms

Authentication	**Pretty Good Privary**	**S/MIME**
Electronic Mail	**Relam**	**Ticket**
Kerberos	**Sequence Number**	**X.509 Certificate**
Nonce	**SubKey**	**ZIP**

Key Points

- Kerberos is a network authentication protocol. It is designed to provide strong authentication for client/server applications by using secret-key cryptography.
- Kerberos Requirements
  - Secure
  - Reliable
  - Transparent
  - Scalable
- Kerberos v4 basic third-party authentication scheme.
- Kerberos environment consists of:
  - A Kerberos server
  - A number of clients, all registered with server
  - Application servers, sharing keys with server
- Kerberos Version 5 is specified in RFC 1510 and provides a number of improvements over version 4 in the areas of environmental shortcomings and technical deficiencies.
- X.509 was initially issued in July 3, 1988 and was begun in association with the X.500 standard. It assumes a strict hierarchical system of certificate authorities (CAs) for issuing the certificates.
- The X.509 certificate is the heart of the standard. There are 3 versions, with successively more info in the certificate - must be v2 if either unique identifier field exists, must be v3 if any extensions are used.
- Multipurpose Internet Mail Extensions (MIME) is an extension to the RFC 822 framework that is intended to address some of the problems and limitations of these uses of SMTP.
- Secure/Multipurpose Internet Mail Extension is a security enhancement to the MIME internet e-mail format standard, based on technology from RSA Data Security. It is ability to sign and/or encrypt messages.

- A reply attack is one which an attacker obtains a copy of an authenticated packet and the later transmits it to the intended destination.
- X.509 also includes three alternative authentication procedures
  1. 1-way for unidirectional messages (like email).
  2. 2-way for interactive sessions when timestamps are used.
  3. 3-way for interactive sessions with no need for timestamps.
- An SSL session is an association between a client and a server. Sessions are created by the Handshake Protocol Sessions define a set of cryptographic security parametes, which can be shared among multiple connections.
- *Transport Mode:* It provides protection for upper layer protocols.
- *Tunnel Mode:* It provides proctection to the entire IP Packet.
- IPsec is implemented by a set of cryptographic protocols for (1) securing packet flows, (2) mutual authentication and (3) establishing cryptographic parameters.
- Main parts of SSL
  - SSL Handshake Protocol
  - SSL Change Cipher Spec Protocol
  - SSL Alert Protocol
  - SSL Record Protocol
- S/MIME functions
  - Enveloped data
  - Signed data
  - Clear-signed data
  - Signed and enveloped data.

Question with Answers *(2 Marks)*

Q. 1. *Why does PGP generates a signature before applying compression?*

Ans. The signature is generated before compression due to 2 reasons

1. It is preferable to sign an uncompressed message so that one can store only the uncompressed message together with the signature for future verification.
2. Even if one were willing to generate dynamically a recompressed message for verification, PGP's compression algorithm presents a difficulty.

Q. 2. *Why is R 64 conversion useful for email generation?*

Ans. The Radix 64 conversion is performed before the segmentation of the messages take place. The use of radix 64 is that it converts the input stream to 33%. The radix 64 converts the input stream to a radix 64 format.

Q. 3. *What is MIME?*

Ans. Multipurpose Internet Mail Extensions (MIME) is an extension to the RFC 822 framework that is intended to address some of the problems and limitations of these uses of SMTP.

Q. 4. *What is S/MIME?*

Ans. Secure/Multipurpose Internet Mail Extension is a security enhancement to the MIME internet e-mail format standard, based on technology from RSA Data Security. It is ability to sign and/or encrypt messages.

Q. 5. *What services are provided by IPSec?*

Ans.
- Access control
- Connectionless integrity
- Data origin authentication
- Rejection of replayed packets

Q. 6. *What is replay attack?*

Ans. A reply attack is one which an attacker obtains a copy of an authenticated packet and the later transmits it to the intended destination.

Q. 7. *List out Authentication Procedures in X.509.*

Ans. X.509 also includes three alternative authentication procedures

1. 1-way for unidirectional messages (like email).
2. 2-way for interactive sessions when timestamps are used.
3. 3-way for interactive sessions with no need for timestamps.

Q. 8. *What is the difference between an SSL Connection and SSL Session?*

Ans. A connection is a transport that provides a suitable type of service. For SSL, such connections are peer-to-peer relationships. The connections are transit. An SSL session is an association between a client and a server. Sessions are created by the Handshake Protocol Sessions define a set of cryptographic security parameters, which can be shared among multiple connections.

Q. 9. *What is the difference between Transport Mode and Tunnel Mode?*

Ans.

	Transport Mode	***Tunnel Mode***
1.	It provides protection for upper layer protocols.	It provides proctection to the entire IP Packet.
2.	Used for end-to-end communication between two host.	It is used when one or both ends of an SA is a security gateway such as firewall or router that implement IPSec.
3.	Authenticates IP payload and selected portions of IP header and Ipv6 extensions header.	Authentications entire inner IP packet plus selected portions of outer IP header and outer IPv6 extensions header.

Q. 10. *List out four requirements were definded for Kerberos.*

Ans. The four requirements were definded for kerberos are Secure, Reliable,Transparent and Scable.

Q. 11. *What entities constitute a full-service Kerveros environment?*

Ans. A full service environment consists of a Kerberos Server, a number of clients and a number of application servers.

Q. 12. *List out S/MIME functions.*

Ans.
- Enveloped data
- Signed data
- Clear-signed data
- Signed and enveloped data

Q. 13. *Why does ESP include a padding field?*

Ans. Padding is added to the ESP to provide partial traffic flow confidentiality by concealing the actual length of the payload.

Q. 14. *List out main parts of SSL.*

Ans.
- SSL Handshake Protocol
- SSL Change Cipher Spec Protocol
- SSL Alert Protocol
- SSL Record Protocol

Q. 15. *What's Inside an X.509 Certificate?*

Ans. Version, Serial Number, Signature Algorithm Identifier, Issuer Name, Validity Period, Subject Name.

Q. 16. *How IPsec is implemented?*

Ans. IPsec is implemented by a set of cryptographic protocols for (1) securing packet flows, (2) mutual authentication and (3) establishing cryptographic parameters.

Q. 17. *How does PGP use the concept of trust?*

Ans. PGP provide a convient means of using trust, associating trust with public keys, and exploiting trust information. Each entry in the public key ring is a public key certificate.

Q. 18. *List out parts of Web Security.*

Ans. Web security includes three parts: security of server, security of client, and network traffic security.

Q. 19. *What is SET?*

Ans. SET is an open encryption and security specification designed to protect credit card transactions on the Internet. SSL secures communications between a client and a server.

Review Questions

1. What is kerberos?
2. Explain secure authentication dialogue of kerberos.
3. What is kerberos realm?
4. Explain X.509 format.
5. What is revocation of certificates?
6. Explain authentication procedure of X.509.
7. Explain characteristics of PGP.
8. Explain PGP operation and its different services.
9. Explain S/MIME and its functionality.
10. Define IPSec (IP Security) and its application.
11. Explain IPSec document.
12. Explain IPSec authentication header.
13. Explain SSL architecture.
14. Explain briefly SET.
15. Explain handshake protocol.

❑❑❑

PART 5

NETWORK AND INTERNET SECURITY

Chapter

CHAPTER 10

SYSTEM LEVEL SECURITY

10.1 INTRUDERS

10.1.1 What is Intrusion Detection?

Process of monitoring the events occurring in a computer system or network and analyzing them for signs of *intrusion*.

A significant security problem for networked systems is hostile, or at least unwanted, trespass being unauthorized login or use of a system, by local or remote users; or by software such as a virus, worm, or Trojan horse.

One of the two most publicized threats to security is the intruder (or hacker or cracker), which **Anderson identified three classes** of:

- **Masquerader**: An individual who is not authorized to use the computer (outsider)
- **Misfeasor:** A legitimate user who accesses unauthorized data, programs, or resources (insider)
- **Clandestine user:** An individual who seizes supervisory control of the system and uses this control to evade auditing and access controls or to suppress audit collection.

10.1.2 Types of Intrusion Detection Systems

- **Information Sources:** the different sources of event information used to determine whether an intrusion has taken place.
  - Network-based IDS
  - Host-based IDS
  - Application-Based IDS
- **Analysis:** The most common analysis approaches are
  - Misuse Detection
  - Anomaly Detection
- **Response:** The set of actions that the system takes once it detects intrusions.
  - **Passive measure:** Reporting IDS findings to humans, who are then expected to take action based on those reports.
  - **Active measure**: Involving some automated intervention on the part of the system.

10.1.3 Intruders History

The intruder threat has been well publicized, particularly because of the famous "Wily Hacker" incident of 1986–1987, documented by Cliff Stoll. Benign intruders might be tolerable, although they do consume resources and may slow performance for legitimate users. However, there is no way in advance to know whether an intruder will be benign or malign. Intruders may use compromised systems to launch attacks on other systems, further degrading performance.

One of the results of the growing awareness of the intruder problem has been the establishment of a number of computer emergency response teams (CERTs). These cooperative ventures collect information about system vulnerabilities and disseminate it to systems managers.

10.1.4 Intrusion Techniques—Password Crackers

Attackers can try to run a password cracker program once they gained access to the system (perhaps using a guest account)

- Better yet: try to guess the password:
- Try default passwords used for standard accounts –many system administrators do not bother to change them when they buy the computer
- Exhaustively try all short passwords (those of one to three characters)
- Try words in the system's online dictionary and also a list of likely passwords
- Collect information about users: full name, names of their spouse and children, pictures in their office, books showing their hobbies, etc
- Try user's phone number, social security numbers, room numbers
- Try all legitimate license plate numbers for this state
- Use a Trojan horse.

10.1.5 Approaches to Intrusion Detection

Can identify the following approaches to intrusion detection:

1. **Statistical anomaly detection:** Collect data relating to the behavior of legitimate users, then use statistical tests to determine with a high level of confidence whether new behavior is legitimate user behavior or not.
   (a) *Threshold detection:* Define thresholds, independent of user, for the frequency of occurrence of events.
   (b) *Profile based:* Develop profile of activity of each user and use to detect changes in the behavior
2. **Rule-based detection:** Attempt to define a set of rules used to decide if given behavior is an intruder
   (a) Anomaly detection: rules detect deviation from previous usage patterns
   (b) Penetration identification: expert system approach that searches for suspicious behavior

10.1.6 Audit Records

A fundamental tool for intrusion detection is the audit record. Some record of ongoing activity by users must be maintained as input to an intrusion detection system. Basically, two plans are used:

- **Native audit records:** Virtually all main O/S's include accounting software that collects information on user activity, advantage is its already there, disadvantage is it may not contain the needed information
- **Detection-specific audit records:** Implement collection facility to generates custom audit records with desired info, advantage is it can be vendor independent and portable, disadvantage is extra overhead involved.

10.1.6.1 Statistical Anomaly Detection

Statistical anomaly detection techniques cover threshold detection and profile-based systems.

Threshold detection involves counting no occurrences of a specific event type over an interval of time, if count surpasses a reasonable number, then intrusion is assumed. By itself, is a crude and ineffective detector of even moderately sophisticated attacks.

Profile-based anomaly detection focuses on characterizing past behavior of users or groups, and then detecting significant deviations. A profile may consist of a set of parameters, so that deviation on just a single parameter may not be sufficient in itself to signal an alert. Foundation of this approach is analysis of audit records.

10.1.6.2 Audit Record Analysis

An analysis of audit records over a period of time can be used to determine the activity profile of the average user. Then current audit records are used as input to detect intrusion, by analyzing incoming audit records to determine deviation from average behavior. Examples of metrics that are useful for profile-based intrusion detection are: counter, gauge, interval timer, resource use. Given these general metrics, various tests can be performed to determine whether current activity fits within acceptable limits, such as: Mean and standard deviation, Multivariate, Markov process, Time series, Operational; as discussed in the text.

The main advantage of the use of statistical profiles is that a prior knowledge of security flaws is not required. Thus it should be readily portable among a variety of systems.

10.1.6.3 Base-Rate Fallacy

To be of practical use, an intrusion detection system should detect a substantial percentage of intrusions while keeping the false alarm rate at an acceptable level. If only a modest percentage of actual intrusions are detected, the system provides a false sense of security. On the other hand, if the system frequently triggers an alert when there is no intrusion (a false alarm), then either system managers will begin to ignore the alarms, or much time will be wasted analyzing the false alarms. Unfortunately, because of the nature of the probabilities involved, it is very difficult to meet the standard of high rate of detections with a low rate of false alarms. A study of existing intrusion detection systems indicated that current systems have not overcome the problem of the base-rate fallacy.

10.1.7 Distributed Intrusion Detection

Until recently, work on intrusion detection systems focused on single-system standalone facilities. The typical organization, however, needs to defend a distributed collection of hosts supported by a LAN or internetwork, where a more effective defense can be achieved by coordination and cooperation among intrusion detection systems across the network.

Porras points out the following major issues in the design of a distributed IDS:

- A distributed intrusion detection system may need to deal with different audit record formats
- One or more nodes in the network will serve as collection and analysis points for the data, which must be securely transmitted to them
- Either a centralized (single point, easier but bottleneck) or decentralized (multiple centers must coordinate) architecture can be used.

10.1.7.1 Distributed Intrusion Detection - Architecture

The following figure shows the overall architecture, consisting of three main components, of the system independent distributed IDS developed at the University of California at Davis. The components are:

- *Host agent module:* Audit collection module operating as a background process on a monitored system.
- *LAN monitor agent module:* Like a host agent module except it analyzes LAN traffic.
- *Central manager module:* Receives reports from LAN monitor and host agents and processes and correlates these reports to detect intrusion.

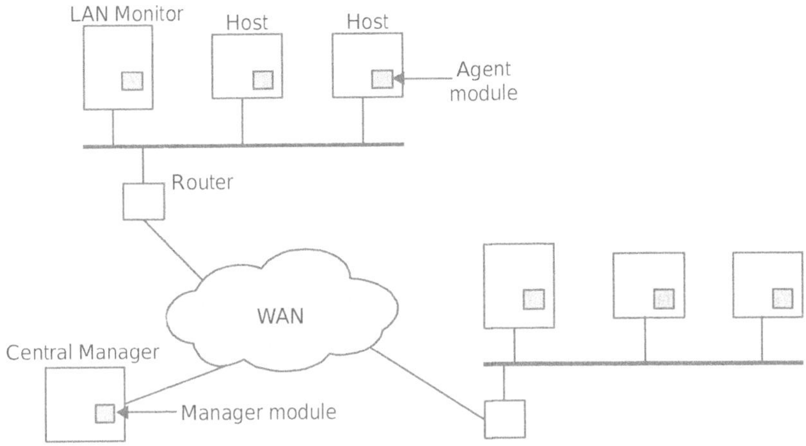

Fig. 10.1. *LAN monitoring system.*

10.1.7.2 Distributed Intrusion Detection—Agent Implementation

The following Fig. 10.2 shows the general approach that is taken. The agent captures each native O/S audit record, and applies a filter that retains only records of security interest. These records are then reformatted into a standardized format (HAR). Then a template-driven logic module analyzes the records for suspicious activity. When suspicious activity is detected, an alert is sent to the central manager. The central manager includes an expert system that can draw inferences from received data. The manager may also query individual systems for copies of HARs to correlate with those from other agents.

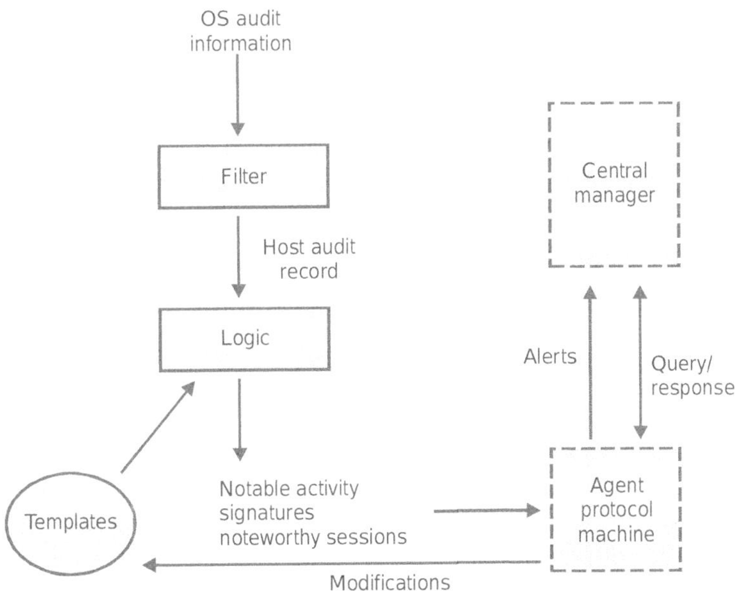

Fig. 10.2. *Distributed intrusion detection.*

10.1.7.3 Honeypots

Honeypots are decoy systems, designed to lure a potential attacker away from critical systems, and:

- divert an attacker from accessing critical systems
- collect information about the attacker's activity
- encourage the attacker to stay on the system long enough for administrators to respond.

These systems are filled with fabricated information designed to appear valuable but which any legitimate user of the system wouldn't access, thus, any access is suspect.

10.2 PASSWORD MANAGEMENT

10.2.1 What is Password?

A **password** is a form of secret authentication data that is used to control access to a resource. The password is kept secret from those not allowed access, and those wishing to gain access are tested on whether or not they know the password and are granted or denied access accordingly.

10.2.2 Password Studies

Studies have shown that users tend to choose poor passwords too often.

A study at Purdue University in 1992 observed password change choices on 104 machines, for 7000 users, and found almost 3% of the passwords were three characters or fewer in length, easily exhaustively searched!

Password length is only part of the problem, since many people pick a password that is guessable, such as their own name, their street name, a common dictionary word, and so forth. This makes the job of password cracking straightforward.

A study by Klein 1990 collected UNIX password files, containing nearly 14,000 encrypted passwords, and found nearly one-fourth of these passwords were guessable.

A strategy is needed to force users to select passwords that are difficult to guess.

10.2.3 Password Guessing

The rate at which an attacker can submit guessed passwords to the system is a key factor in determining system security. Some systems impose a long time out (several seconds) after a small number (*e.g.*, a maximum of three) of failed password entry attempts. Absent other vulnerabilities, such systems can be secure with relatively simple passwords, if they are not easily guessed. Examples of passwords that are easily guessed include the name of a relative or pet, an automobile license plate number, and such default passwords as *admin*.

Other systems store or transmit a cryptographic hash of the password in a manner that makes the hash value accessible to an attacker. When this is done, and it is very common (to most observers' surprise or despair), an attacker can work off-line, rapidly testing candidate passwords against the true password's hash value.

Lists of common passwords are widely available and can further speed the process. (See Password cracking.) A sufficiently complex password used in a system with a good hash algorithm can defeat such attacks as the work factor imposed on such an attacker can be made impossible in practice. Passwords that are used to generate cryptographic keys, *e.g.*, for disk encryption or Wi-Fi security, are also subject to high rate guessing. Stronger passwords are needed in such systems.

10.2.4 Password Capture

There is also a range of ways of "capturing" a login/password pair, from the low-tech looking over the shoulder, to the use of Trojan Horse programs (*e.g.*, game program or nifty utility with a covert function as well as the overt behavior), to sophisticated network monitoring tools, or extracting recorded info after a successful login—say from web history or cache, or last number dialed memory on phones etc. Need to educate users to be aware of whose around, to check they really are interacting with the computer system (trusted path), to beware of unknown source s/w, to use secure network connections (HTTPS, SSH, SSL), to flush browser/phone histories after use etc.

10.2.5 Password Cracking

Attempting to crack passwords by trying as many possibilities as time and money permit is a brute force attack. A related method, rather more efficient in most cases, is a dictionary attack. In a dictionary attack, all words in one or more dictionaries are tested.

There are several programs available for password auditing and recovery such as LophtCrack, John the Ripper, and Cain; some of which use password design vulnerabilities (as in the Microsoft LANManager system) to increase efficiency. Some are useful to system administrators as any password which can be found using one of these programs is most definitely a weak password and should be rejected as an unacceptable password choice.

10.2.6 Protecting the Passwords

- In UNIX, the 8 characters of the password are converted to a 106-bit string that serves as key for (modified with 12-bit "salt"value) DES –start with 64-bits all 0 and iterate DES encryption 210 times: the result will be the hash of the password and will be stored in the file. The following diagram shows Loading new password.

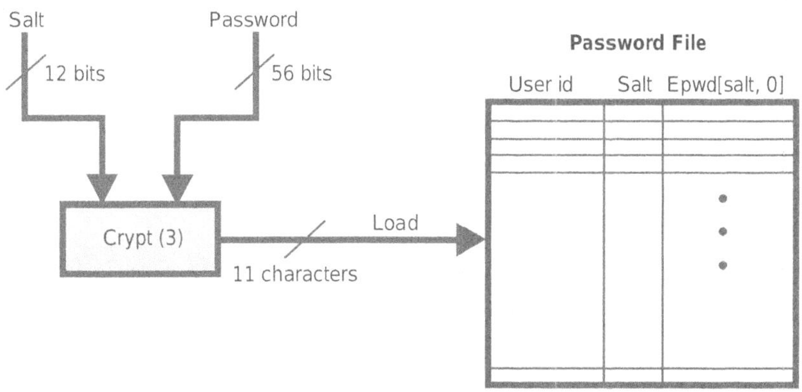

(a) Loading a new password

The salt prevents duplicate passwords from showing in the password file (chosen based on the time when the password was assigned to the user). The following diagram shows verifying password in Unix systems.

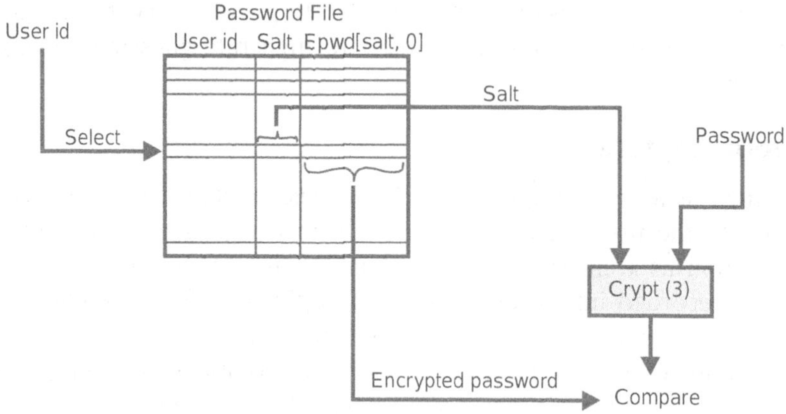

(b) Verifying a password

Fig. 10.3. *Password management system.*

10.2.7 Managing Passwords—Education

Computer-generated passwords create a password for the user, but have problems. If the passwords are quite random in nature, users will not be able to remember them. Even if the password is pronounceable, the user may have difficulty remembering it and so be tempted to write it down. In general, computer-generated password schemes have a history of poor acceptance by users. FIPS PUB 181 defines one of the best-designed automated password generators. The standard includes not only a description of the approach but also a complete listing of the C source code of the algorithm, which generates words by forming a random set of pronounceable syllables and concatenating them to form a word.

10.2.8 Managing Passwords—Computer Generated

Computer-generated passwords create a password for the user, but have problems. If the passwords are quite random in nature, users will not be able to remember them. Even if the password is pronounceable, the user may have difficulty remembering it and so be tempted to write it down. In general, computer-generated password schemes have a history of poor acceptance by users. FIPS PUB 181 defines one of the best-designed automated password generators. The standard includes not only a description of the approach but also a complete listing of the C source code of the algorithm, which generates words by forming a random set of pronounceable syllables and concatenating them to form a word.

10.2.9 Managing Passwords—Reactive Checking

A reactive password checking strategy is one in which the system periodically runs its own password cracker to find guessable passwords. The system cancels any passwords that are guessed and notifies the user. Drawbacks are that it is resource intensive if the job is done right, and any existing passwords remain vulnerable until the reactive password checker finds them.

10.2.10 Managing Passwords—Proactive Checking

The most promising approach to improved password security is a proactive password checker, where a user is allowed to select his or her own password, but the system checks to see if it is allowable and rejects it if not. The trick is to strike a balance between user acceptability and strength.

The first approach is a simple system for rule enforcement, enforcing say guidelines from user education. May not be good enough. Another approach is to compile a large dictionary of possible "bad"passwords, and check user passwords against this disapproved list. But this can be very large and slow to search. A third approach is based on rejecting words using either a Markov model of guessable passwords, or a Bloom filter. Both attempt to identify good or bad passwords without keeping large dictionaries. See text for details.

10.3 VIRUSES AND RELATED THREATS

A program that can infect other programs by modifying them, including a copy of the virus program.

- Similar to biological viruses.
- Can do anything that other programs can.
- Attaches itself to another program and executes when the program executes.
- The stages of a virus life are.
- **Dormant phase:** Virus is idle, will be awaken by a certain trigger–a date, the presence of another program or file, the capacity of the disk exceeding some limit, etc. Not all viruses have this phase.
- **Propagation phase:** Virus places an identical copy of itself into other programs or into certain system areas on the disk –each infected program will carry a clone of the virus which itself will enter a propagation phase.
- **Triggering phase:** Virus is activated to perform its function, can be triggered by a number of events, including a count of its clones.
- **Execution phase:** Function is performed.

10.3.1 Malicious Software

The terminology used for malicious software presents problems because of a lack of universal agreement on all terms and because of overlap. It can be divided into two categories: those that need a host program (being a program fragment e.g., virus), and those that are independent programs (*e.g.,* worm); alternatively you can also differentiate between those software threats that do not replicate (are activated by a trigger) and those that do (producing copies of themselves). Will now survey this range of malware.

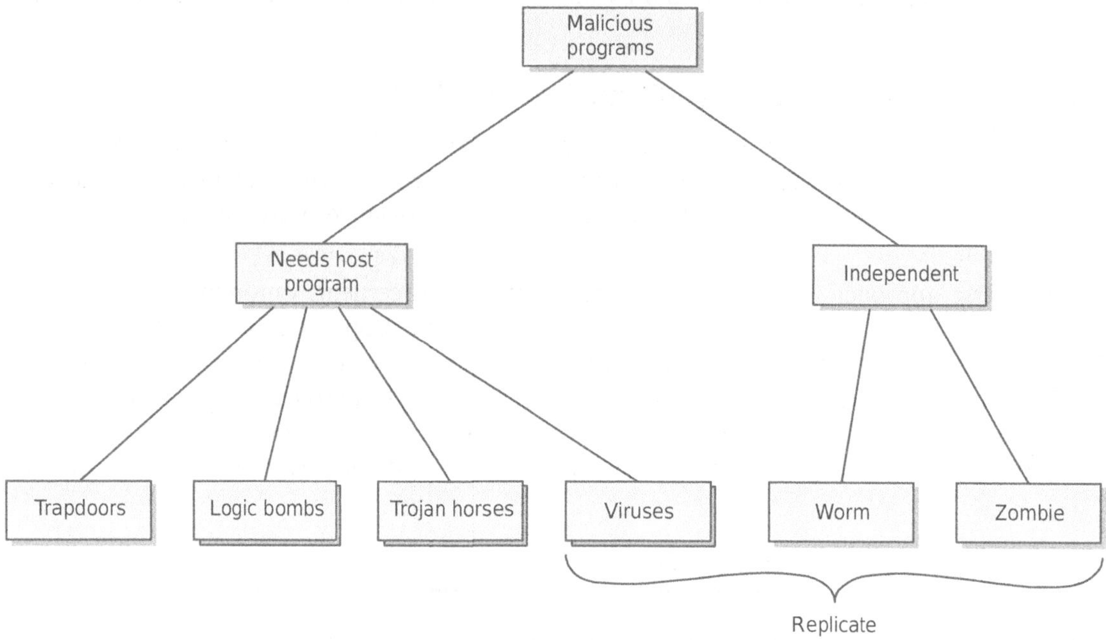

Fig. 10.4. *Structure of malicious software.*

10.3.2 Backdoor or Trapdoor

- Secret entry point into a program
- Allows those who know access bypassing usual security procedures
- Have been commonly used by developers
- A threat when left in production programs allowing exploited by attackers
- Very hard to block in O/S
- Requires good s/w development and update.

10.3.3 Logic Bomb

- One of oldest types of malicious software
- Code embedded in legitimate program
- Activated when specified conditions met
  - *e.g.,* presence/absence of some file
  - particular date/time
  - particular user
- When triggered typically damage system
  - modify/delete files/disks, halt machine, etc.

10.3.4 Trojan Horse

- Program with hidden side-effects
- Which is usually superficially attractive
  - *e.g.*, game, s/w upgrade etc
- When run performs some additional tasks
  - allows attacker to indirectly gain access they do not have directly
- Often used to propagate a virus/worm or install a backdoor
- Or simply to destroy data.

10.3.5 Zombie

- Program which secretly takes over another networked computer.
- Then uses it to indirectly launch attacks.
- Often used to launch distributed denial of service (DDoS) attacks.
- Exploits known flaws in network systems.

10.3.6 Virus Operation

During its lifetime, a typical virus goes through the following four phases:

- **Dormant phase:** Virus is idle, waiting for trigger event (*e.g.*, date, program or file, disk capacity). Not all viruses have this stage.
- **Propagation phase:** Virus places a copy of itself into other programs/system areas.
- **Triggering phase:** Virus is activated by some trigger event to perform intended function.
- **Execution phase:** Desired function (which may be harmless or destructive) is performed.

Most viruses work in a manner specific to a particular operating system or even hardware platform, and are designed to take advantage of the details and weaknesses of particular systems.

10.3.7 Virus Structure

```
program V:=
   {goto main;
   12341067;
   subroutine infect-executable:=          {loop:
                  file:= get-random-executable-file;
                  if (first-line-of-file = 12341067) then goto loop
                  else prepend V to file; }
   subroutine do-damage:= {whatever damage is to be done}
```

```
    subroutine trigger-pulled:= {return true if condition holds}
    main: main-program:=        {infect-executable;
                                 if trigger-pulled then do-damage;
                                 goto next;}
    next:
}
```

The above program shows a general depiction of virus structure. The virus code (V) is prepended to infected programs (assuming the entry point is the first line of the program). The first line of code jumps to the main virus program. The second line is a special marker for infected programs. The main virus program first seeks out uninfected executable files and infects them. Then it may perform some action, usually detrimental to the system, depending on some trigger. Finally, the virus transfers control to the original program. If the infection phase of the program is reasonably rapid, a user is unlikely to notice any difference between the execution of an infected and uninfected program. This type of virus can be detected because the length of the program changes. More sophisticated variants attempt to hide their presence better, by for example, compressing the original program.

10.3.8 Types of Viruses

There has been a continuous arms race between virus writers and writers of antivirus software, with the following categories being among the most significant types of viruses:

- **Parasitic virus:** Traditional and still most common form of virus, it attaches itself to executable files and replicates when the infected program is executed.
- **Memory-resident virus:** Lodges in main memory as part of a resident system program, and infects every program that executes.
- **Boot sector virus:** Infects a master boot record and spreads when a system is booted from the disk containing the virus.
- **Stealth virus:** A virus explicitly designed to hide itself from detection by antivirus software.
- **Polymorphic virus:** Mutates with every infection, making detection by the "signature"of the virus impossible.
- **Metamorphic virus:** Mutates with every infection, rewriting itself completely at each iteration changing behavior and/or appearance, increasing the difficulty of detection.

Macro viruses: Make up now-a-days two thirds of all viruses Platform independent Infect documents not executable code.

E-mail viruses: Send itself to all people on the local address book and then do some local damage.

10.3.9 Worms

- Replicating but not infecting program
- Typically spreads over a network
  - cf Morris Internet Worm in 1988
  - led to creation of CERTs
- Using users distributed privileges or by exploiting system vulnerabilities
- Widely used by hackers to create **zombie PC's**, subsequently used for further attacks, esp DoS
- Major issue is lack of security of permanently connected systems, esp PC's.

10.3.9.1 Worm Operation

A network worm exhibits the same characteristics as a computer virus: a dormant phase, a propagation phase, a triggering phase, and an execution phase. The propagation phase generally:

1. Searches for other systems to infect by examining host tables etc.
2. Establishes a connection with a remote system.
3. Copies itself to the remote system and cause the copy to be run.

10.3.9.2 Recent Worm Attacks

- New spate of attacks from mid-2001
- Code Red - used MS IIS bug
  - Probes random IPs for systems running IIS
  - Had trigger time for denial-of-service attack
  - 2nd wave infected 360000 servers in 14 hours
- Code Red 2 - installed backdoor
- Nimda - multiple infection mechanisms
- SQL Slammer - attacked MS SQL server
- Sobig.f - attacked open proxy servers
- Mydoom - mass email worm + backdoor.

10.3.9.3 Worm Technology

The state of the art in worm technology includes the following:

- **Multiplatform:** Not limited to Windows, can attack a variety of O/S's, esp UNIX.
- **Multiexploit:** Penetrate systems in a variety of ways
- **Ultrafast spreading:** Using prior scan to get addresses of vulnerable machines
- **Polymorphic:** Adopt virus polymorphic technique to evade detection
- **Metamorphic:** Change both appearance and behavior patterns
- **Transport vehicles:** To spread other distributed attack tools, *e.g.,* zombies
- **Zero-day exploit:** Exploit unknown vulnerability

10.4 VIRUS COUNTERMEASURES

The ideal solution to the threat of viruses is prevention, but in general this is impossible to achieve. The next best approach is to be able to do the following:

- **Detection:** determine that infection has occurred and locate the virus.
- **Identification:** of the specific virus that has infected a program.
- **Removal:** of all traces of the virus from the infected program and restore it to its original state; or discard infected program and reload a clean backup version.

10.4.1 Antivirus Software

As the virus arms race has evolved, both viruses and, necessarily, antivirus software have grown more complex and sophisticated. See four generations of antivirus software:

- **First generation:** Simple scanners use a virus signature to identify a virus, limited to known viruses; or use length of program to detect changes to it.
- **Second generation:** Heuristic scanners use rules to search for probable virus infection, *e.g.*, for code fragments; or use crypto hash of programs to detect changes.
- **Third generation:** Activity traps which identify a virus by its actions rather than its structure.
- **Fourth generation:** Full-featured protection using packages consisting of a variety of antivirus techniques used in conjunction, including scanning and activity trap components.

The arms race continues. With fourth-generation packages, a more comprehensive defense strategy is employed, broadening the scope of defense to more general purpose computer security measures.

10.4.2 Antivirus Approaches

- Detection, identification, removal
- Use heuristics instead of looking for a signature
- Activity traps
- Access control capability.

10.4.3 Advanced Antivirus Techniques

More sophisticated antivirus approaches and products continue to appear, such as:

- **Generic decryption**
  - Use CPU simulator to check program signature and behavior before actually running it.
- **Digital immune system** (IBM)
  - General purpose emulation and virus detection.
  - Any virus entering org is captured, analyzed, detection/shielding created for it, removed.

10.4.4 Digital Immune System

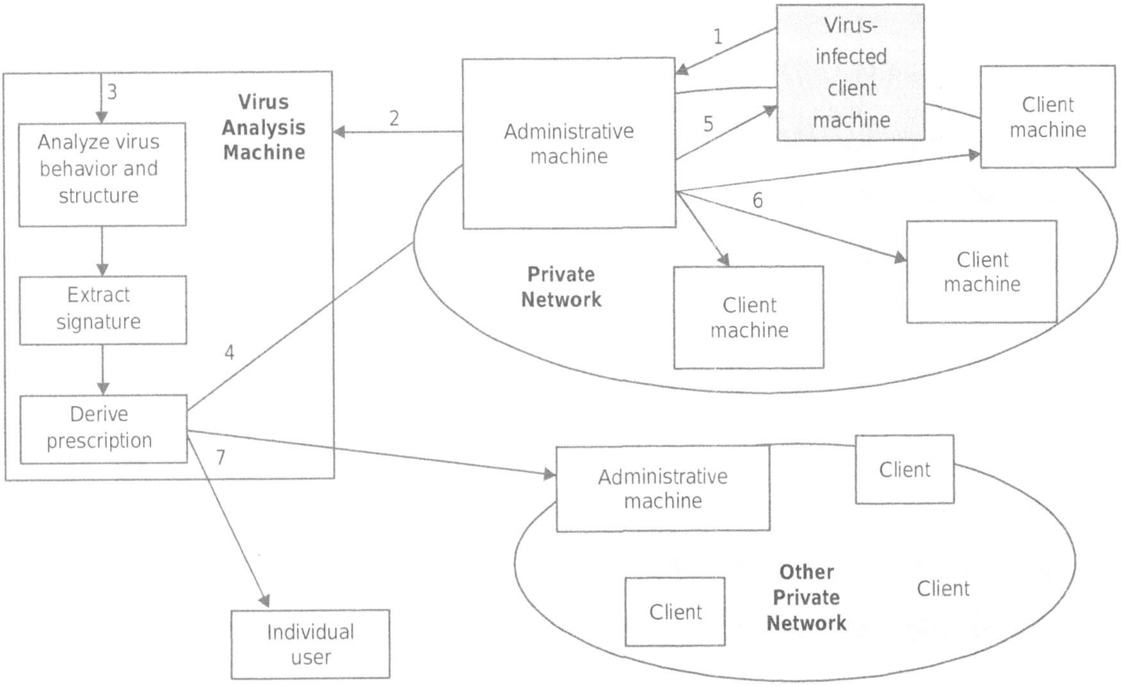

Fig. 10.5. *Digital immune system operation.*

The above figure illustrates the typical steps in digital immune system operation:

1. A monitoring program on each PC uses a variety of heuristics based on system behavior, suspicious changes to programs, or family signature to infer that a virus may be present, and forwards infected programs to an administrative machine.
2. The administrative machine encrypts the sample and sends it to a central virus analysis machine.
3. This machine creates an environment in which the infected program can be safely run for analysis to produces a prescription for identifying and removing the virus.
4. The resulting prescription is sent back to the administrative machine.
5. The administrative machine forwards the prescription to the infected client.
6. The prescription is also forwarded to other clients in the organization.
7. Subscribers around the world receive regular antivirus updates that protect them from the new virus.

10.4.5 Behavior-Blocking Software

Behavior-blocking software integrates with the operating system of a host computer and monitors program behavior in real-time for malicious actions. and blocks potentially malicious actions before they have a chance to affect the system. Monitored behaviors can include the following:

- Attempts to open, view, delete, and/or modify files.
- Attempts to format disk drives and other unrecoverable disk operations.
- Modifications to the logic of executable files or macros.
- Modification of critical system settings, such as start-up settings.
- Scripting of e-mail and instant messaging clients to send executable content.
- Initiation of network communications.

If the behavior blocker detects that a program is initiating would-be malicious behaviors as it runs, it can block these behaviors in real-time and/or terminate the offending software.

The behavior blocker has a fundamental advantage over such established antivirus detection techniques since it can intercept all suspicious requests, and can identify and block malicious actions regardless of how obfuscated the program logic appears to be. But this does mean the malicious code must actually run on the target machine before all its behaviors can be identified.

10.4.6 Distributed Denial of Service Attacks (DDoS)

Distributed denial of service (DDoS) attacks present a significant security threat to corporations and the threat appears to be growing. DDoS attacks make computer systems inaccessible by

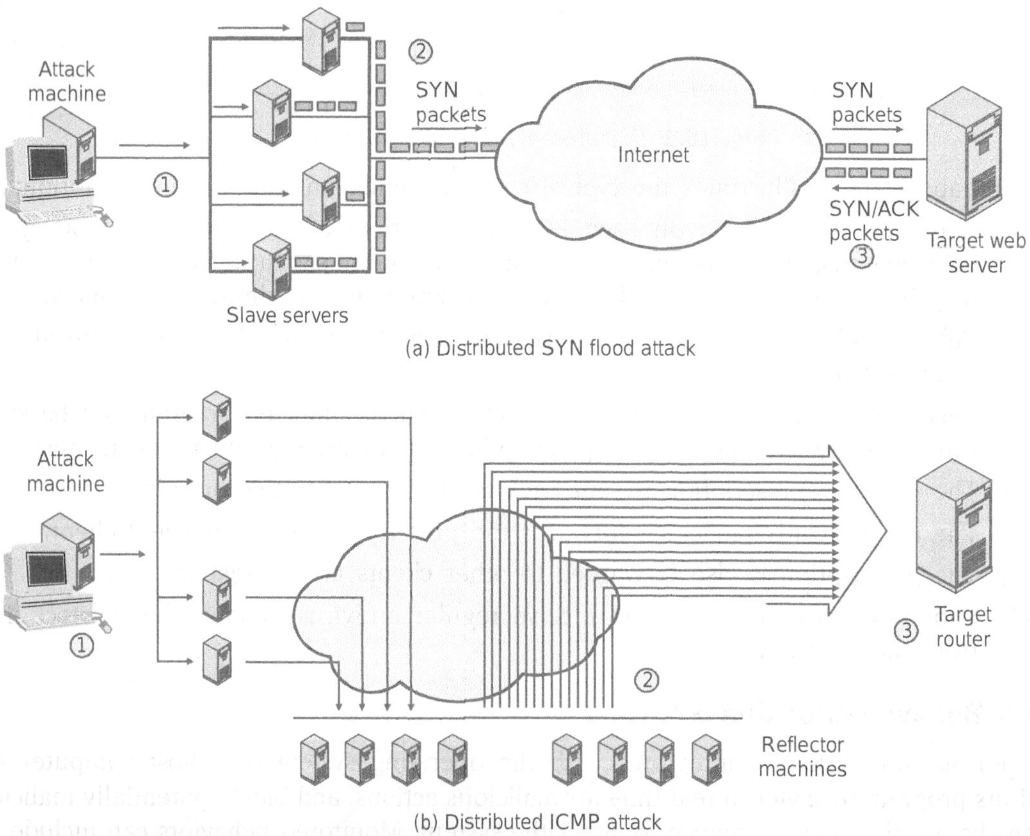

Fig. 10.6. *Distributed system.*

flooding servers, networks, or even end user systems with useless traffic so that legitimate users can no longer gain access to those resources. In a typical DDoS attack, a large number of compromised (zombie) hosts are amassed to send useless packets. In recent years, the attack methods and tools have become more sophisticated, effective, and more difficult to trace to the real attackers, while defense technologies have been unable to withstand large-scale attacks.

A DDoS attack attempts to consume the target's resources so that it cannot provide service. One way to classify DDoS attacks is in terms of the type of resource that is consumed, either an internal host resource on the target system, or data transmission capacity in the target local network.

Fig. 10.6 (*a*) shows an example of an internal resource attack—the SYN flood attack. 1. The attacker takes control of multiple hosts over the Internet. 2. The slave hosts begin sending TCP/IP SYN (synchronize/initialization) packets, with erroneous return IP address information, to the target 3. For each such packet, the Web server responds with a SYN/ACK (synchronize/acknowledge) packet. The Web server maintains a data structure for each SYN request waiting for a response back and becomes bogged down as more traffic floods in.

Fig. 10.6 (*b*) illustrates an example of an attack that consumes data transmission resources. 1. The attacker takes control of multiple hosts over the Internet, instructing them to send ICMP ECHO packets with the target's spoofed IP address to a group of hosts that act as reflectors. 2. Nodes at the bounce site receive multiple spoofed requests and respond by sending echo reply packets to the target site. 3. The target's router is flooded with packets from the bounce site, leaving no data transmission capacity for legitimate traffic.

10.4.6.1 Contructing the DDoS Attack Network

The first step in a DDoS attack is for the attacker to infect a number of machines with zombie software that will ultimately be used to carry out the attack. The essential ingredients are:

1. Software that can carry out the DDoS attack, runnable on a large number of machines, concealed, communicating with attacker or time-triggered, and can launch intended attack toward the target.
2. A vulnerability in a large number of systems that many system admins/users have failed to patch.
3. A strategy for locating vulnerable machines, known as scanning, such as:
   - Random: probe random IP addresses in the IP address space
   - Hit-list: use a long list of potential vulnerable machines
   - Topological: use info on infected victim machine to find more hosts
   - Local subnet: look for targets in own local network

10.5 FIREWALL DESIGN PRINCIPLES

Introduction

Information systems in corporations, government agencies, and other organizations have undergone a steady evolution from mainframes to LANs. Internet connectivity is no longer optional, with information and services essential to the organization. Moreover, individual users want and need Internet access. However, while Internet access provides benefits, it enables the outside world to reach and interact with local network assets, creating a threat to the organization. While it is possible to equip each workstation and server on the premises network with strong security features, this is not a practical approach in general. Firewalls can be an effective means of protecting a local system or network of systems from network-based security threats while at the same time affording access to the outside world via wide area networks and the Internet. However they need to be part of a wider security strategy including host security.

10.5.1 What is a Firewall?

A firewall is inserted between the premises network and the Internet to establish a controlled link and to erect an outer security wall or perimeter, forming a single choke point where security and audit can be imposed. A firewall:

1. Defines a single choke point that keeps unauthorized users out of the protected network, prohibits potentially vulnerable services from entering or leaving the network, and provides protection from various kinds of IP spoofing and routing attacks.
2. Provides a location for monitoring security-related events
3. A convenient platform for several Internet functions that are not security related, such as NAT and Internet usage audits or logs
4. A firewall can serve as the platform for IPSec to implement virtual private networks.

The firewall itself must be immune to penetration, since it will be a target of attack.

10.5.2 Firewall Limitations

Firewalls have their limitations, including that they:

1. Cannot protect against attacks that bypass the firewall, *e.g.*, PCs with dial-out capability to an ISP, or dial-in modem pool use
2. Do not protect against internal threats, *e.g.*, disgruntled employee or one who cooperates with an attacker
3. Cannot protect against the transfer of virus-infected programs or files, given wide variety of O/S and applications supported.

10.5.3 Types of Firewall

Have three common types of firewalls: packet filters, application-level gateways, and circuit-level gateways.

1. Packet Filters

A packet-filtering router applies a set of rules to each incoming and outgoing IP packet to forward or discard the packet. Filtering rules are based on information contained in a network packet such as src and dest IP addresses ports, transport protocol and interface. Some advantages are simplicity, transparency and speed.

If there is no match to any rule, then one of two default policies are applied:

- That which is not expressly permitted is prohibited (default action is discard packet), conservative policy
- That which is not expressly prohibited is permitted (default action is forward packet), permissive policy

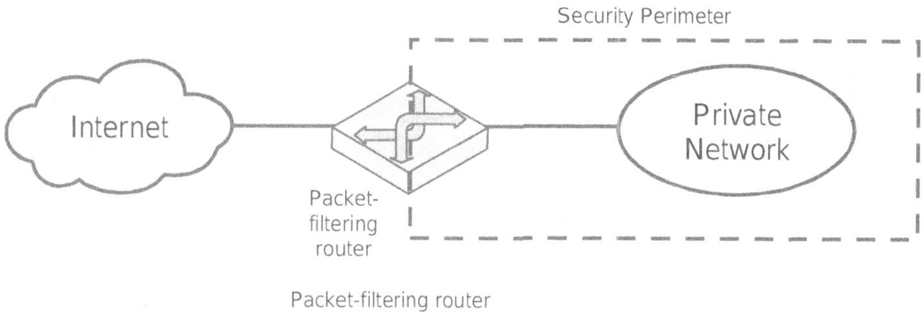

Fig. 10.7. *Packet filter firewall.*

The above Fig. 10.7 illustrates the packet filter firewall placement in the border router, on the security perimeter, between the external less-trusted Internet, and the internal more trusted private network.

2. Application Level Gateway

- Have application specific gateway/proxy
- Has full access to protocol
  - User requests service from proxy
  - Proxy validates request as legal
  - Then actions request and returns result to user
  - Can log/audit traffic at application level
- Need separate proxies for each service
  - Some services naturally support proxying
  - Others are more problematic

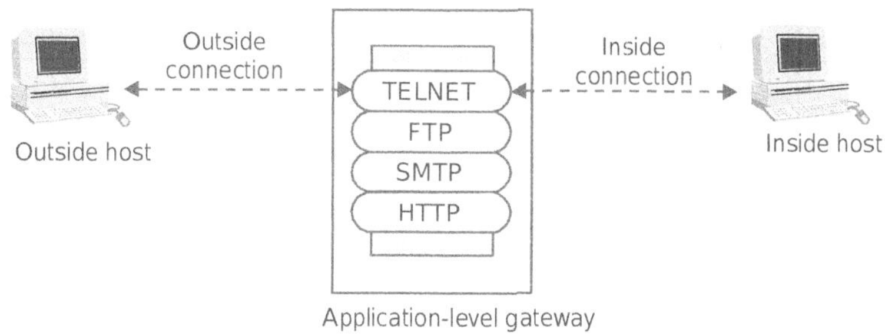

Fig. 10.8

The above Fig. 10.8 illustrates an application-level gateway (or proxy server), emphasizing that it only supports a specific list of application services.

3. Circuit Level Gateway

A circuit-level gateway relays two TCP connections, one between itself and an inside TCP user, and the other between itself and a TCP user on an outside host. Once the two connections are established, it relays TCP data from one connection to the other without examining its contents. The security function consists of determining which connections will be allowed. It is typically used when internal users are trusted to decide what external services to access.

One of the most common circuit-level gateways is SOCKS, defined in RFC 1928. It consists of a SOCKS server on the firewall, and a SOCKS library and SOCKS-aware applications on internal clients.

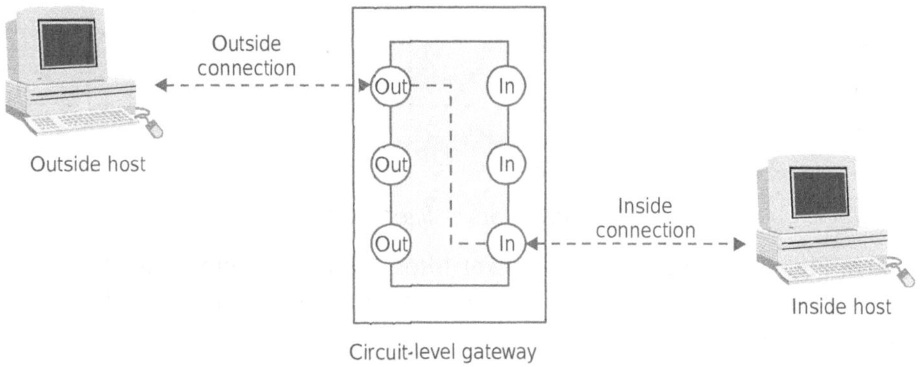

Fig. 10.9

The above Fig. 10.9 illustrates a circuit-level gateway, showing how it relays between 2 TCP connections. Note that it can be implemented in a stand-alone system or can be a specialized function in an application-level gateway for certain applications. Note also that relaying UDP packets is more problematical, because of the lack of connection context, and require a parallel TCP connection to provide these details.

10.5.4 Firewall Configurations

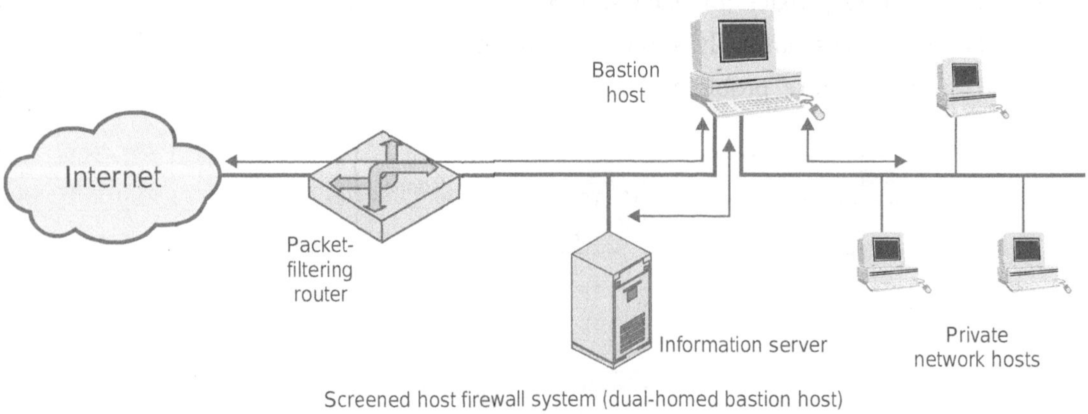

Fig. 10.10

The above Fig. 10.10 illustrates the "screened host firewall, dual-homed bastion configuration" which physically separates the external and internal networks, ensuring two systems must be compromised to breach security. The advantages of dual layers of security are also present here. Again, an information server or other hosts can be allowed direct communication with the router if this is in accord with the security policy, but are now separated from the internal network.

10.6 TRUSTED SYSTEMS

Trusted system is a system that is relied upon to a specified extent to enforce a specified security policy. As such, a trusted system is one which failure may break a specified security policy.

10.6.1 Access Control

Following successful logon, a user has been granted access to one or a set of hosts and applications. Associated with each user there can be a profile that specifies permissible operations and file accesses, which the operating system can then enforce.

A general model of access control is that of an access matrix, the basic elements of which are:

- **Subject:** An entity (typically a process) capable of accessing objects.
- **Object:** Anything to which access is controlled, *e.g.*, files, portions of files, programs, memory segments.
- **Access right:** The way in which an object is accessed by a subject, *e.g.*, read,write and execute.

One axis of an access matrix consists of identified subjects that may attempt data access, the other lists objects that may be accessed, and each entry in the matrix indicates the access rights of that subject for that object. In practice, an access matrix is usually sparse and is implemented by decomposition in one of two ways. If decomposed by columns, you have access control lists, which list users and their permitted access rights for each object. If decomposed by rows it yields capability tickets, which specify authorized objects and operations for a user.

10.6.2 Trusted Computer Systems

- Information security is increasingly important
- Have varying degrees of sensitivity of information
  - Military info classifications: confidential, secret etc
- Subjects (people or programs) have varying rights of access to objects (information)
- Known as multilevel security
  - Subjects have **maximum** and **current** security level
  - Objects have a fixed security level **classification**
- Want to consider ways of increasing confidence in systems to enforce these rights.

10.6.3 Reference Monitor

The following Fig. 10.11 illustrates the reference monitor as a controlling element in the h/w and O/S of a computer. It regulates access of subjects to objects on the basis of their security parameters. It has access to the security kernel database, which lists the access privileges (security clearance) of each subject and the protection attributes (classification level) of each object. The reference monitor enforces the security rules (no read up, no write down). It must have properties of:

- **Complete mediation:** Security rules are enforced on every access.
- **Isolation:** Reference monitor and database are protected from unauthorized modification.
- **Verifiability:** Reference monitor's correctness must be provable.

These are stiff requirements, usually met only by a trusted system.

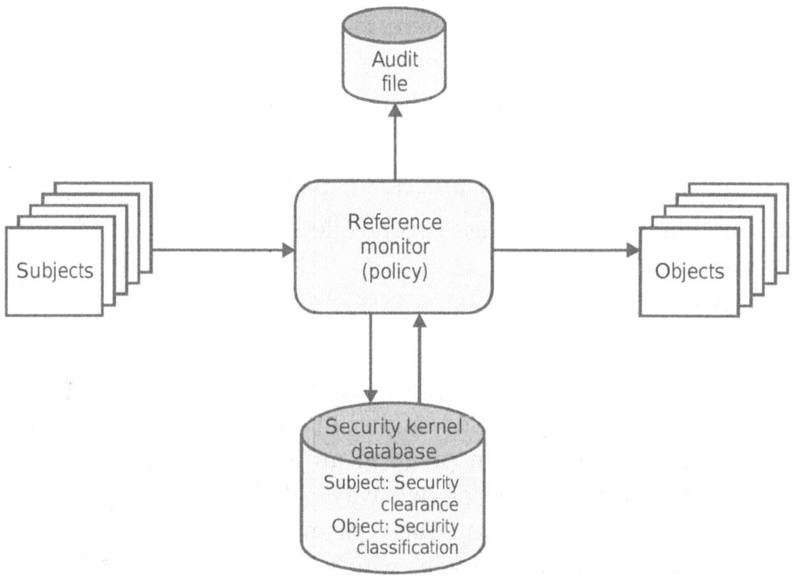

Fig. 10.11. *Reference monitor.*

10.6.4 Evaluated Computer Systems

Trusted systems need to be evaluated against a suitable set of criteria by an approved government agency. The original standard developed by the US DoD and NSA was TCSEC in the early 80's. Later standards were developed by other countries, harmonized in the EU with IPSEC (which was also used in Australia), and now internationally with the Common Criteria. These standards define a number of "levels" of evaluation with increasingly stringent checking, to which an evaluation center evaluates commercially available products as meeting the security requirements specified, within a given functionality area. These evaluations are needed for Defense procurements but are published and freely available, and can serve as guidance to commercial customers for the purchase of commercially available, off-the-shelf equipment.

10.7 KEY TERMS, KEY POINTS AND REVIEW QUESTIONS

Key Terms

Access Control List	**Circuit Level Gateway**	**Packet-Filtering Router**
Access Matrix	**Firewall**	**Reference Monitor**
Access Right	**Multilevel Security**	**Trusted System**
Application Level Gateway		

Key Points

- The most serious threat to computer security is unauthorized intrusions into a computer system.
- Fundamental tool for intrusion detection is audit report.
- Intrusion detection system gives early warning of an intrusion so that defensive action can be taken to prevent or minimize damage.
- Malicious programs are intentionally inserted in a system for damaging.
- Example of malicious programs: viruses, worms, torjan horses.
- Virus is a program that infect the other programs by modifying them.
- Worm is a program that replicate itself and send copies to other computers across network.
- Denial of service attack is an attempt to prevent legitimate users of a service from using it.
- Firewall is a barrier through which all traffic passes.
- A firewall is designed to operate as a filter at the level of IP packets or at higher protocol layer.
- Trusted system is computer and operating system that can be verified to implement a given security policy.

Question with Answers *(2 Marks)*

Q. 1. *What is intruder?*

Ans. Accessing a network unauthorized is as intrusion.

Q. 2. *What is intrusion detection system?*

Ans. An intrusion detection system (IDS) is a system for detection unauthorized access to the system.

Q. 3. *What are audit reports? Give its forms.*

Ans. Audit report is a fundamental tool for intrusion detection. Two forms of audit records are:

1. Native audit records
2. Detective audit records.

Q. 4. *Define password protection.*

Ans. Password protection is the front line protection against intruder to the system. A password authenticate the ID and provide security to the system.

Q. 5. *What is Malicious program?*

Ans. A program that is intentionally included or inserted in a system for harmful purpose is malicious program.

Q. 6. *Define Virus.*

Ans. A virus is a piece of program code that can infect other programs by modifying them.

Q. 7. *What is Worm?*

Ans. A worm is program designed to copy itself and send copies from a computer to other computer across the network.

Q. 8. *Define Trojan horse.*

Ans. A Trojan horse is a computer program that appears to be useful but that actually does damage.

Q. 9. *What is logic bomb?*

Ans. A logic bomb is a software embedded in some legitimate progarms and is set to explode under certain conditions.

Q. 10. *List out 4-types of viruses.*

Ans.
- Parasitic virus
- Memory resident virus
- Boot Sector virus
- Stealth virus

Q. 11. *List out steps in virus removal process.*

Ans.
- Detection of virus
- Identification of virus
- Removal of traces of virus

Q. 12. *List out Antivirus approaches.*

Ans.
- General Decryption
- Digital Immune System
- Behavior-Blocking Software.

Q. 13. *What is denial of service?*

Ans. A denial service is an attempt to prevent a genuine user of service from using it.

Q. 14. *List out main goals of firewall.*

Ans.
- All the traffic is allowed to pass
- Firewall itself is immune to penetration.
- Only authorized traffic is allowed to pass.

Q. 15. *List out Commonly used firewalls from threats of security.*

Ans. (*a*) Packet filtering router.

(*b*) Application level gateway.

(*c*) Circuit level gateway.

Review Questions

1. What is an intruder? What are its classes?
2. Define intrusion detection. Explain distributed IDS.
3. What are audit reports?
4. What is mean by password protection? Give strategies of password selection.
5. What is malicious program? Give examples.
6. Define: 1. Torjan Horse, 2. Logic bomb.
7. What is generic decryption technology?
8. Briefly explain digital immune system.
9. Explain briefly distributed denial of service attacks.
10. What are firewall design principles?
11. Explain packet filtering router.
12. Explain application level gateway.
13. What is circuit level gateway?
14. Define Virus. Specify the types of virus.
15. Discuss in detail the packet – filtering router firewall.
16. List and brief the different generations of antivirus software.
17. Discuss on behavior – Blocking software.

❑❑❑

APPENDICES

APPENDIX 1 THE IMPORTANCE OF STANDARDS

In evaluating the many options for network security solutions, it is essential to understand and consider the role of security standards. The growth in distributed computing and the ensuing increase in computer crime has led to legislation and regulations that establish legal requirements for network and data security. The various ANSI, FIPS and ISO network security standards have undergone extensive peer review and represent the strongest security design thinking available in the commercial marketplace. Use of standards-compliant network security provides the best assurance of high quality, strong security for your network, conforming to legal requirements and standards of "due care." This white paper summarizes legal considerations and security standards, security services and standards, and considerations in the selection of standards.

Commercially reasonable security standards have been defined by the international banking community through adoption of ANSI and ISO standards. These standards provide methods of data encryption, message authentication and user identification to protect against the risks encountered during electronic funds transfers. Use of the ANSI X9 standards, developed under the auspices of the American Banking Association, is the best way to assure "commercial reasonableness," the best protection against legal liability, and the best protection for data that is transmitted during funds transfers.

In the corporate world, organizations and employees are required to meet their fiduciary responsibility by protecting assets, including information assets. Again, the use of standards-based security provides excellent evidence that "due care" has been exercised by employing methods endorsed by national, government and international standards bodies and in use by "similarly situated" corporations. In the Federal Government environment, compliance with FIPS (Federal Information Processing Standards) standards is a procurement requirement. FIPS are adopted and promulgated by the National Institute of Standards and Technology (NIST).

❑❑❑

Appendix 2

Standards and Regulations

STANDARD

The following network security standards provide the minimum requirements for providing secure and seamless interconnection of communications networks and systems while protecting the State's computing resources and information whether that is through existing budget unit network infrastructure or through the states AZNET program for network services. Multi-layered protection shall be deployed at the Internet gateway, the network server, and the desktop levels to prevent introduction of malicious code or unauthorized access into the State's information systems.

1. **Network Perimeter Security:** Firewall technology shall be employed at the edge of a budget unit's network including the Internet Gateway, to protect sensitive internal information assets and infrastructure from unauthorized access. External (inbound and outbound) traffic shall be routed through secure gateways, such as firewalls.
2. **End Point Security:** Client platform devices, including State-owned assets, client devices used by remote workers and telecommuters, as well as third-party entities, connected to the budget unit's internal network should be protected from sending or receiving hostile threats from unauthorized network traffic or software applications.
3. **Access to Internetworking Devices and Shared Platforms:** Internet working devices (including routers, firewalls, switches, etc.) and shared platforms (including mainframes, servers, etc.) provide both access to and information about networks. They shall be controlled to prevent unauthorized access.
4. **Patch Management:** Budget units shall develop and implement written procedures that identify roles and responsibilities for implementing patch management that include the following activities:
5. **Demilitarized Zone:** Services provided through the Internet (Web-enabled applications, FTP, Mail, DNS, VoIP, etc.) shall be deployed on a Demilitarized Zone (DMZ) or proxied from the DMZ.

6. **External connection to networks:** External connections to networks shall be routed through secure gateways (as required above) and protected by at least one of the following encryption methods, as appropriate:
7. **Inter-network Transport Services:** Generally and commercially available transport services, commonly referred to as carrier services, are defined in *Statewide Standard P710-S710, Network Infrastructure*. Based on budget unit business requirements, these services should be configured and implemented to allow for automatic re-routing of communications when critical nodes or links fail, or fall-back to alternate transport services, including the provision of duplicate or alternate secure gateways and external exchanges or switching centers.
8. **Wireless Network Access:** The 802.1x security standards having centralized user authentication in accordance with *Statewide Standard P800-S820, Authentication and Directory Services*, encryption technologies with automated key distribution, and VPN technologies shall be used as appropriate with standard wireless networks: IEEE 802.11x (Wireless Local Area Network (WLAN)), IEEE 802.15 (Wireless Personal Area Network (WPAN)), and IEEE 802.16 (Wireless Metropolitan Area Network (WMAN)).
9. **Intrusion Detection/Prevention:** Intrusion detection mechanisms or intrusion prevention tools should be incorporated into all servers connected to WANs and to all internetworking devices that serve as gateways between WAN network segments.
10. **Vulnerability Scanning:** Network and host vulnerability scanners should be used to test for the vulnerabilities of internal systems and of network perimeter defenses, as well as adherence to security policy and standards. Vulnerability scanners should be components of the State's comprehensive network security solutions. Such components allow security administrators to measure security, manage risk, and eliminate vulnerabilities, providing a more secure network environment.
11. **Destruction of Network Documentation:** Destruction of hardcopy and electronic documentation of network device configurations, network diagrams, etc., shall be destroyed, when superseded, or no longer needed. Such destruction may be completed on-site by the use of a commercial strength document shredder and/or the use of a secure recycling container. The secure container shall contain a pad lock or other similar locking mechanism and the contents of the container must be securely disposed of either through the document shredder and/or recycled by a third party contractor to destroy such documentation.

❑❑❑

Appendix 3

Internet Standards and the Internet Society

The following organizations set security standards for national and international network applications.

- **ANSI** - American National Standards Institute sets standards for the banking industry.
- **FIPS** - Federal Information Processing Standards. This organization sets standards for U.S. Government use.
- **ISO/IEC** - International Standards Organization and the International Electrotechnical Commission set international standards.
- **IETF** - Internet Engineering Task Force. This organization is responsible for setting standards for Internet users.

Security Services

Security services are used to achieve a desired business outcome. Business goals for network applications and the corresponding security services are:

Business Goal	Security Service
• Keep communications private	• Data Encryption
• Information that is received is exactly what was sent	• Authentication
• You are who you claim to be	• User Authentication
• Legally binding electronic transactions	• Digital Signatures

The table below identifies the various areas of security standardization. It also illustrates the standards that are in common across the different standards bodies:

Security Service	Standards			
	ANSI	FIPS	ISO/IEC	IETF
Data Encryption Standard	X3.92; X3.106	FIPS 46, 74, 81	8372, 10116	1829
User Authentication	X9.26	FIPS JJJ (draft)	9798, 11131	1334
Message Authentication	X9.9, X9.19	FIPS 113, 180-1	9797, 8731	1826, 1827, 1828, 1852
Key Management–Secret	X9.17, X9.24	FIPS 171	8732, 11568	–
Key Management–Public	X9.42 (draft)	–	9494-8, 11770-3	Oakley + ISAKMP (IPSEC drafts)

The standard for automated key management, accepted worldwide, is ANSI X9.17/ISO DIS 8732/FIPS 171. This standard provides for secure automatic, periodic, electronic changes of encryption and authentication keys.

ANSI X9.17/ISO DIS 8732/FIPS 171 has been formally reviewed and adopted by both standards organizations and the major users of commercial encryption technology, large banks and financial institutions. ANSI X9.17 is in use for applications such as:

- Electronic Funds Transfers.
- Payment Authorization.
- Automated Clearinghouse Transactions.
- Secure Remote Access for users such as Auditors, Law Enforcement Agencies (FBI, Secret Service), Diplomats, Sales Organizations.
- Securities Trading.

Public key management standards are now emerging, but have not yet been accepted. ANSI 9.42 and IETF Oakley+ISAKMP exist only in draft form and have not been approved through the peer review process. A working group of the IETF is revising the ISAKMP+Oakley draft (no RFC number is yet assigned) so that it may be proposed and formally adopted later in 1997.

Encryption Standards

Data Encryption/Confidentiality (keeping communications private): Protects data from unauthorized disclosure. Data encryption is a process in which the data is "scrambled or coded" before it passes through the network. The information is decoded at the receiving location and read "in the clear." It is based on encryption algorithms such as the Data Encryption Standard (ANSI X3.92) or the Rivest-Shamir-Adleman (RSA) or IDEA algorithm. Encryption algorithms are the series of mathematical steps that are employed to transform data into encrypted form or are used to generate a Message Authentication Code (MAC).

User Authentication: This is a process for identifying a user prior to initiating a secure session and/or randomly during the session (*i.e.,* to make sure you are still talking to the same user). Standards in this area include ANSI X9.26 in the banking environment and Challenge Handshake Authentication Protocol (CHAP) and Password Authentication Protocol (PAP) in the Internet community. The CHAP and PAP are protocols for authenticating a user to a central hub/site when dialing into a network, but not end-to-end or a host. ANSI X9.26 is a challenge-response protocol that carries out the exchange using DES encryption. CHAP is based on a similar process using an algorithm called MD5. PAP is a weak authentication protocol lacking encryption and passing passwords in the clear. A draft Federal Information Processing Standards (FIPS) – currently called JJJ - is being made available by NIST to use the Digital Signature Standard for user authentication (X9.30).

Message Authentication: ANSI X9.9 (based on DES) and FIPS JJJ are examples of authentication algorithms. These algorithms are a sort of cryptographic check sum – simply put, this is another way of authenticating data (not to be confused with an arithmetic checksum that is easily spoofed or impersonated).

Non-Repudiation: This service is implemented using Digital Signatures. Two standards exist in this arena: DSS, the Digital Signature Standard (ANSI X9.30); and, RSA Signatures (ISO 9796). Digital signatures bind the user with the data file, providing both proof of data integrity and the origin of data that can be verified by any third party at any time. This function is critical for audit control in an electronic commerce environment.

❑❑❑

APPENDIX 4 NATIONAL INSTITUTE OF STANDARDS AND TECHNOLOGY'S

NIST, an agency of the U.S. Department of Commerce, was founded in 1901 as the nation's First Federal Physical Science Research Laboratory. Over the years, the scientists and technical staff at NIST have made solid contributions to image processing, DNA diagnostic "chips," smoke detectors, and automated error-correcting software for machine tools. Just a few of the other areas in which NIST has had major impact include atomic clocks, X-ray standards for mammography, scanning tunneling microscopy, pollution-control technology and high-speed dental drills.

NIST General Information

From automated teller machines and atomic clocks to mammograms and semiconductors, innumerable products and services rely in some way on technology, measurement and standards provided by the National Institute of Standards and Technology.

Founded in 1901, NIST is a non-regulatory federal agency within the U.S. Department of Commerce. NIST's mission is to promote U.S. innovation and industrial competitiveness by advancing measurement science, standards, and technology in ways that enhance economic security and improve our quality of life.

NIST carries out its mission in four cooperative programs:

- The NIST Laboratories, conducting research that advances the nation's technology infrastructure and is needed by U.S. industry to continually improve products and services.
- The Baldrige National Quality Program, which promotes performance excellence among U.S. manufacturers, service companies, educational institutions, health care providers, and nonprofit organizations; conducts outreach programs and manages the annual

Malcolm Baldrige National Quality Award which recognizes performance excellence and quality achievement.

- The Hollings Manufacturing Extension Partnership, a nationwide network of local centers offering technical and business assistance to smaller manufacturers.
- The Technology Innovation Program, which provides cost-shared awards to industry, universities, and consortia for research on potentially revolutionary technologies that address critical national and societal needs.

❑❑❑

Appendix 5

Standards and Specifications Cited in this Book

ANSI Standards

Number	*Title*	*Year*
X9.17	Financial Institution Key Management	1995

Internet RFCs

Number	*Title*	*Year*
RFC 822	Standard for the format of ARPA Internet text message	1982
RFC 1510	The Kerberos Network Authentication Service	1993
RFC 1750	Randomness Recommendations for Security	1994
RFC 2026	The Internet Standard Process	1996
RFC2246	The TLS Protocol	1999
RFC 2402	IP Authentication Header	1998

ITU-T Recommendations

Number	*Title*	*Year*
X.509	The Directory: Public Key and Attribute Certificate Frameworks	2000
X.800	Security Architecture for Open System Interconnection	1991

NIST Federal Information Processing Standards

Number	*Title*	*Year*
FIPS 46-3	Data Encryption Standard (DES)	1999
FIPS 81	DES Mode of Operation	1980
FIPS 180-1	Secure Hash Standard	1995
FIPS 180-2	Secure Hash Standard	2001
FIPS 186-2	Digital Signature Standard	2000
FIPS 197	Advanced Encryption Standard	2001
FIPS 181	Automated Password Generator	1993

❑❑❑

ANNEXURE I

ANNEXURE OF CHAPTER-1

INTRODUCTION

A basic understanding of computer networks is requisite in order to understand the principles of network security. In this section, we will cover some of the foundations of computer networking then move on to an overview of some popular networks. Computer networking is the engineering discipline concerned with the communication between computer systems. Computer networking is sometimes considered a sub-discipline of telecommunications, computer science, information technology and/or computer engineering since it relies heavily upon the theoretical and practical application of these scientific and engineering disciplines.

What is Network?

A network is any set of computers or devices connected to each other with the ability to exchange data.

The three types of networks are: the Internet, the intranet, and the extranet. Examples of different network methods are:

- Local area network (LAN), which is usually a small network constrained to a small geographic area. An example of a LAN would be a computer network within a building.
- Metropolitan area network (MAN), which is used for medium size area. Examples for a city or a state.
- Wide area network (WAN) that is usually a larger network that covers a large geographic area.
- Wireless LANs and WANs (WLAN and WWAN) are the wireless equivalent of the LAN and WAN.

All networks are interconnected to allow communication with a variety of different kinds of media, including twisted-pair copper wire cable, coaxial cable, optical fiber, power lines and various wireless technologies. The devices can be separated by a few metres (*e.g.*, via Bluetooth) or nearly unlimited distances (*e.g.*, via the interconnections of the Internet). Networking, routers, routing protocols, and networking over the public Internet have their specifications defined in documents called RFCs.

❑❑❑

ANNEXURE **II**

ANNEXURE OF CHAPTER-4

ADVANCED ENCRYPTION STANDARD (AES)

The Advanced Encryption Standard (AES) was published by NIST (National Institute of Standards and Technology) in 2001. AES is a symmetric block cipher that is intended to replace DES as the approved standard for a wide range of applications. The AES cipher (and other candidates) forms the latest generation of block ciphers, and now we see a significant increase in the block size – from the old standard of 64-bits up to 128-bits; and keys from 128 to 256-bits. In part this has been driven by the public demonstrations of exhaustive key searches of DES. Whilst triple-DES is regarded as secure and well understood, it is slow, especially in s/w. In a first round of evaluation, 15 proposed algorithms were accepted. A second round narrowed the field to 5 algorithms. NIST completed its evaluation process and published a final standard (FIPS PUB 197) in November of 2001.

NIST selected Rijndael as the proposed AES algorithm. Rijndael was designed characteristics as follow:

1. Resistance against all known attacks.
2. Speed and code compactness on a wide range of platforms.
3. Design simplicity.

Description of the cipher

AES is based on a design principle known as a Substitution permutation network. AES does not use a Feistel network. The AES cipher is specified as a number of repetitions of transformation rounds that convert the input plaintext into the final output of ciphertext. Each round consists of several processing steps, including one that depends on the encryption key. A set of reverse rounds are applied to transform ciphertext back into the original plaintext using the same encryption key.

High-level Description of the Algorithm

1. Key Expansion—round keys are derived from the cipher key using Rijndael's key schedule

2. Initial Round
   (*i*) Add Round Key—each byte of the state is combined with the round key using bitwise xor
3. Rounds
   (*i*) Sub Bytes—a non-linear substitution step where each byte is replaced with another according to a lookup table.
   (*ii*) Shift Rows—a transposition step where each row of the state is shifted cyclically a certain number of steps.
   (*iii*) Mix Columns—a mixing operation which operates on the columns of the state, combining the four bytes in each column.
   (*iv*) Add Round Key
4. Final Round (no Mix Columns)
   (*i*) Sub Bytes
   (*ii*) Shift Rows
   (*iii*) Add Round Key

AES Parameters

A number of AES parameters depend on the key length. Here we assume the key length of 128-bits. The following Table 1 shows various parameters of AES.

Table 1. AES Parameters

Key size (words/bytes/bits)	4/16/128	6/24/192	8/32/256
Plaintext block size (words/bytes/bits)	4/16/128	4/16/128	4/16/128
Number of rounds	10	12	14
Round key size (words/bytes/bits)	4/16/128	4/16/128	4/16/128
Expanded key size (words/bytes)	44/176	52/208	60/240

GLOSSARY

- **Antivirus software** or an intrusion prevention system (IPS) help detect and inhibit the action of such malware.
- **Authentication** is any process by which you verify that someone is who they claim they are.
- **Advanced Encryption Standard** (AES), which should have security strength equal to or better than DES, and significantly improved efficiency.
- **AES** must be a symmetric block cipher with a block length of 128-bits and support for key lengths of 128, 192 and 256-bits.
- **AES key expansion algorithm** takes as input a 4-word (16-byte) key and produces a linear array of 44 words (156 bytes).
- **Asymmetric encryption** can be used for confidentiality, authentication or both.
- **AES** Cipher Designed by Rijmen-Daemon in Belgium
- **Add Round Key** is a form of Vernam cipher and by itself would not be formidable.
- **Brute-Force attack** is every possible key is tried until an intelligible translation into plaintext is obtained. On average, half of all possible keys should be tried to achieve success.
- **Cryptanalysis** is the study of recovering communications by those other than the intended receiver.
- **Computer Security** is more like providing means to protect a single PC against outside intrusion.
- **Computer Security** is an integral element of sound management.
- **Caesar Cipher** involves replacing each letter of the alphabet with the letter standing three places further down the alphabet.
- **Differential Cryptanalysis** attack is first published attack that is capable of breaking DES in less than 2^{55} complexity.
- **Diffusion** refers to the property that the statistics structure of the plaintext is dissipated into long range statistics of the ciphertext.
- **Discrete Logarithms** are group-theoretic analogues of ordinary logarithms.

- **Diffie-Hellman Key** agreement was invented in 1976 during a collaboration between Whitfield Diffie and Martin Hellman.
- **Diffie-Hellman (D-H)** key exchange is a cryptographic protocol that allows two parties that have no prior knowledge of each other to jointly establish a shared secret key over an insecure communications channel.
- **Diffie-Hellman Key Exchange** is vulnerable to a man-in-the-middle attack.
- **Electronic Code Book Mode** has each 64-bit plaintext is mapped to respective 64-bit ciphertext, and each such possible pair represents 1 page of the codebook.
- **Elliptic Curve Arithmetic** can be used develop a variety of elliptic curve cryptography schemes, including key exchange, encryption and digital signature.
- **Fermat's Theorem** states that, if **p** is prime number and a postive integer not divisible by p then $a^{p-1} = 1 \pmod{p}$.
- **Firewall** is a barrier through which all traffic passes.
- **Kerberos** is a network authentication protocol. It is designed to provide strong authentication for client/server applications by using secret-key cryptography.
- **Kerberos Version 5** is specified in RFC 1510 and provides a number of improvements over version 4 in the areas of environmental shortcomings and technical deficiencies.
- **MD5** (**Message-Digest Algorithm 5**) is a widely used cryptographic hash function with a 128-bit hash value.
- **Multipurpose Internet Mail Extensions** (**MIME**) is an extension to the RFC 822 framework that is intended to address some of the problems and limitations of these uses of SMTP.
- **Network Security** starts from authenticating the user, commonly with a username and a password.
- **Number Theory** is the branch of pure mathematics concerned with the properties of numbers in general.
- **RSA** involves a public key and a private key.
- **RSA** is block cipher in which the plaintext and ciphertext are integers between 0 and n – 1 for same n.
- **Random Numbers** play an important role in the use of encryption for various network security applications.
- **Steganography** is the science of hiding information.
- **Security Services** is the services to implement security policies and implemented by security mechanism.
- **Symmetric Encryption** also referred to as conventional encryption or single-key encryption was the only type of encryption in use prior to the development of public key encryption.

- **Substitution Technique** is one in which the letters of plaintext are replaced by other letters or by numbers.
- **Trapdoor** one-way function is a one-way function for which the inverse direction is easy given a certain piece of information, but difficult otherwise.
- **Traffic Analysis** is monitoring of communications flows between parties
- **True Random Number Generator** (TRNG) uses a nondeterministic source to produce randomness.
- **Trusted System** is computer and operating system that can be verified to implement a given security policy.
- **X.509** was initially issued in July 3, 1988 and was begun in association with the X.500 standard. It assumes a strict hierarchical system of certificate authorities (CAs) for issuing the certificates.
- **X.509 Certificate** is the heart of the standard. There are 3 versions, with successively more info in the certificate - must be v2 if either unique identifier field exists, must be v3 if any extensions are used.

❑❑❑

INDEX

❑❑❑